Humanistic Studies in the Communication Arts

Editorial and Persuasive Writing:

Opinion Functions of the News Media

Humanistic Studies in the Communication Arts

A TAXONOMY OF
CONCEPTS IN COMMUNICATION
by Reed H. Blake and Edwin O. Haroldsen

COMMUNICATIONS AND MEDIA
Constructing a Cross Discipline
by George N. Gordon

ETHICS AND THE PRESS
Readings in Mass Media Morality
Edited by John C. Merrill and Ralph D. Barney

DRAMA IN LIFE
The Uses of Communication in Society
Edited by James E. Combs and Michael W. Mansfield

INTERNATIONAL AND INTERCULTURAL COMMUNICATION
Edited by Heinz-Dietrich Fischer and John C. Merrill

EXISTENTIAL JOURNALISM
by John C. Merrill

THE COMMUNICATIONS REVOLUTION
A History of Mass Media in the United States
by George N. Gordon

COMMUNICATION ARTS IN THE ANCIENT WORLD
Edited by Eric A. Havelock and Jackson P. Hershbell

EDITORIAL AND PERSUASIVE WRITING
Opinion Functions of the News Media
by Harry W. Stonecipher

Humanistic Studies in H|S C|A *the Communication Arts*

Editorial and Persuasive Writing:

Opinion Functions of the News Media

by

Harry W. Stonecipher

COMMUNICATION ARTS BOOKS

HASTINGS HOUSE, PUBLISHERS

New York 10016

Library of Congress Cataloging in Publication Data

Stonecipher, Harry W.
Editorial & persuasive writing:
Opinion functions of the news media
(Humanistic studies in the communication arts)
(Communication arts books)
Includes index.
1. Editorials. 2. Persuasion (Rhetoric)
I. Title.
PN4778.S8 070.4'12 78-26974
ISBN 0-8038-1953-6
ISBN 0-8038-1954-4 pbk.

Published simultaneously in Canada by Copp Clark Ltd., Toronto

Designed by Al Lichtenberg
Printed in the United States of America

Contents

Preface

The opinion ingredient of the news media seemingly grows more ubiquitous with each passing year. This is true in part because the growing complexity of the news during the 1970's has made interpretation and illumination of the issues of increasing importance to readers. It is true also because of the increasing volume of news and information. The opinion function of the news media, one journalism educator has noted, serves a vital need of the consumers of news who "these days are drowning in data." Numerous sources could be cited to establish the need for the mass media to extend the news columns and newscasts to tell what it all means, to put complex issues into perspective, to attempt to persuade readers, listeners, and viewers to accept this or that point of view as being in the public interest. Once the need for the opinion function is established, two general questions remain: (1) how well do the news media perform this vital persuasive function, and (2) how might they perform their persuasive function more effectively?

In answering these questions, the author has turned to both conventional wisdom (as practiced and expressed by media professionals) as well as the extensive research literature dealing with attitude formation and attitude change as these findings relate to mass media persuasion. The author's long experience in teaching a course in opinion writing—or critical and persuasive writing as it is called in a few schools of journalism—has brought him to the realization that while shop talk and the views of professionals are important, it is also important that the student journalist gain a better theoretical and conceptual basis for such a course of study.

The volume of shop talk about editorial writing and commentary is extensive. The author's participation in the National Conference of Editorial Writers during the past six years, his twelve years' experience as newspaper editor and publisher prior to that, and his general orientation toward the news media have made it a pleasure to probe the conventional wisdom of professionals. *The Masthead,* the official quarterly publication of the NCEW, has been relied upon as an important reference source. Other professional journals have also been consulted. The compulsion to illustrate every writing and persuasive technique discussed in the book with an editorial or column from the work of media professionals, however, has been resisted. In the first place, the teacher can better illustrate many of the persuasive techniques discussed in the book with examples from local or regional media which should be more meaningful to students. Secondly, a textbook which relies too heavily upon current events commentary becomes too scrapbookish and is too soon out of date.

What the book does do is to use selected examples from the work of Pulitzer Prize winning editorialists during the past decade. With the cooperation of the newspapers concerned, at least one editorial has been used from each of the following winners:

1977—Warren Lerude, Foster Church, and Norman Cardoza of the *Nevada State Journal* and the *Reno Evening Gazette.*
1976—Philip Kerby of the *Los Angeles Times.*
1975—John Daniell Maurice of the *Charleston* (W. Va.) *Daily Mail.*
1974—F. Gilman Spencer of *The Trentonian,* Trenton, N.J.
1973—Roger B. Linscott of the *Berkshire Eagle,* Pittsfield, Pa.
1972—John Strohmeyer of the *Bethlehem* (Pa.) *Globe-Times.*
1971—Horance G. Davis, Jr., of the *Gainesville* (Fla.) *Daily Sun.*
1970—Philip L. Geyelin of *The Washington Post.*
1969—Paul Greenberg of the *Pine Bluff* (Ark.) *Commercial.*

Various conceptual and theoretical aspects of persuasive writing are dealt with in Chapters 7 through 10. The research literature, though often technical and conditional, provides numerous insights into attitude formation and attitude change which should be helpful to the mass media editorialist. Source credibility, for example, is important if one is to be an effective persuader, but what are the dimensions of credibility? How does one become a more credible editorialist? Chapter 8 deals with the research findings relating to these questions. Various message characteristics which have been found to enhance persuasion is the subject of Chapter 9. The obstinate nature of the mass media audience and various theories about audience persuasibility is the subject of Chapter 10. Various other conceptual and theoretical insights from communications research, from social and psychological research, and from other research areas are reported in other portions of the book where their inclusion seems to be most appropriate.

While the primary focus of the book is upon newspapers, many of the principles discussed also apply to the broadcast media. For this reason, the similarities and the differences among the various media are discussed at appropriate points throughout the book. Indeed, much of the experimental research discussed in Chapters 8 through 10 deal with oral rather than written communication. Likewise, in the discussion of such problems as that of access to the media, the differences between the print and electronic media have been delineated. It is important that even the student who has no other plans but to work on a newspaper be aware of these differences.

The interdisciplinary approach taken in this book has flowed from the author's teaching effort to draw together information from various sources, as well as from his media experience. A debt of gratitude is owed to my students who were first exposed to many of the theoretical concepts in this book. Numerous faculty colleagues have also been helpful and have encouraged the research and writing of this book. I wish particularly to thank Dr. Douglas Anderson, assistant professor of journalism at the University of Nebraska at Omaha, a former Nebraska newspaper editor, for his careful reading and suggestions while the manuscript was in the preparation stage, and Dr. Ralph Johnson, a former faculty colleague and now an associate editor and editorial writer for the *Toledo Blade,* for his encouragement and counsel. I also wish to thank the various editors of *The Masthead,* quarterly publication of the National Conference of Editorial Writers, for their encouragement by publishing from time to time articles based upon my research into attitude formation and attitude change as it affects the role of the media editorialist.

A special thanks goes to my wife, Helen Marie, for her assistance in typing, proofreading, and editing, and for her patience and understanding during the months this manuscript was in preparation. For these reasons this book is dedicated to her.

HARRY W. STONECIPHER
Carbondale, Illinois

January 1979

Foreword

Journalists dislike facing the fact. Broadcasters pretend not to understand. In the academy, we shrug our shoulders. These days we eschew rhetorical questions.

Reactions vary, but none of us can deny that the American "press" mentioned in the First Amendment of the Bill of Rights is fundamentally a different sort of cultural institution from today's newspaper or radio-television news organization. Nor do most of us want to grapple with the question of whether or not, were our Constitution written by men who could peer into the future and understand how American journalism would change in 200 years, anything like the specific clause guaranteeing freedom of the press would be (a) needed or (b) affirmed by Congress and the voters of the various states.

In the Colonial period and after the revolution—until, I would say, about 1840 or so—the American press was a snarling *weimaraner*. Newspapers indeed dealt in what we now call "hard news," but it was often slanted and usually partisan. The print press mentioned in our Bill of Rights was an extension of public political life in a vigorous new country—contentious, sometimes libelous, opinionated and fierce, nursed to maturity by the same men who had made an armed revolution and fired the shot that is still being heard around the world. This was the press and these were the newspapers, magazines and pamphlets that were given broadside constitutional protection by the Bill of Rights.

Freedom of the press meant largely freedom to express opinions, mostly in a political context, and to bring to the literate populace political platforms and the policies of people who were running for public offices of all sorts. Without a First Amendment to protect the circulation of these various and many biases, how could the mechanisms of democracy, so painfully spelled out in the main body of the Constitution itself, possibly work? Free speech and a free press was not one bit a luxury; they were a necessity if, in any manner, the American voter (male, white, propertied and literate—a fraction of the population) was to cast an enlightened and useful vote at the next election. An absolute prerequisite, in fact!

Over the past two centuries, the press in the United States has grown and broadened in scope and assimilated to itself many new technologies and new constituencies to a mind-boggling degree. But the words of the First Amendment remain unchanged. Whatever their original rationale, it has been all but lost in this staggering proliferation of contemporary mass media that, between the covers of magazines and books, in newspapers and on the air, purport to tell the public what is "new"—in itself a comparatively recent construction of the term "news." The once snarling cur has become a fat and amiable police dog, well fed and groomed, the property of the "best people" (by their own published definition), responding, in large measure, to their commands and theirs alone. It stands sleepily on guard to prevent societal dirty work, mostly in government, growling loudest and best when an incredibly visible, vulnerable blunderer—a Boss Tweed or a Richard Nixon—fouls the nest of government so foolishly and obviously that the ringing of burglar alarms wakes him up well after the fact.

So much for canine metaphors. For better or worse, the American press has been devoting itself during much of the past century to an ideal of objectivity in news coverage that has amused many sophisticated journalists in Western Europe and elsewhere. Broadcast journalists have followed in their path, often with refreshing and candid *caveats* that the voodoo of their peculiar media cannot handle objectivity as well as the printed page to the degree that the Federal Communications Commission has been willing to settle for mere tokens of "fairness" (in lieu of objectivity) from radio and television newsrooms and documentary units. Print editorials meanwhile are probably the least read and least effective columns printed in our daily and weekly press. Once in a while, a radio or television station manager will read an editorial message, usually a strong statement that comes down hard in favor of virtue and against vice. Walter Lippmann is dead. Certainly, some readers now search out columns by writers like James Reston or William Buckley, but mostly to confirm their own inviolable previous opinions, that is, if they search them out at all. Despite Nixonian cries of "foul," broadcast commentators still analyze in hasty fashion the great issues of the moment with thoughtful statements to the effect that things may either get better or worse and that possible outcomes of the immediate situation will either be good or bad, depending on many factors including whether the principal parties mean what they say or say what they mean. ("And now back to you, Walter, in New York . . .")

I shall resist the all too facile temptation to place the blame for the current curious blandness of the "opinion function" of the American press of print, spoken words and pictures upon professors of journalism, mainly because the men who today make the policies for our newspapers and broadcasting networks are not graduates of schools of journalism, nor have they even studied journalism in any kind of classroom. In the print media, these folks are, by and large, ivy league-educated members of publishing dynasties, large and small, into which they were either born or married. In broadcasting, they are a weird combination of public relations, businessmen and lawyer types, also for the most part, beneficiaries (or victims) of so-called liberal arts educations, not necessarily given at the sort of schools where the best people send their young. At the middle and lower levels of journalistic enterprise in the United States, real live journalism school graduates moil and are hard pressed to challenge, not only company policy but also institutional higher truths, even if some of them feel so inclined. All the rebellious youngster can do (when and if one exists) is go off somewhere and start another newspaper (certainly not a new radio or television network), which, while often attempted, succeeds once in a blue moon, if that frequently.

What I cannot resist, however, is the observation that the American press of tomorrow *may* well be able to restore to American journalism some of the early vigor that once characterized its pages if, and only if, relevant educators make it their business to teach thoroughly and with requisite passion forceful lessons in what I still consider one of the most important tasks of any type of newspaper or news organization anywhere: to act as the conscience of its constituency and to treat almost every bit of so-called "hard" news as the equivocal matter it will probably turn out to be, if it is important enough. Armies do not invade neighboring countries. Men do, and they carry with them political, religious and economic ideas that will affect the lives of their grandchildren and possibly yours and mine. Auditoriums do not simply collapse from the weight of too much rain or snow on the roof. Certain schools of architecture are dominated by near idiots, as a trip to your local shopping center will demonstrate. Corrupt contractors put too much sand in the cement and skimp on steel, and so on and so on and so on.

True enough possibly, but all matters of interest to investigative reporters, you may say. Detective work is fine and dandy, but, taken alone, it is useless. The reporter or writer or editor who is unable or unwilling to crystalize his facts and data into a requisite quantum of opinion is neither a full man nor woman. Some day he will be replaced by a machine; in fact, he probably has been already, for the most part, if we can believe the noted pollster who tells us that the average American gets about two-thirds of his news from the TV set and probably buys newspapers to scan advertisements, gossip and obituaries.

Nor is it enough for broadcasters to point their cameras at an event and claim with dead pans they are merely televising visual "truths" which they have little or no obligation to qualify, explain or, if necessary, view with alarm or outrage. If ever this matter was in dispute, it was settled once and for all time at the Democratic Party convention in Chicago in 1968. But memories are as short or as long in the broadcasting world as they need to be, more or less like television news stories. Most broadcast reporters are still living in the light of Ed Murrow's bravest moment, when he turned in his chair to the viewers of *See It Now* in the 1950's and gave them his thoughtful, hammer-like opinions, in characteristically spare prose, of Senator Joe McCarthy in a style that had been until that moment a bit too sharp for the proper gentlemen and ladies of the printed page. A blue moon also rose over *The Selling of the Pentagon* and *The Guns of Autumn,* but most of the rest has been silence or silliness.

One matter of transcendent importance, however, remains the pivotal and bitter truth: nobody can and will write or speak forceful and meaningful words of editorial opinion in any context unless he or she knows precisely how to do it. In *Editorial and Persuasive Writing,* Dr. Stonecipher provides no magic formula, nor does one exist. What Stonecipher offers is a wealth of experience with the editorial aspects of journalism, an impressive and inspiring galaxy of case-study material and a passion of his own that I think it well behooves the neophyte journalist and student to attempt to try to emulate. I believe it was St. Francis, a visible living monument to his own self-denial, who, having passed through a town, was asked by a disciple when he was going to preach his sermon. "I have already preached my sermon!" was the reply.

A good teacher teaches best by example. So does a good book. This is exactly the kind of approach to this most difficult and testing aspect of the numerous journalistic professions that attracted me first to Dr. Stonecipher's work and the one that impels me now to recommend to you a considered and careful reading of it.

This is my opinion as an editor, and I hope it has been suitably persuasive.

George N. Gordon

The Quarterly Publication of
The National Conference of Editorial Writers

The NCEW's
BASIC STATEMENT OF PRINCIPLES

(Adopted in Philadelphia, October 10, 1975)

Editorial writing is more than another way of making money. It is a profession devoted to the public welfare and to public service. The chief duty of its practitioners is to provide the information and guidance toward sound judgments that are essential to the healthy functioning of a democracy. Therefore, editorial writers owe it to their integrity and that of their profession to observe the following injunctions:

1. The editorial writer should present facts honestly and fully. It is dishonest to base an editorial on half-truth. The writer should never knowingly mislead the reader, misrepresent a situation, or place any person in a false light. No consequential errors should go uncorrected.
2. The editorial writer should draw fair conclusions from the stated facts, basing them upon the weight of evidence and upon the writer's considered concept of the public good.
3. The editorial writer should never use his or her influence to seek personal favors of any kind. Gifts of value, free travel and other favors that can compromise integrity, or appear to do so, should not be accepted.

   The writer should be constantly alert to conflicts of interest, real or apparent, including those that may arise from financial holdings, secondary employment, holding public office or involvement in political, civic or other organizations. Timely public disclosure can minimize suspicion.

   Editors should seek to hold syndicates to these standards.

   The writer, further to enhance editorial page credibility, also should encourage the institution he or she represents to avoid conflicts of interest, real or apparent.

4. The editorial writer should realize that the public will appreciate more the value of the First Amendment if others are ac-

corded an opportunity for expression. Therefore, voice should be given to diverse opinions, edited faithfully to reflect stated views. Targets of criticism—whether in a letter, editorial, cartoon or signed column—especially deserve an opportunity to respond; editors should insist that syndicates adhere to this standard.

5. The editorial writer should regularly review his or her conclusions. The writer should not hesitate to consider new information and to revise conclusions. When changes of viewpoint are substantial, readers should be informed.
6. The editorial writer should have the courage of well-founded convictions and should never write anything that goes against his or her conscience. Many editorial pages are products of more than one mind, and sound collective judgment can be achieved only through sound individual judgments. Thoughtful individual opinions should be respected.
7. The editorial writer always should honor pledges of confidentiality. Such pledges should be made only to serve the public's need for information.
8. The editorial writer should discourage publication of editorials prepared by an outside writing service and presented as the newspaper's own. Failure to disclose the source of such editorials is unethical, and particularly reprehensible when the service is in the employ of a special interest.
9. The editorial writer should encourage thoughtful criticism of the press, especially within the profession, and promote adherence to the standards set forth in this statement of principles.

The Masthead, Spring 1978
Reprinted by permission.

Los Angeles Times

HARRISON GRAY OTIS, 1882-1917
HARRY CHANDLER, 1917-1944
NORMAN CHANDLER, 1944-1960

OTIS CHANDLER
Publisher and Chief Executive Officer

TOM JOHNSON
President and Chief Operating Officer
WILLIAM F. THOMAS
Executive Vice President and Editor

CHARLES C. CHASE, Vice President—Operations
ROBERT L. FLANNES, Vice President and Assistant to the Publisher
JAMES B. GRIDER, Vice President—Production
ROBERT C. LOBDELL, Vice President and General Counsel
DONALD S. MAXWELL, Vice President and Controller
VANCE L. STICKELL, Vice President—Sales

GEORGE J. COTLIAR, Managing Editor
ANTHONY DAY, Editor of the Editorial Pages
JEAN SHARLEY TAYLOR, Associate Editor

TARGET: THE PUBLIC

In resisting gag orders that are now issued almost routinely by trial judges, the press has found itself in a circular trap. It works this way, as illustrated by a recent murder trial in Austin, Tex.:

The judge ordered the news media "not to carry the name or address of any juror selected to serve on the case"; in turn, the trial judge, the Texas Supreme Court, Justice Lewis F. Powell Jr. of the U.S. Supreme Court and, finally, the Supreme Court itself (5 to 2) declined a newspaper's application for a stay of the order.

The trial ended the day after the U.S. Supreme Court denial, and the issue in this particular case became moot. With what results? Direct restraint was imposed on the press, despite the guarantees of the First Amendment.

The original court order originated in a highly whimsical, if not bizarre, set of circumstances: The jurors' names and addresses were made known in the courtroom. In addition, the names and addresses of the entire panel from which the jury was chosen were on record. The judge declined to sequester the jury to protect it from possible outside influence. This was done for the convenience of the jury and to save the county some $500 a day. So, in effect, the First Amendment protections of the public's right to be fully informed were bargained away for frivolous reasons.

It may be argued that disclosure in the press of the identities of the jury had no significance, but how far-reaching will the next gag order be, and the next, and the next?

We have already gone far down along this path. A New York judge asserted the right to hold a secret trial, and a Los Angeles judge attempted to ban all comment on a murder case by "all agencies of the public media . . ." Other examples of judicial undercutting of the First Amendment are too numerous to review here. The point to be understood here is this: When judicial censorship is imposed, its target is the public, not the press. The press is only the intermediary.

It is a curious trend that has developed in the courts in the past decade.

Such direct restraint on the press and the public, if attempted by the legislative or the executive branch, would be found, as it has been by the courts, plainly unconstitutional.

But when the power of judges is concerned, an increasing number of judges at the trial level are deciding that their authority is unchecked by the constitutional restraints imposed on the other branches. As one constitutional lawyer has said, "Judges have had a taste of authority in deciding what can and cannot be reported about trial proceedings, and they like it."

In fighting judicial orders to restrict public information, the press is in the anomalous position of seeking a judgment from its adversary. Lower court judges in increasing number find little difficulty ruling in their own behalf.

It is true, since the beginning, that judges have been among the foremost expositors and defenders of the principles underlying the First Amendment. Yet the current trend in the courts represents a departure from that great tradition, and reflects a loss of confidence in freedom, which is the essence of the First Amendment.

These two editorials, spanning the geographical breadth of the United States, are representative of the work of Pulitzer Prize winning editorialists during the past decade whose work has been used to illustrate various techniques of editorial writing at appropriate points throughout this book. "Mission Incredible," written by Philip L. Geyelin, Editorial Page Editor of the *Washington Post* and winner of the Pulitzer Prize in 1970, was the first Watergate editorial published by the *Post*. Its fortuitous reference to tapes not being allowed to self-destruct gives the editorial a stunning prescience. "Target: The Public," written by Philip Kerby of the *Los Angeles Times,* was one in a series of incisive editorials dealing with press freedom which won the *Times* a Pulitzer Prize for editorial writing in 1976.

The Washington Post

AN INDEPENDENT NEWSPAPER

MISSION INCREDIBLE

"As always, should you or any of your force be caught or killed, the Secretary will disavow any knowledge of your actions. This tape will self-destruct in five seconds . . . good luck . . ."
—From the CBS-TV show, *Mission Impossible*

As an example of life imitating art—of a sort—we have not for some time seen anything like the Watergate caper now unfolding in weird and scarcely believable detail, right down to the taped locks, the rubber gloves, the tear gas pens, the array of electronic equipment, and the crisp new hundred dollar bills in the hands of the five men who stole into Democratic Party headquarters the other night under cover of darkness and something less than impenetrable aliases. *Mission Impossible* it wasn't; experts in these matters all agree that the job was bungled at almost every step of the way. *Mission Incredible* it certainly is, both in terms of execution and, more important, in terms of the motives that could conceivably have prompted so crude an escapade by such a motley crew of former Central Intelligence Agency operatives and Miami-based, anti-Castro activists.

Mr. Ronald L. Ziegler, the White House spokesman, has already dismissed it as a "third-rate burglary attempt" and warned that "certain elements may try to stretch this beyond what it is." The implication of that last statement is that he knows what it is and if so, we wish he would tell us, because frankly it doesn't shape up as your ordinary, garden variety burglary—however "third-rate" its execution. An attempt to implant electronic surveillances in the headquarters of a major political party strikes us as something much more resembling what the Democratic National Chairman, Mr. Lawrence O'Brien, has called an "act of political espionage." And that, for all its comic, melodramatic aspects, is not quite so easy to dismiss.

In fact, without wishing to stretch things one bit beyond the demonstrable facts, there are certain elements here which could raise questions in even the least suspicious or skeptical minds. This is, for example, an election year, and while it is possible to suppose that this deed was done by a foreign government or even some extra-terrestrial interests, the finger naturally points, in a time of intense and developing political combat, to the Democrats' principal and natural antagonist; that is to say, it points to somebody associated with or at least sympathetic to—we may as well be blunt about it—the Republicans.

We do not so allege; we merely note that this is what some people are going to be saying, or thinking, and that their speculations, dark as they may sound, are going to be encouraged by word of various connection between several of the suspects and one part or another of the Republican power structure. For example, Mr. James W. McCord, one of the five men arrested, has worked on security problems both for the Republican National Committee and the Committee for the Re-Election of the President. Two of the group had in their personal effects the address of a Mr. Howard E. Hunt, another former CIA agent, who serves as a consultant to White House consultant Charles W. Colson. Other more tenuous links have been developed between the arrested suspects and elements of the Republican Party.

Mr. John Mitchell, the former Attorney General who is heading the committee for Mr. Nixon's re-election, has stoutly denied any knowledge of the affair as has the Chairman of the Republican National Committee, Senator Dole, as well as Mr. Ziegler. So life has imitated art up to a point; the "force" has been "caught"; "the Secretary" has "disavowed any knowledge" of its actions. What remains now to be seen—what is, in short, the crucial question in a time of waning confidence in the processes of government—is whether a Republican administration can bring itself to use every means at its command to prosecute perpetrators of the Watergate raid. From the sound of it, there would seem to be an abundance of evidence in the captured equipment and freshly-minted currency. It ought not to be left to the Democrats to dig into *Mission Incredible* by pressing a civil suit. In short, this particular tape ought not to be allowed to self-destruct.

1

The Opinion Function: *An Introduction*

THE MODERN NEWSPAPER editorialist, carefully composing his thoughts upon the screen of a video display terminal, performs an important function in mass communications. It's a communications function which has been exercised, in one way or another, for centuries. Indeed, the origins and forerunners of the newspaper editorial, according to one journalism historian, include the sixteenth century handwritten newsletters and ballads in England which often failed to differentiate between fact and opinion. Later followed the English newsbooks, the corantos, the diurnals and mercuries, various types of pamphlets, and the use of prefatory commentaries. During the Revolutionary War period in America the potency of the editorial form was repeatedly demonstrated and various stylistic devices were further developed. There were, for example, Thomas Paine's brilliant wartime series, the "Crisis Papers," which were instrumental in maintaining military and civilian morale, Isaiah Thomas' graphic evaluative account of the Battle of Lexington; and the incisive political arguments in the Federalist Papers urging the adoption of the Constitution.[1]

During the 1790's, however, when a new breed of hired editors came upon the American scene, editorial expression of a less responsible nature emerged. This period produced some of the most invective writing and billingsgate ever published by the American press. These attacks, one writer has observed, included such name-calling as "pert and prating popinjay," "hackneyed guttersnip, "maggot of corruption," "wad on a dungheap," and "sniveling, sophisticated hound." Despite such vindictive language, however, the colonial press apparently gave editorial support and printed political opinion influential and powerful enough to help sway a people to form a new nation.[2] The modern newspaper editorial, in fact, emerged during the year following the American Revolution.

On the 200th anniversary year of American independence, John B. Oakes, editorial page editor of the *New York Times,* speaking to members of the National Conference of Editorial Writers, found the country's editorial pages "alive and kicking"—still performing their basic function of maintaining a posture of constructive criticism of the social, political, economic, and sometimes even moral dilemmas of society. Criticizing partisan political editorials written by some of the most eminent editors during the nineteenth and early twentieth century, Oakes appealed for a more responsible criticism, noting:

> It seems to me that we have no real purpose if we do not provide, or at least try to provide, constructive, responsible criticism of every aspect of public affairs that we ourselves are capable of writing about. In this fantastically complex society in which we are living, no one can be an expert on all matters; but each of us by virtue of the position we hold—whether supreme boss of a small-town daily or a small but significant cog in a huge publicity empire—is capable of having some effect on the public policies of his community and his country.[3]

To carry out that responsibility, however, requires independence and integrity of editor and publisher alike. The editor, Oakes said, cannot be isolated from what's going on in the world around him; he must be insulated, nonetheless, from the pressures of business, social, political, or otherwise—this protection must be provided by the publisher.

Philip L. Geyelin, editorial page editor of the *Washington Post,* who shared the 200th anniversary NCEW program with Oakes, found the modern American editorial page much like a bugle call. The page, Geyelin said, is too authoritative, too rigid, too stereotyped—and not nearly versatile enough to be as effective as it might be in the age of the communications explosion when the attention span of the average newspaper reader is increasingly overtaxed. Part of that communications explosion, of course, is television, which Geyelin termed both all-pervasive and "phantasmagorical," a medium which bombards the viewer with a "shifting series of illusions and deceptive appearances." Geyelin noted that

> newspaper readers, now more than ever, need somebody to follow along and tidy things up, to take these phantasms and examine them and rearrange them so that they begin to make some sense. Readers, I think, don't any longer want to be told by newspapers who to vote for or what to be in favor of, or to be against, as much as they want to know what matters. They want to know, not what *we* think but what *they* ought to be thinking about.[4]

And the newspaper editorial writer has a far wider range of instruments to choose from than merely blowing a bugle, Geyelin concluded. They include such techniques as

> humor, analysis, the raising of tough questions that even *we* can't answer, the making of orderly patterns out of meaningless mosaics, the job of simply keeping the record straight. And we are going to have to make more and better use of these instruments. It isn't just a question of whether one wants to spend one's life blowing bugle calls. The real question is whether, if that's all you're blowing, anybody is going to be listening.

Broadcast Editorializing

In contrast to the long history of editorializing through the various forms of written communications—from the newsletter to the electronically composed, photo-set, offset-printed newpaper editorial—broadcast editorializing is of much more recent origin. As recently as 1941 the Federal Communications Commission, ruling on a construction permit and license renewal for Station WAAB in Boston, effectively discouraged broadcast editorials.[5] The FCC, however, had a change of mind in 1949 when the so-called "Fairness Doctrine" was enunciated, encouraging stations to express their editorial views on the air.[6] Fifteen years later in a primer clarifying the applicability of the Fairness Doctrine in the handling of controversial issues of public importance, the FCC summarized the case history of various aspects of the doctrine: the affording of a reasonable opportunity for the presentation of contrasting viewpoints, the personal attack principle, and licensee editorializing.[7]

Even though the fairness doctrine on the surface encourages editorializing, the FCC's personal attack rule requires stations to give free time to any individual or group criticized in their editorials. Likewise, broadcasters who endorse a political candidate must give free time to all opponents. Such government regulation, without doubt, tends to discourage more active broadcast editorializing. Ted Landphair, manager of news and public affairs of Radio Station WMAL, Washington, D.C., for example, found broadcasters "fed up" with intrusions into the daily work of editorial judgments by the need to worry about the specter of the bureaucrat in the newsroom. Referring to the Fairness Doctrine as an "Apple Pie" doctrine difficult to oppose because of its "fairness" implications, Landphair emphasizes that most persons engaged in broadcast news do oppose it. One of the problems the doctrine poses, he noted, is in the political arena:

> Under the political equal-time provisions, a violation of Section 315 means equal time for lots of candidates (maybe as many as 100 declared or would-be candidates in 1976), ranging from Lar (America First) Daly, who has run for president seven times going back to 1948 . . . to Merril Riddick, an 80-year-old Montana prospector who be-

> lieves in the Puritan ethic and turning garbage into electricity. Giving time, and lots of it, to these minor figures, no matter how pure their motives, is what keeps us from a repetition of broadcasts like the Kennedy-Nixon debates of 1960.[8]

A nationwide survey for *Broadcasting Yearbook* in 1977 indicated, however, that 58 percent of the television stations responding to the survey and 70 percent of the AM radio stations responding do editorialize, at least occasionally. Of these, only about 22 percent of the television stations and 16 percent of the radio stations editorialize daily. Other sources place the total number of television stations editorializing daily at only about 10 percent of all stations on the air. Even when broadcasters do editorialize, some critics point out, they often choose noncontroversial topics like "Support Your Local Red Cross."[9] It may also be true, as some critics point out, that broadcasters avoid strong editorial stances because such statements make enemies. Such criticism is often applied, with some justification, to newspaper editorial pages as well.

Criticism of Media Editorials

Criticism of the editorial effort of the news media ranges from condemnation of media owners for their failure to provide "a service adequate to the needs of the society" to recommendations calling for "the abandonment of the practice of refraining from mutual comment and the adoption instead of a resolute policy of criticism of the press by the press."[10]

One line of criticism views the content of a newspaper, for example, as the product of the conflicting goals of the reader (to be entertained), the reporter, and presumably the editorialist (to change the world), and the publisher (to make money). In this conflict, some critics hold, the reporter and editorialist usually lose. For one thing, the reader and the publisher have most of the power; for another, their goals are more compatible. The reporter and editorialist, on the other hand, represent a minority viewpoint. The decline of the editorial page may thus be viewed as an example of the publisher-reader coalition at work. Many readers find today's editorial page either too heavy or too bland for their tastes, which is of little concern to most publishers, critics say, because:

> They use the edit page to praise the weather, pontificate on the latest news from Afghanistan, and urge everyone to vote in the next election. There are very few newspapers left in the country that regularly publish strong editorials on local controversies, thus risking the reader's anger.[11]

Ben H. Bagdikian, journalist, author, and one of the most articulate critics of the press, said, more than a decade ago after examining the editorial pages of some eighty-eight daily newspapers for a given day, that though he found plenty of things to criticize, there were some signs that the American daily newspaper editorial page had begun to emerge from its "Know-Nothing" period. However, he still found a number of weaknesses: (1) poor factual background and too simplistic an approach to foreign affairs, (2) editorials which lacked an effective point of view, (3) too many "dear-me" editorials which presented a parade of facts, allowing the conclusion to escape, and (4) editorials which asked questions but provided no answers.

For too many years, Bagdikian said, "the editorial page staff was a substitute for a pension plan. It was a company-paid nursing home for geriatric cases." But he saw changes coming:

> Today there is a growing knowledge and relevance in editorial pages. But it is too slow in changing. Already the power of public explanation lies largely with the news-magazines and the television documentaries. Papers are changing, but the world and the country's population are changing faster.[12]

Curtis MacDougall, professor emeritus at Northwestern University, a panelist on a National Conference of Editorial Writers program in 1974, also found newspaper editorial pages plagued by a number of faults and shortcomings. He found editorials too conservative, too chauvinistic and super-patriotic, too slow to support the underdog or to endorse an unpopular issue or candidate. Editorialists, MacDougall charged, too often exhibit a "blind acceptance of the status quo." Editorials, found to be ill researched, were characterized as being too dull, too bland, too ineffective.[13]

One of the often repeated criticisms of the press is that it does not engage sufficiently in mutual self-criticism. Editorialists, however, have benefited from such criticism for more than thirty years. The catalyst for this self-examination is usually identified as the National Conference of Editorial Writers which was founded in 1947.[14] *The Masthead,* the quarterly publication of the NCEW, has been filled with criticism of editorial pages through the years. The National Broadcast Editorial Association, organized in 1975 to stimulate high standards in broadcast editorializing and to encourage more stations to take up the editorial challenge, also publishes a newsletter which engages in self-criticism from time to time. The *Radio-TV Editorial Journal,* published by the Foundation for American Communications, has also been engaged in working toward improvement of both electronic and print editorials, including sponsorship of seminars for the working press as well as members of the scientific community.

James Reston of the *New York Times,* in a lecture, "The Press Under Fire," recently came to the defense of both the print and electronic media. He pointed out that:

> There is now more self-criticism and institutional criticism in the newsrooms of the TV and radio stations as well as in the newspaper offices than at any time in my years as a reporter. I would even defend the provocative thought that the moral tone of the newspapers is usually better than the moral tone of the communities in which they are published. But our responsibilities are obviously greater than our talents and our judgment, and our critics are quite right to keep after us. In short, our wrongs are there for all to see, but I believe we're moving in the right direction.[15]

If the editorialist's talents and judgment often do not measure up to the task of illuminating the issues and commenting upon the problems of the day, and if taking a strong editorial stance is so damaging to good business practice, why do the mass media continue to engage in such a hazardous exercise?

The Need for Editorializing

One basic argument for the press, both the print and electronic media, to engage in editorializing—illuminating the intelligence of the day, arguing the merits or demerits of a public issue, seeking the answer to some complex problem of public concern—is that the First Amendment demands it. Thomas I. Emerson, professor of law at Yale University and a First Amendment scholar, has pointed out that:

> A system of freedom of expression, operating in a modern democratic society, is a complex mechanism. At its core is a group of rights assured to individual members of the society. This set of rights, which makes up our present-day concept of free expression, includes the right to form and hold beliefs and opinions on any subject, and to communicate ideas, opinions, and information through any medium—in speech, writing, music, art, or in other ways. . . . From the obverse side it includes the right to hear the views of others and to listen to their version of the facts. It encompasses the right to inquire and, to a degree, the right of access to information.[16]

Press freedom, therefore, carries with it concomitant responsibilities for the mass media to assist individual members of society to engage in what Justice Wendell Holmes has called a marketplace of ideas. In fact, "the best test of truth," he concluded, "is the power of the thought to get itself accepted in the competition of the market."[17] Justice Holmes, of course, was not the first public figure to utter such a "marketplace" philosophy. John Milton stated in the *Areopagitica,* first published in 1644, that

> though all the winds of doctrine were let loose to play upon the earth, so Truth be in the field, we do injuriously by licensing and prohibiting to misdoubt her strength. Let her and Falsehood grapple; who ever knew Truth put to the worse in a free and open encounter?

And Justice Hugo Black, replying to an argument that the First Amendment prohibited the application of antitrust legislation to the press, emphasized the affirmative aspects of the First Amendment. Justice Black said:

> It would be strange indeed . . . if the grave concern for freedom of the press which prompted adoption of the First Amendment should be read as a command that the government was without power to protect that freedom. . . . That Amendment rests on the assumption that the widest possible dissemination of information from diverse and antagonistic sources is essential to the welfare of the public, that a free press is a condition of a free society. . . . Freedom of the press from governmental interference under the First Amendment does not sanction repression of that freedom by private interests.[18]

While the courts have never held that the First Amendment mandates press responsibility,[19] an independent inquiry by the Commission on Freedom of the Press headed by Robert M. Hutchins, then Chancellor of the University of Chicago, found numerous requirements for a free press if it is to be responsible. The Commission concluded that if freedom of the press was "freighted with the reponsibility of providing the current intelligence needed by a free society," at least five requirements must be met:

> Today our society needs, first, a truthful, comprehensive, and intelligent account of the day's events in a context which gives them meaning; second, a forum for the exchange of comment and criticism; third, a means of projecting the opinions and attitudes of the groups in the society to one another; fourth, a method of presenting and clarifying the goals and values of the society; and fifth, a way of reaching every member of the society by the currents of information, thought, and feeling which the press supplies.[20]

The argument that the press should take affirmative action to meet the basic requirements of a free society has developed into the so-called "social responsibility theory" of the press. Clearly the Hutchins' Commission requirements go far beyond the news function of the mass media. Comment and criticism, from both the media and the individual members of society, for example, is clearly a requirement which can only be fulfilled by the editorial, opinion function of the press. (For a discussion of the need for the press to afford an open forum, see Chapter 12.)

One modern-day editorialist, however, viewing the editorial page as a stranger might, didn't like what he saw. "Why do we continue, most of us, to serve up this thin gruel when the world needs vitamins in its diet?" he asked. His answer: too many editorialists "have a disabling case of the 'responsibles.' " One of the cares which weigh too many editorialists down, he noted, is the obligation never to be wrong. As a result, editorials are often compromising and dull, but safe.

> Yet it is not our job to be dull and safe, any more than it is our job to be all-knowing, wise, objective, and long-suffering. Some of this is baggage brought in from the newsroom, whence most of us came. Some of it is plain pomposity. All of it gets in the way. Our job is to move readers, to arouse in them some response above the level of a yawn. It may not be much, but it is the only work we have.[21]

Can the mass media editorialist help serve the function ascribed by Justice Holmes, Justice Black, and the Hutchins' Commission? Can he move the members of his audience to some response above the "level of a yawn"? The findings of empirical researchers in the social sciences would indicate that he can.

Persuasive Effect of Editorials

Most of the resources of newspapers and the news staffs of broadcast stations admittedly are devoted to the communication of information, not persuasive communication. The typical newspaper in the United States devotes about four percent of its non-advertising space to editorial comment. Another 12 percent is devoted to various kinds of columns, some dealing with politics and public affairs. On the same day the television networks are likely to devote about 16 percent of their evening newscasts to commentary. Local stations, however, only rarely include editorial comment in local programming.[22] Despite this focus on providing the audience with information, much of the early communications research dealt with the persuasive function of the media and with attitude change. Since the editorial pages of the nation's newspapers are often filled with political comment and fulminations—some of it thoughtful, scholarly, analytical; some of it shrill, partisan, even obtrusive—it should not be surprising that many researchers dealt with the effect of such political communication on readers. A benchmark study on voting behavior—the ultimate test of political persuasion—during the 1940 presidential campaign indicated that the news media failed to make a significant change in voter attitudes toward Roosevelt and Willkie.[23] Indeed, this and other early research by social scientists into political influence documented so well the pervasive influence of personal factors—the argument that, more than anything else, people influence people—that the likelihood of newspaper endorsements, for example, having any real influence was almost dismissed out of hand. This view has been greatly modified by more recent research, as pointed out in the next section, which finds the media a more effective persuasive agent.

Other researchers, however, have taken issue with placing the mass media in such a persuasive role. They argue that press coverage, perhaps even to include editorial endorsements, generally fails to change a voter's position on a candidate or issue. What the press accomplishes, these researchers argue, is to make people more aware of the issues. In a political campaign, for example, studies have shown that press coverage determines which issues voters feel are important. Under this so-called "agenda-setting" function, it is asserted, the press not only makes the public aware of the issues of a campaign but also sets the public's priorities.[24] In setting the agenda, in determining the priorities in an ongoing debate about an election campaign or a local public issue, the mass media editorialist, therefore, may become an important determinant in the ultimate outcome of the campaign or debate. Research findings pointing to the agenda-setting function of the mass media, in other words, do not lessen the importance of the role played by the press. The findings, indeed, tend to emphasize the overall importance of the communications function of the mass media in the persuasive process.

Editorial Endorsements Do Count

How much is an editorial endorsement worth? Findings by the Institute for Social Research at the University of Michigan indicate that the political stances taken by newspapers in the United States may be among the most underestimated forces in campaign politics. A study of the 1968 presidential campaign, for example, found support for the notion that undecided voters—those who do not have strong alternative forces acting upon them, such as party loyalty—may be influenced by editorial endorsements of even national candidates.[25] The same researcher found that in the 1972 presidential election both Independents and Democrats voted differently depending upon what candidate was endorsed by the newspaper they read most often. Republicans, for some reason, did not appear to be influenced significantly by editorial endorsements.[26] What the research findings on the last five presidential political campaigns demonstrated, according to this researcher, is that political endorsements by newspapers do count and do influence voters at the polls.[27] Other research findings indicate that editorial endorsements may be even more effective at the state and local level. Such endorsements, as might be expected, were found to have the most influence on voters who make up their minds at the last moment.[28]

Arguments about the relative effectiveness of newspaper endorsements of political candidates, about the impact of television on political coverage, about the relationship of this variable and that variable on political persuasion as compared to newspaper endorsements continue unabated. One researcher sees little evidence, for example, that television has a demonstrable impact on voting behavior. In contrast, editorial endorsement by newspapers is seen as making sense out of the glut of partisan campaign appeals, much of it transmitted by television.[29] Even when other factors are taken into account, voters' choices during the 1956, 1960, 1964, 1968, and 1972 presidential campaigns were related to endorsements by newspapers to which they had been exposed. One researcher concluded that "Given the pervasive influences of the newspaper that have recently been isolated in the present data, the time seems ripe for both research investigators and decision-makers to reconsider their disregard of the printed media."[30]

There is little doubt that the impact of editorial endorsements is more highly regarded by social science researchers today than was true when the question was first posed and empirically studied more than a decade ago. This trend, combined with ongoing research stressing the importance of the agenda-setting function of the mass media, further emphasizes the apparently growing importance of the editorial endorsement in the complex process of political persuasion.

The Editorial Function

While the social science researcher may focus his attention on the editorial endorsement, the one aspect of political communication he can best measure, obviously such a press function is episodic, at best. Elections just do not occur that frequently. What are the primary editorial functions of the editorial page or of the broadcast editorial? One may get a different answer wherever he turns.

A newspaper functions as "a lamp of enlightenment to the people," says one editor.

> It can be, and should be, a beacon to illuminate the course of progress for the community it serves. The lamp of enlightenment shines in the news columns. The beacon glows in the editorial pages. It is a torch fed by the vision and wisdom of the editorial policy.[31]

A journalism educator and editorial textbook author views mass media editorials as providing a "gyroscope function," serving as a rudder and compass for the reader or listener, bringing meaning out of the jumble of news and events. Acknowledging that it would be ludicrous to suggest that the opinion function of the mass media provides any universal, one-size-fits-all answer to the daily bewilderment and confusion of the news, he notes that

> it is *not* ludicrous, it is *not* unreasonable, to argue that the gyroscope effect of the opinion function constitutes one of our best remaining hopes of achieving a sense of balance and perspective in the fact of towering apprehensions and a suffocating glut of information and ideas.[32]

The function of the editorial is sometimes viewed as a means of prophesying. It is the prophet's job not only to explain the world but to warn the people when they sin, or stray after false gods, one editor noted. He further observed:

> Editorial writing remains the soul of journalism, and journalism falls down on the job if it doesn't turn its prophets loose. Who ever heard of a gagged Isaiah, a mealy-mouthed Jeremiah? Yet many of today's editorial writers are not allowed the self-disciplined freedom that a confused and troubled country could use.[33]

Horace Greeley's publisher, it has been pointed out, allowed the *New York Tribune* prophet to pursue his anti-slavery, anti-hanging, Socialistic, and other frequent aberrant arguments. The *Tribune* prophet's journalistic voice of a century ago is still remembered, while the publisher, Thomas McElrath, is all but forgotten.

Louis M. Lyons, former curator of the Nieman Foundation, speaking to the National Conference of Editorial Writers, concluded with this advice, and charge, to editorialists:

> Finally, if one needed an excuse for an editorial page, or to try to define the primary role of the page, I think it would be to express the tone of the paper. This even more than the policy of the paper. It's a chance to represent the institution itself, as a civilized and civilizing force, as a concerned and considerate citizen, as a moderate and moderating influence, as a thoughtful person, a good neighbor, one who cares. The tone reflects the character of the paper. Whatever else, whatever encroachments, this does remain your charge.[34]

Similarly, others have referred to the editorial page as the conscience of the medium as well as the community and as a showcase effort for the enlightenment of the public.

Others view the function of mass media editorials much more critically. The editorialist's efforts to explain, to interpret, to illuminate, to advocate, to argue a point of view, for example, are sometimes viewed as too confusing and biased, too windy and pontifical, too detached and irrelevant, too bland and dull, or too shrill and loud. Or, as the comedian Fred Allen said of radio several years ago, some critics view editorials as being ineffectual, as being "as fleeting as a butterfly's cough."

The Media Editorialist

The American editorial writer, what manner of man is he? This and related questions were put to 630 editorial writers for the nation's daily newspapers in a survey conducted for the National Conference of Editorial Writers in 1971.[35] The study was similar but broader in scope than a study conducted by the NCEW a decade earlier. Editorial writers, according to the 1971 survey, appeared to be slightly younger (a mean age of 48.4 as compared to 50 in 1962), happier in their jobs, and comparatively better educated than they were a decade earlier. Although active in public affairs organizations, they expressed a reluctance to engage in partisan political memberships for fear of jeopardizing their impartiality. They viewed their job as highly prestigious, ranking below only high public office holders, nuclear physicists, novelists, and physicians.

Responses to a question about political party preferences indicated that the often expressed view that the nation's editorial pages are overwhelmingly conservative and Republican, if true, occurs despite the personal views of editorial writers. More than 48 percent, for example, reported their political leanings were Independent, 30 percent Democrat, and 17 percent Republican. In response to a statement: "the editorial writer, in order to preserve the ability to make impartial judgments, should avoid membership in partisan political organizations," 50 percent marked strongly agree, 28 percent agreed, 12 percent disagreed, 3 percent strongly disagreed, and 6 percent had no feelings one way or the other. One question inevitably raised by the data, however, is whether or not a conflict exists between the opinions expressed on partisan political activity and the editorialist's actual behavior.

A long-standing debate has continued for many years within American journalism, one group of researchers observes, over the definition of what constitutes a responsible role for the journalist. The debate involved two polar values often posed as questions: (1) Should the journalist be a "neutral" observer, an impartial transmission link dispensing information to the public, or (2) Should he be a "participant," playing a more active role by interpreting and interrelating the information he reports. In the neutral image, news is seen to emerge naturally from the events and occurrences of the real world with the journalist, as a spectator, faithfully and accurately reporting what he observes. The journalist's relationship to information is thus one of detachment and neutrality. In the participant image, the journalist must play a more active, watchdog role, assuming a personal responsibility for the information he reports. The active-passive dimension is further differentiated in terms of the controls exercised over the content of the news story. The neutral observer allows control to be vested in the events observed while the participant orientation sees the control as vested in the journalist himself.[36]

The factors found to delineate the journalist's conception of professional responsibility (his "neutral" or "participant" image), as reported in the above research, may give some insight into the values of the mass media editorialist. The editorialist is, without doubt, more associated with the participant image than the neutral. It is interesting to note that the participant newsman was found to be better educated than the neutral journalist. The editorialist is usually better educated than the newsman with more than 82 percent of the NCEW sample holding baccalaureate degrees, 20 percent with master's degrees, and an additional 19 percent with some graduate work. Participant values are also related positively with the level of income and with the larger news organizations located in larger cities.

It is also interesting that the participant newsman's journalistic responsibility appears to be reinforced by informal relationships with other journalists, not with attachments and integration into the social structure of the community—as is often true with those holding the neutral image. This independence of the journalist from community ties better enables him to investigate, analyze, even crusade. Formal allegiances with news sources, both with public figures and individuals not involved directly in the news, might compromise the journalist's ability to exercise such independent judgment. The editorialist, likewise, needs to maintain such an independent stance.

It should be remembered, however, that this younger, happier, better educated, participant-oriented mass media editorialist as described above is but the image of a composite profile which emerges from only two empirical studies. Such a profile may or may not be accurate when projected to the present membership lists of the National Conference of Editorial Writers or the National Broadcast Editorial Association. It should be remembered also that a common complaint of the mass media editorialist is that he labors on a staff that is often too small to meet the challenges which his role demands. It is possible that this understaffing problem may have more effect on the ultimate role performed by the mass media editorialist than any of the profile characteristics discussed above.

Rising to the Editorial Challenge

The overall editorial performance of newspapers has been both lavishly praised and soundly condemned by segments of the public during the past decade. Newspapers, for example, have been called "the greatest medium yet devised for making all the people of a community alive to the common interests and problems they face each day."[37] The editorial page has also been linked with the news pages of newspapers to being the subject of frequent complaints in correspondence to the National News Council. Such complaints place the newspaper editorialist "on the firing line," according to Ned Schnurman, associate director of the Council, and affords a "kind of barometer of public reaction on this sensitive subject."[38] One of the complaints is a growing public sense of discontent over the rapidly blurring lines between what is news and what is editorial comment in the print media. Schnurman observed that it is a relatively simple matter for the News Council to dispose of critics who rail against editorial pages that they don't like and complain that newspapers have no right to their own opinions or to print the opinions of syndicated columnists with which they do not agree. He pointed out:

> No doubt the volume of such anti-editorial mail has remained constant for generations. But the new voice of opposition parallels the rise of the new journalism, which, in the case of some entire publications, means advocacy journalism (editorializing) on any and all sub-

> jects covered. The traditional dailies have generally resisted this trend, but those same papers also often carry syndicated columns that are not easy to distinguish—typographically at least—from news stories in their pages.[39]

Even though these complaints are usually dismissed by the News Council, the problem of such identification is one that should be met and dealt with by the editors charged with the make-up of the paper's opinion pages, Schnurman said.

Many editors have recognized the frustration of readers who have a difficult time distinguishing between the newspaper's factual news content and its opinion and commentary. The *Louisville* (Ky.) *Times,* for example, publishes a letter-from-the-editor from time to time about such matters. In a recent letter headed "Why we must print commentary," Michael J. Davies, managing editor of the *Times,* in a prefatory note, said: "Newspapers are in the business of helping readers understand their world. But we feel that readers often don't understand their newspapers. This is another in a series of articles in which editors and company executives explain what our papers do, and why."

Although the opinion function of the mass media is often challenged, the need for such an effort is frequently supported. One defender of the press, noting that there is a profound difference between reportage and journalism, concluded:

> An evolving communications technology is rapidly finding new ways to compete with the newspaper's function as a routine record of the day's events. But no technological change can ever challenge the newspaper's command of big ideas, its traditions of deep inquiry, sweeping synthesis, and inspired advocacy. Tomorrow's newspaper must be not merely a register, but a tribune, not merely a ledger, but a clarion.[40]

How can the American newspaper page become a "clarion" rather than merely a "ledger"? One approach is through the fostering of more professional methods and goals to enhance both the literary excellence of the editorial output as well as boosting the prestige of the mass media editorialist and commentator. Dwight Sargent, former editorial page editor of the *New York Herald Tribune,* former curator of the Nieman Foundation, and president of the Freedom of Information Foundation at the University of Missouri, noted more than a decade ago:

> The nation's editorial pages address themselves to a larger congregation than all our preachers, bend the ear of more people than all our bartenders, counsel more customers than our barbers and taxi drivers and speak to a bigger classroom than our teachers. A sobering thought, this.[41]

The National Conference of Editorial Writers has devoted its efforts to finding ways for its members to live up to their responsibilities through a continuing commitment to the profession's highest traditions of civic leadership, Sargent contended. Its members take seriously its "Basic Statement of Principles," revised after extended debate in 1975. The preamble and nine "injunctions" to editorial practitioners provide excellent guidelines for the mass media editorialist, whether he is employed by the print or electronic media. The preamble states:

> Editorial writing is more than another way of making money. It is a profession devoted to the public welfare and to public service. The chief duty of its practitioners is to provide the information and guidance toward sound judgments that are essential to the healthy functioning of a democracy. Therefore, editorial writers owe it to their integrity and that of their profession to observe the following injunctions:
>
> (For a listing of the entire "Basic Statement of Principles," including the injunctions, see page 15.)

Katharine Graham, publisher of the *Washington Post,* a strong editorial voice in the nation's capital, commenting upon the editorial role of a newspaper, took note that the editorial and op-ed pages of a newspaper are fundamentally different than any of the other pages of the paper. Here the publisher, the editorial page editors, the editorial writers, the syndicated columnists, guest writers and readers themselves pass judgment, offer their views and openly give expression to their views and opinions, both individually or collectively. In the editorials, Mrs. Graham noted, the newspaper, as an institution, speaks directly and usually anonymously to its audience. But, the *Washington Post* publisher observed:

> That editorial voice may be olympian or chatty. It may thunder, exhort or chide. At best it will be eloquent, perceptive and persuasive; at worst capricious, uninformed or dull. Whatever its nature, it is that voice, more than any other single aspect of a newspaper, which day by day expresses the institution's convictions and conveys its personality.[42]

It is this editorial voice, this opinion function of the mass media—as exercised by the newspaper editorialist and broadcast commentator, the critical reviewer and the syndicated columnist, the personal columnist and the letter writer—with which the following chapters deal.

NOTES for Chapter 1

[1] See Jim Allee Hart, *Views on the News: The Developing Editorial Syndrome, 1500–1800* (Carbondale, Ill.: Southern Illinois University Press, 1970).

[2] *Ibid.*, pp. 178–96.

[3] See John B. Oakes, "Pages Are Alive—and Kicking," *The Masthead* 28 (Winter 1976): 17–20.

[4] Philip L. Geyelin, "Who Listens to Your Bugle Calls?" *The Masthead* 28 (Winter 1976): 14–17.

[5] See "In the Matter of the Mayflower Broadcasting Corp. and the Yankee Network, Inc. (WAAB)," 8 F.C.C. 333, 338 (January 16, 1941).

[6] "In the Matter of Editorializing by Broadcast Licenses," 13 F.C.C. 1246 (June 1, 1949).

[7] "Applicability of the Fairness Doctrine in the Handling of Controversial Issues of Public Importance," 29 *Fed. Reg.* 10415, adopted July 1, 1964; printed July 25, 1964.

[8] Ted Landphair, "The Apple Pie Doctrine," *Radio-TV Editorial Journal* 2 (January-February 1977): 24–25.

[9] See, e.g., Peter M. Sandman, David M. Rubin, and David B. Sachsman, *Media: An Introductory Analysis of American Mass Communications,* 2d ed. (Englewood Cliffs, N.J.: Prentice-Hall, 1976), p. 317.

[10] For a general statement of the shortcomings of the press as surveyed in the 1940's, see The Commission on Freedom of the Press, *A Free and Responsible Press* (Chicago: University of Chicago Press, 1947).

[11] Sandman, Rubin, and Sachsman, *Media,* p. 266.

[12] Ben H. Bagdikian, "Editorial Pages Change—But Too Slowly," *The Masthead* 19 (Summer 1967): 96–100.

[13] For a report on MacDougall and other panelists, see Paul B. Hope, "We're the Problem," *The Masthead* 26 (Winter 1974–75): 6–8.

[14] For a discussion of the history of NCEW, see Dwight Sargent, "The Goal of Self-Criticism Endures," *The Masthead* 27 (Fall 1975): 17–18.

[15] James Reston, "Criticizing Ourselves," *The Masthead* 28 (Spring 1976): 42.

[16] Thomas I. Emerson, *The System of Freedom of Expression* (New York: Random House, 1970), p. 3.

[17] Abrams v. United States, 250 U.S. 616 (1919).

[18] Associated Press v. United States, 326 U.S. 1 (1945).

[19] Chief Justice Warren Burger, writing for the majority of the Court in *Miami Herald Publishing Co. v. Tornillo,* noted that "A responsible press is an undoubtedly desirable goal, but press responsibility is not mandated by the Constitution and like many other virtues it cannot be legislated." 418 U.S. 241, 256 (1974).

[20] Commission on Freedom of the Press, *A Free and Responsible Press,* pp. 20–21.

[21] William P. Cheshire, "A Memo to Editorial Boards," *The Masthead* 24 (Summer 1972): 1–2.

[22] See Lee B. Becker, Maxwell E. McCombs, and Jack M. McLeod, "The Development of Political Cognitions," in *Political Communication: Issues and Strategies for Research,* ed: Steven H. Chafee (Beverly Hills, Calif.: Sage Publications, 1975), p. 21.

[23] Paul Lazarsfeld, et al., *The People's Choice* (New York: Duell, Sloan and Pearce, 1944).

[24] For a discussion of the agenda-setting function, see William Glavin, "Political Influence of the Press," *ANPA News Research Bulletin* 4 (November 10, 1976).

[25] See John P. Robinson, "Perceived Media Bias and the 1968 Vote: Can the Media Affect Behavior After All?" *Journalism Quarterly* 49 (Summer 1972): 239–46.

[26] John P. Robinson, "The Press as King-Maker: What Surveys from the Last Five Campaigns Show." *Journalism Quarterly* 51 (Winter 1974): 587–94.

[27] See "Endorsements Do Count," *The Masthead* 26 (Summer 1974): 64–66.

[28] Maxwell McCombs, "Editorial Endorsements: A Study of Influence," *Journalism Quarterly* 44 (Autumn 1967): 545–48.

[29] See Robinson, "The Press as King-Maker," p. 587.

[30] *Ibid.*, p. 594.

[31] William H. Heath, "Editorial Policy," *The Masthead* 19 (Summer 1967): 66–70.

[32] John L. Hulteng, *The Opinion Function: Editorial and Interpretive Writing for the News Media* (New York: Harper & Row, 1973), pp. 179–80.

[33] Herbert Brucker, "The Prophet Motive," *The Masthead* 22 (Summer 1970): 9–12.

[34] Louis M. Lyons, "What's Left for Editorial Writers?" *The Quill* (March, 1971): p. 11.

[35] For distribution tables of responses, see Cleveland Wilhoit and Dan Drew, "A Profile of the Editorial Writer," *The Masthead* 23 (Fall 1971): 2–14.

[36] See John W. C. Johnstone, Edward J. Slawski, and William W. Bowman, "The Professional Values of American Newsmen," *Public Opinion Quarterly* 36 (Winter 1972–73): 522–40.

[37] Leo Bogart, "Changing News Interests and the News Media," *Public Opinion Quarterly* 32 (Winter 1968–69): 450–74.

[38] Ned Schnurman, "The Blurring Lines," *The Masthead* 26 (Summer 1974): 61–63.

[39] *Ibid.*, p. 61.

[40] Bogart, "Changing News Interests," p. 574.

[41] Dwight E. Sargent, "National Conference of Editorial Writers: 'A Working Group, and No joking,' " *The Bulletin of the American Society of Newspaper Editors* (Jan. 1, 1964): 6–7, 10.

[42] Katharine Graham, " 'We': A Preface," in *The Editorial Page*, ed.: Laura Longley Babb (Boston: Houghton Mifflin, 1977), p. 1.

2

The Editorial: *An Attempt Toward Defining & Classifying*

SOMEONE ONCE DESCRIBED the editorial writer as "He who after the battle is over descends from the mountain and slays the wounded." There are countless more flattering, and hopefully, more functional and accurate definitions and classifications of the editorial. Several such definitions and classifications will be examined in this chapter. Such a discussion should serve two functions: (1) it should help to distinguish and clarify for journalism students the various forms and types of opinion writing, and (2) it should afford the media professional a few ideas on how to better inform and educate his readers or listeners concerning both the recognition of and the distinction between opinion writing and the more factual news reports.

In regard to the first function, it should be noted that not every article, column, or item which appears on the newspaper editorial page is necessarily opinion, nor does every feature labeled "column," wherever it appears, necessarily guarantee that it is largely opinion. Nor is the opinion in a broadcast news program limited to that portion labeled "editorial." A more functional approach to distinguishing between news and opinion writing is to view the content of the mass media as a continuum rather than to attempt a dichotomous objective-subjective classification. At one end of the continuum is the straight, factual news report relatively free of any assertions from the writer; at the other end is the more formal editorial which deals almost entirely with case-making and the expression of opinion. In between these two polar points, from the more objective to the more subjective, is the feature article which seeks to highlight human interest; the interpretative and background stories which explain the more complex news or place the events being reported in a more meaningful frame of reference; news analyses and commentary which may often engage in attempts to persuade the reader of the rightness of the writer's point of view; and various critical reviews of literary and artistic efforts. Once such a continuum has been established, it can be said that the opinion function of the mass media lies in those types of writing located on the subjective end of the news-editorial continuum.

The second function listed above may be served if the definitions and classifications arrived at by the mass media editorialist can be disseminated to the reader or listener so that he may better understand the policies being followed by the newspaper or broadcast station. As noted in Chapter 1, the National News Council receives frequent complaints indicating a growing public sense of discontent over the often blurred distinctions between what is news and what is editorial comment in the print media. Former Vice President Spiro T. Agnew, in his attacks on the press in 1969, was critical of both the print and electronic media, but he was particularly critical of the failure of television to separate its comment—particularly the "instant analysis" of speeches by the President—from its news reports. Others have noted that the audiences of both the print and electronic media often do not distinguish between the medium's factual reports and its commentary.

To overcome such misunderstanding, newspapers have taken various approaches in explaining editorial policy to their readers. Some use the "Letter From the Editor" approach as noted above in regard to the *Louisville* (Ky.) *Times.* A number of newspapers have adopted a reader's advocate or ombudsman approach, as has the *St. Louis Post-Dispatch* in its "Readers Advocate" column. One of the duties of an ombudsman is to explain editorial policy, as well as *faux pas* by the newspaper, to its readers. Other newspapers periodically explain to readers in an editorial page box or feature just where the opinion content of the newspaper is located. The Carbondale, Illinois, *Southern Illinoisan,* for example, publishes this information from time to time on the editorial page:

NEWS AND VIEWS

The Southern Illinoisan presents the newspaper's opinions, the viewpoints of readers and the opinions of staff members clearly marked as such.

—The newspaper's opinions are carried on the editorial page, marked as "Editorials—Our Opinions."

—The views of readers who wish to express their own opinions are carried in the "Letters to the Editor" column on the Editorial Page.

—The personal opinions of members of the staff run in the signed columns, "From Where I Sit," "Byline BG," "M.E. Too" and in the personal columns on the sports pages. The opinions are not necessarily those of the newspaper.

—News background, commentary and news analysis articles are marked as such to alert you they are different in nature from the usual news stories.

In our other material, whether taken from the wire services or written by our staff, we try to be as objective and as fair as is humanly possible, to report all of the facts as accurately as we can get them.

Broadcast commentary on network news programs is usually designated as commentary, both through lead ins and, on television, by graphic means. Often the commentary is given by someone other than the news announcer, for example, Eric Sevareid on the CBS evening news. On local news programs, however, the handling of commentary often brings complaints from listeners or viewers who fail to note any difference between the commentary designated as editorial, which members of the audience can answer, and commentary given as a part of the news program, which they may be refused a right to answer. This problem will be discussed further below.

If it is granted that the journalism student needs to become aware of the various classifications of materials falling under the opinion content of the mass media and that the various audiences of the news media frequently need to be informed about the classification and location of such materials, then the task remains to probe efforts to define and classify these various types of opinion.

What Is an Editorial?

An editorial may be thought of as a journalistic essay which either attempts (1) to inform or explain, (2) to persuade or convince, or (3) to stimulate insight in an entertaining or humorous manner. As an essay the editorial may be thought of as having an introduction, a body, and a conclusion. In terms of the various forms of composition, it may employ exposition, narration, description, or argumentation. In fact, many of the definitions examined below have elements of the various characteristics attributed to essays.

William Allen White, editor and publisher of the *Emporia* (Kan.) *Gazette,* possibly one of the best known editorial writers of the so-called "Golden Age" of journalism, said:

> . . . generally speaking, an editorial is an expression of opinion based upon a selection of facts which present a truth in a new light—something that everyone knows which no one before ever thought of![1]

Leon Flint begins his editorial writing textbook, *The Editorial,* used for many years in journalism schools throughout the United States, with this definition:

> The editorial—the published expression of the opinions of an editor—is one of the many mediums through which men have satisfied their instinct to spread ideas. Storm centers of thought furnish its natural habitat.[2]

M. Lyle Spencer, the author of *Editorial Writing,* another standard textbook for many years, wraps up the editorial in a neat, compact package:

> An editorial may be defined as a presentation of fact and opinion in concise, logical, pleasing order for the sake of entertaining, of influencing opinion, or of interpreting significant news in such a way that its importance to the average reader will be clear.[3]

Borrowing from these sources, Jim Allee Hart, reporting upon the historical forerunners, precursors, roots, and derivations of the newspaper editorial in his book, *Views on the News: 1500–1800,* said:

> The modern editorial is a presentation of fact and opinion in a concise, logical, pleasing order for the sake of entertaining, of influencing opinion, or of interpreting significant news in such a way that its importance is clear to the average reader.[4]

He noted, however, that such an interpretation of events is viewed from the standpoint of certain principles or policies adopted or advocated by the newspaper publishing it. In this sense an editorial is largely biased; it becomes the mouthpiece, the very personality of the newspaper. Hart observed:

> If we accept this explanation of the editorial and if we recognize that the term "editorial" was originally an adjectival modifier of the word "article" and meant an article written by the editor, it becomes easier for us to understand its evolution. Origins and forerunners of the modern editorial begin to stand out from the welter of newspaper opinion writing before 1800.[5]

However, only on the smaller newspapers, for example, those in the less than 100,000 circulation category, would editorials likely be written by the publisher or corporate publisher today. But the concept of the editorial as the newspaper's institutional voice largely remains. For this reason, editorials—in contrast to opinion columns, critical reviews, or news-analysis type articles—are usually published anonymously. The views expressed in unsigned editorials, therefore, are theoretically those of the newspaper as an institution. Editorial anonymity is based upon myth-making, according to one critic of the practice, and its use should be re-examined by editorialists.[6] The practice, however, is still prevalent in newspapers throughout the United States.

Questions regarding the definition and classification of opinion writing, however, may still remain, for example: How does one distinguish between news, interpretation, and opinion? Lester Markel, former Sunday editor of the *New York Times,* once delineated the concepts in this fashion: What someone says is news; why it was said is interpretation; whether or not it should have been said is opinion. On another occasion Markel commented: What you see is news; what you know is background; what you feel is opinion. All of which may be another way of saying that the concept of news and opinion being viewed as a dichotomy should give way to a news-opinion or objective-subjective continuum. The formal newspaper editorial—usually separated and labeled as the opinion of the newspaper and published anonymously—might then be considered as that segment of writing which falls at the extreme subjective end of the news-opinion continuum.

Classified as to Parts

Most editorials, as essays generally, have three parts. For the essay it is the introduction, the body, and the conclusion. The editorial essay's three parts are (1) the statement of the subject, issue, or thesis, (2) comment about the subject, issue, or problem, and (3) a conclusion or solution drawn from the comment. Unlike the essay, the editorial's parts are not necessarily in that order. An editorial, for example, may open with the conclusion, or an aspect of the conclusion. And the statement of the subject and the comment may be interspersed. Indeed, the skillful editorial writer will often comment on the facts of the event or issue as they are presented, meshing fact with opinion in every sentence where possible. The fact that an editorial has three parts, however, does not mean that it is necessarily lengthy. This classic comment by Editor White, of the *Emporia Gazette,* written as one paragraph, has the essential elements of a three-part editorial. White wrote:

> Frank Munsey, the great publisher, is dead. Frank Munsey contributed to the journalism of his day the great talent of a meat packer, the morals of a money changer and the manners of an undertaker. He and his kind have about succeeded in transforming a once great profession into an eight per-cent security. May he rest in trust! [7]

The first sentence is a factual statement of the subject with no comment except for the satiric use of "great." The next two sentences are comment. The last sentence, "May he rest in trust!," is an explicit conclusion.

Most effective editorials have three parts. An editorial, however, may have only two parts: a statement of the subject, and comment, but no conclusion. Such an editorial, as noted in Chapter 9, isn't likely to be very persuasive. It is possible, of course, to write a one-part editorial using description as comment, for example, of the beauty of a landscape with no stated subject and no conclusion.

Classified as to Purpose

Various of the definitions discussed above make reference to the purpose of editorial comment, for example, Flint's reference to interpretation, influencing opinion, and entertainment. A more recent textbook in editorial writing used three similar categories as classifications for the pigeonholing and discussion of editorials by type: (1) editorials that inform or explain, (2) editorials that try to convert, and (3) editorials that amuse or amaze.

The editorial written for the purpose of informing the reader or explaining to him the meaning of some complex event or issue of general or public interest is related to the expository essay. Its purpose is to interpret or to illuminate, but not necessarily to argue a point of view. Such editorials may be only one step beyond the more objective treatment of the event or issue as reported in the news columns, extending those reports where needed to put them in a better perspective for the reader. This extension may be to place the event or issue in an historical perspective, relating it to what has gone before. It may be to relate the news event or issue to other previously reported events or issues, placing the recent development in a more meaningful frame of reference, illuminating its importance for the reader. It may be to discuss a question or problem raised by the news event or issue presented in the news columns in terms of alternative solutions or answers for the purpose of illuminating the problem or the significance of the question for readers. An editorial written for the purpose of informing and explaining, however, would theoretically stop short of advocating or arguing that a preferred solution or answer be accepted by the reader.

During the textbook adoption controversy in the Kanawha County, West Virginia, schools, John Daniell Maurice, editor of the *Charleston Daily Mail,* wrote more than fifty editorials trying to provide leadership in the turmoil. The series won him the 1975 Pulitzer Prize for editorial writing. The following editorial from the series first explores some agreements underlying the differences held by those engaged in the controversy. Then the editorial suggests "some new consensus," but the overall editorial approach is a plea for understanding, not an argument.

CAN TOM JEFFERSON BE SAVED FOR POSTERITY?

From a mile or so behind the battle lines, there is much that is encouraging in this prolonged war over textbooks.

Underlying all the difference, there is a unanimous agreement that literacy is better than illiteracy. It is so much better that there is no objection whatever to a compulsory attendance law which says to the child that he must attend school.

Beyond all dispute there is a unanimous agreement that as the child is compelled to try it makes a great difference what he reads. When he grows up, he may read what he pleases—or nothing at all. But during his minority, as he studies under public auspices, what he reads is just as important as the skill itself. No one learns to read in a vacuum.

There is still another agreement, by and large. English literature remains the source from which this "what" must be drawn. Where else can an English-speaking people turn for the source material which preserves their traditions, refines their tastes and shapes their sense of identity and common purpose?

But along about here the agreement breaks down. It breaks down because there is no longer any consensus on what constitutes the body of English literature and how it may be distinguished from trash in the instruction of the young.

Horatio Alger, as someone has noted, is out. Allen Ginsburg has taken his place. Oddly, Shakespeare survives, although he was as thoroughgoing a humanist as Western civilization has produced—the first great poet who was not a deeply religious man. Mark Twain hangs on by the skin of his teeth. He was surely a skeptic and probably a racist as well. Admiral Farragut is done for. In the heat of battle, he said "Damn the torpedoes." "Damn," as everyone ought to know, is a no-no.

One awaits the shattering discovery that Thomas Jefferson was not altogether what he seemed to be. He was a deist, at best, and something of an anti-clerical. Besides, there was a dark chapter in his private life which American history has chosen to gloss over. Can the Declaration of Independence be saved—and with it the luxurious freedom to debate these issues and learn from them?

And one says this from a personal conviction that a skilled teacher could introduce Genesis, the Book of Job, the story of David, the Psalms into the public school curriculum—without offense to the Constitution and to the great improvement of the literature texts. This same skilled teacher could save Shakespeare, although he was a dark and troubled man whose counsel may be read as the religion of nihilism and despair.

In short, there is a need for some new consensus and a base for it. Eventually, among people who wish to preserve their freedom from both ignorance and indoctrination, it will emerge. The object, remember, is an adult who can live with himself and his neighbors without making an obsolute nuisance of his life and a wreckage of his social order.

It cannot emerge in the heat of battle, under the threat of terror, on some pretense that the cause of education is served by enforcing some non-attendance law at which everyone grows older wiser by staying home from school.

Charleston (W. Va.) *Daily Mail,* November 4, 1974
Reprinted by permission.

The editorial which attempts to persuade, which attempts to influence, or which attempts to convert a reader to the point of view being expounded is the type dear to the editorialist's heart. Such an editorial is clearly at the polar point on the objective-subjective continuum. As discussed in Chapter 10, editorials written to persuade and influence may have greater success in reinforcing opinions and attitudes already held than in converting readers holding views initially opposed to those being advocated by the editorialist. The emphasis, perhaps, should be on the word "try" or "attempt" in the category heading rather than upon the word "convert." Or, editorials in this category might better be identified as those which argue or advocate a point of view. While the point of view being advocated, the solution being offered, or the action being called for may not be accepted by readers holding contrary views, such an editorial effort still may be worthwhile if it does nothing more than to reinforce the opinions of those who look favorably toward the views being advocated. Such a reinforcement function is important, if for no other reason than it inoculates readers against future counterarguments.

A series of twenty editorials published in the *Nevada State Journal* and the *Reno Evening Gazette* attacking the alleged political influence of brothel operator Joe Conforte won Pulitzer Prize awards in 1977 for three Reno newspaper editorialists: Warren L. Lerude, Foster Church, and Norman F. Cardoza. The following is representative of the hard-hitting argumentative editorials in the series, this one written by Lerude.

CONFORTE POWER MUST BE ENDED FOR PUBLIC GOOD

"He is no longer a 'colorful local character.' His tactics are undesirable in our community and are serously undermining our credibility."

Joe Conforte is the subject.

Businessmen and women serving on the Greater Reno Chamber of Commerce Board of Directors, under the leadership of Bill Kottinger, are addressing Conforte with the above words.

These respected business leaders are to be praised for speaking out.

For far too long Conforte has been tolerated in Reno and Sparks by persons who like to smile and say, ah, what the heck, he's just another businessman.

He is not just another businessman.

He runs a whorehouse. Nothing wrong there in Storey County, whose officials have agreed to legalizing prostitution.

But he pushes for heavy influence over the public officials in Reno and Sparks, two cities whose residents have declared Conforte's business to be illegal.

Conforte is not to be opposed because he operates a brothel. In most of Nevada, brothels are quite well accepted from a pragmatic point of view.

Conforte is to be opposed because he sweeps into his influence public officials who, generally speaking, are ashamed to admit their relationship with him.

How many officials in the Nevada Legislature and other governmental bodies are in political debt to Conforte, perhaps we will never know because most of them are hiding their financial ties to the brothel operator. They are afraid of public opinion and won't own up to their acceptance of his money.

The only time officials seem to acknowledge the facts are when the newspapers or a grand jury expose the truth.

Then the officials try to shrug off Conforte as just another businessman.

A rather large group of business people is speaking out today and making it quite clear they don't believe Conforte is any such thing.

These businessmen delivered to the *Gazette* and *Journal* a statement on Friday afternoon which they wished to share with the community, and the news in that statement is published on the front page.

Including their reference to Conforte's quote that "everybody's laughing" at the Washoe County Grand Jury for issuing a report critical of public officials who allow themselves to be tied in with Conforte.

The businessmen and women call Conforte's view "unbelievably arrogant." And they go on to say: "If people are laughing, it is appalling that we would allow any individual to so insinuate himself into the community that we would laugh at his insults to our intelligence. Perhaps this silence is due to a fear of retribution against decent law-abiding citizens. No one individual would want to subject himself to possible public embarrassment or private harassment—or worse, but if the populace speaks with a unified voice, perhaps Mr. Conforte will get the message that his philosophy is bad for the community and completely unacceptable."

Bravo.

It's refreshing to see the business leaders of those two cities coming out and opposing Conforte's influence in city hall.

The news of their opposition to Conforte will be well received, we're sure, in other communities across the country whose residents have cast bitter glances at Reno and Sparks because of the Conforte political power.

This is a positive day for Reno and Sparks.

The Gazette suggests more of the same strong opposition should continue to be voiced by the citizenry until Conforte's influence in our city halls is eliminated and the politicians of Washoe County are served notice that a whorehouse operator who wants to pick police chiefs is not just another businessman but, in fact, is an arrogant and intolerable influence against the public good.

Conforte wishes to run a whorehouse. Fine. Let him stay in one. And let the city halls of Reno and Sparks be restored to places of a greater respect.

Nevada State Journal and *Reno Evening Gazette,* March 20, 1976.
Reprinted by permission.

The third category of editorials, those written to amuse or amaze, may have a serious purpose, may attempt to illuminate an issue, or may even attempt to advocate, but the approach taken by such an editorial will likely be different. The serious, straightforward approach, for example, may be abandoned for a change-of-pace piece which relies upon satire or irony for its effect. The tone may be sprightly and humorous, if the subject matter allows for such treatment. Or the editorialist may become a personal columnist writing more informally, more personally, more folksy. He may rely upon his narrative skills to try to capture a mood, to depict the color of an event, to render the essence of a scene through whatever appropriate literary devices or techniques he can marshal. The editorialist who possesses a light touch or a quick wit, or who is infected with a sense of humor and a desire to write more creatively, can work toward brightening the editorial page just as the feature writer can bring a spark of life to the often dreary news columns.

Here is an example of an editorial, this one from the *Detroit Free Press,* written primarily to entertain the reader. Unlike many change-of-pace efforts, it is not satiric or humorous, nor does it deal with an unusual happening or set of facts. The editorialist simply reminisces about the winter rainfall, describing its effect upon Detroit and the Michigan midlands, rendering the scene—the blazing fireplace within, wondering about the past effect of the rain upon the primitive cave dweller, capturing the mood which the rain casts upon city dwellers.

THE VAGABOND RAIN

Rain. Splink. Splank. Splunk. It comes hesitantly at first, then the splinks and the splanks run into each other, and form a staccato drumming on the roof.

If it's dark, and the wind is soughing through the winter-denuded elms, all the elements are present to make a blazing fireplace seem the fulfillment of all that is good and beautiful. Primitive man must have felt the same urgings, and the soot from his fires still darkens the roofs of caves from the Dordogne to Ajanta and Ellora.

It's easy to imagine that the cave art spreading across the walls of these stony sanctuaries was drawn and painted, many times, when it was raining outside.

The rain is a vagabond. It comes to us from distant places, so that when we read one morning that it is raining in Minneapolis or Milwaukee, it's not surprising if rain from that same frontal system reaches Detroit that night.

Rain speaks to us not only of the upper reaches of Ol' Man River in Minnesota and the sand counties of Wisconsin, but of storms and squalls ruffling the waters of Superior, mixed with the first soft snows of the Ontario lake country.

It speaks of thunder clouds rolling across Grand Traverse Bay, of sheets of lightning sweeping the Michigan midlands, of rain over Bad Axe, Fargo and Flat Rock.

In Detroit the upper stories of skyscrapers are obscured by the rain clouds, and seeing the skyline on a rainy morning, its dips and rises shorn even by a blanket of mist, approximates the leveling process done by storm clouds to great mountain ranges. Skyscrapers and mountains both are reminded of their earthly origins in a storm.

The faint cackling of Canada geese overhead on a rainy night resurrects immediately the old story that the geese must be lost, circling tirelessly to try to get their bearings. A flock of sparrows, or one or two doves, driven by the wind into a refuge of shrubbery, is taken as a sign of foreboding for the intensity of the storm that is to follow.

The strange light that precedes a good rain flattens out details. And puts an edge of electricity on the air. And then the rain . . .

And after it's over, the world smells clean again—not soapy-clean but, well, just clean.

Splink. Splank. Splunk. The dripping rain completes the circle, and the earth is reborn.

Detroit Free Press, November 4, 1975
Reprinted with permission.

The Editorial Paragraph

Related to the change-of-pace editorial written to amuse or amaze is the news-slant editorial paragraph used by many newspapers, either as editorial fillers or, in some instances, to be combined in a panel with a column heading as an editorial page feature. Paragraphing, once practiced by hundreds of editorialists on a regular basis for publication in both daily and weekly newspapers, has gone into decline since its wide use during the 1920's and 1930's. Two reasons are given for the decline of the paragraph: (1) syndication has afforded newspapers a more economical supply of such material, discouraging the development of local talent, and (2) modern readers, because of disparate cultural and educational interests, no longer find the paragraphs as desirable as was true during the pre-World War II period. One of the most successful syndicated paragraphers, Bill Vaughan of the *Kansas City Star,* and author of the "Senator Soaper" syndicated column of paragraphs, commenting upon the paragrapher's declining audience, observed:

> The causes, I think, are several. One is that the good paragraph presupposes a certain literacy on the part of the reader—a familiarity with current events, coupled with enough background of history (and not

> textbook history, exclusively, but the history of baseball, beer and burlesque, as well) and a willingness to be amused by words. In this sense our people are becoming less literate. They seem largely unable to decide by themselves if a thing is funny; they need the roar of a studio audience to reassure them.[8]

Editorial paragraphs may be identified by their brevity and epigrammatic structure. The best of them are no more than twenty to thirty words long which briefly restate some news fact or news event and make a quip or comment about the event. The comment may be a bright, witty thought tersely and ingeniously expressed; it may be a pun, or it may be amusing or humorous because of the statement's incongruity, because of the juxtaposition of contrasting elements, because of exaggeration, or because of some other method of eliciting humor.

Rufus Terral, former editorial writer for the *St. Louis Post-Dispatch,* defined the editorial paragraph as "a piece of editorial ordnance . . . It is a spitball lovingly fired out of a rubber band, a tack placed thoughtfully in a chair. But though it is a small, lowly modest item of the journalistic arsenal, it has its uses."[9] Terral's advice for writing editorial paragraphs is as brief as are his "spitballs." He noted that as few words as possible should intervene between the subject and the comment, and that the word or phrase that explodes the comment should be the last word or phrase in the paragraph. Here are three modern-day, student-written, news-slant paragraphs which Terral might approve of and which might have appealed to the national audience of a "Senator Soaper":

> Idi Amin is not really dead; he is just holding out for a bigger contract.
>
> The trans-Alaskan pipeline is not only designed to help the nation's fuel hogs, the first oil was led down the pipeline by a pig.
>
> Anita Bryant may lose her job as a result of her anti-gay campaign; her orange juice sponsors fear she may have had one o.j. too many.

The news-slant paragraph, as other forms of condensation, is often difficult to write well. Such writing, however, may serve not only to brighten up the editorial page, but a paragraph may become just the filler needed to justify an editorial column during the makeup process.

Other Editorial Classifications

In addition to classification by purpose, editorials also may be classified (1) by form of composition, (2) by appeal, (3) by source, and (4) by content.

Expository writing is more likely to constitute the primary form of composition in editorials written to inform and to explain. Clarity and precision in the use of language, however, are necessary if the editorialist accomplishes his goal of illuminating and interpreting complex news events or ambiguous public issues. Argumentation as a form of composition likewise parallels another of the categories of editorials classified as to purpose—editorials written to influence or argue a point of view or course of action. Editorial argumentation as a form of composition strives to persuade, to convince readers of the rightness of the position being advocated by logical force, even by emotion of expression. Narration and description are used, of course, in all aspects of editorial writing, but primarily in editorials whose purpose is to amaze or amuse. It is possible, for example, to write an editorial as a narrative, using the fictional devices of dialogue, the rendering of scene, and various other techniques of the short story writer. It is also possible to comment upon a landscape in wholly descriptive terms. While the editorialist may employ all four forms of composition, expository and argumentative composition are his daily forte.

Most editorial messages appeal to the intellect. They are usually straightforward in approach, marshaling evidence and documentation for the judgments and conclusions being expressed. The audience of such editorial messages is perceived as being made up of intelligent, open-minded persons who will respond to logical appeals, who will evaluate the evidence rationally, and who will respond accordingly. Editorials may appeal, of course, to the emotions. For short term results where the end may justify the means, an appeal based upon fear arousal would be an instance of an emotional appeal. For short term results, fear arousal may spur an audience into action, but over the longer period the effectiveness of such an appeal will diminish. For example, the historical hell-fire-and-brimstone approach of many evangelists in making their altar calls might get a person to the altar, but such a fear appeal may not do much toward correcting the lifestyle of the penitent, the long-term goal of the evangelist. Research findings regarding emotional appeals are discussed further in Chapter 9.

Editorial messages may be classified by content, for example, those dealing with political subjects, economic issues, scientific developments, human rights, business interests, cultural events, etc. The mass media should be dealing with all types of subjects and issues, limited only by the interests of members of the medium's audience. A newspaper editorial page, for example, should not be limited to the discussion of political subjects exclusively.

Editorial messages may also be classified as to geography and as to source. Local subjects should be of most importance to the community newspapers and the smaller broadcast stations. However state, regional, national, and international issues are often as pertinent as subjects closer to home as the planet earth continues to decrease in temporal, if not spatial, dimensions. The opinion content of newspapers may likewise be classified by source. The editorials, as the institutional view of the newspaper, are segregated and labeled though the author is usually anonymous. The columnists are identified. Other contributors on the editorial or op-ed pages are designated. The letter writers' effort is set off in a separate column. The reprinted opinions from other media sources are identified.

All these methods of classification, though they have their limitations and are admittedly artificial, do serve to show the unlimited opportunities open to a versatile editorial page editor and, to a lesser extent, the broadcast editorialist.

Classifying Broadcast Commentary

Various provisions arising from the so-called "Fairness Doctrine" make defining the broadcast editorial a more complex and, at the same time, a more exacting process. The Fairness Doctrine, first adopted by the Federal Communications Commission and later by Congress, grew out of two premises: (1) that the airwaves are inherently restricted to use by a few persons and (2) that broadcasters have an obligation to inform their listeners about public issues. In 1949 the FCC ruled that:

> [I]t is evident that broadcast licensees have an affirmative duty generally to encourage and implement the broadcast of all sides of controversial public issues over their facilities, over and beyond their obligation to make available on demand opportunities for the expression of opposing views. It is clear that any approximation of fairness in the presentation of any controversy will be difficult if not impossible of achievement unless the licensee plays a conscious and positive role in bringing about balance presentation of the opposing viewpoints.[10]

Congress finally recognized this doctrine in 1959 by adding the following wording to Section 315 of the Communications Act:

> Nothing in the foregoing sentence [concerning equal opportunities for political candidates] shall be construed as relieving broadcasters . . . from the obligation imposed upon them . . . to operate in the public interest and to afford reasonable opportunity for the discussion of conflicting views on issues of public importance.

Generally, then, the Fairness Doctrine is meant to insure that a broadcast licensee is not able to present only one side of public issues. Further, he cannot avoid issues altogether, thus freeing himself from the fairness doctrine; rather there is an affirmative obligation to seek out and broadcast information about matters of concern to his audience.

While the 1949 FCC ruling encouraged electronic editorializing, the Fairness Doctrine does not require it. Stations which do editorialize, however, usually set such broadcasts off from news programming and notify listeners and viewers that replies will be broadcast. The Fairness Doctrine gives no person or group an absolute right of reply; rather it leaves such matters to the reasonable judgment of the broadcaster. If the editorial makes a personal attack, however, the person attacked must be notified, furnished copies of the editorial, and afforded an opportunity to reply. If the editorial endorses a political candidate, the station must give an opportunity of reply to all the candidate's opponents. Editorial comment in these categories is usually well defined by content if not in the broadcast format.

It is the commentary and viewpoint sections often interposed in the news programs which become a point of controversy. Is such commentary subject to the Fairness Doctrine's right of reply as are editorials? It is if the content of such commentary or viewpoint expression meets the "controversial issue" category of the Fairness Doctrine. It has been held, for example, that "under the Fairness Doctrine, if there is a presentation of a point of view on a controversial issue of public importance over a station (or network), it is the duty of the station (or network), in its overall programming, to afford a reasonable opportunity for the presentation of contrasting views as to that issue. This duty applies to all station programming and not merely to editorials stating the station's position."[11] The problem often becomes one of balancing the demands of viewers to reply with concerns of the station to use wisely the limited resources available for news and entertainment programs. In the process of balancing, critics sometimes charge that broadcast commentary is being woven into news programs rather than being segregated and designated as editorial to avoid the reply requirement.

Problem-Solving Editorials

Editorials which analyze and present solutions to problems, or editorials which tackle tough questions evolving from current events and seek answers to those questions should be considered in a class by themselves. In the first place, such editorials, whether for the print or electronic media, require much effort in both research and creative thought. Problem-solving thinking follows three general steps: (1) the problem must be recognized, (2) the problem must be analyzed, and (3) a solution must be found. In the process, the problem must be pulled apart into its various elements for examination and analysis. Alternative solutions must be formulated and tested. The solution offered must be documented and presented in such a way that the skeptical reader or viewer will be satisfied.

One source suggests that asking the right question is the most important ingredient of problem solving. As Gertrude Stein lay dying, according to legend, she asked, "Does anybody know the answer?" When nobody replied, she asked, "Does anybody know the question?" What questions the editorialist asks to a marked degree determines what he learns. What question he determines is central to the problem at hand

and will ultimately determine the kind of solution he comes up with in his editorial. Problems, indeed, are often directly related to questions—questions of fact, questions of meaning, questions of probability, questions of value, questions of policy.[12] Not all editorial subjects, of course, involve problem solving and the seeking of answers to questions.

Personalizing Editorial Comment

An extension of the personal journalism of the early nineteenth century is the modern-day personal columnist who plys his art in hundreds of community as well as in many urban newspapers. He has the advantage of identity which his colleague, the editorialist, often is denied. He often has more freedom than the editorialist, even an editorialist writing to amuse or amaze, since the columnist can inject himself into his commentary, can be more informal, more chatty, more personal. The personal columnist may be a humorist, or an essayist, or a muckraker, or a reformer, or an investigative reporter, or a social critic. He may be a newspaper opinion writer or he may be a broadcast commentator. He may capture the largest audience of any media opinion writer and be the most loved and revered, or he may be the object of the most criticism and the most audience feedback. He is often in a class by himself in the function he performs.

The product of the personal columnist, however, almost defies definition. It may range from the philosophical commentary of a Harry Golden, former editor of the *Carolina Israelite,* a syndicated columnist, and author of books, to the more pointed social and political criticism of a Nat Hentoff of the *Village Voice* or an impassioned outraged I. F. (Izzy) Stone who for years decried the goings on in Washington in his tiny newsletter, *I. F. Stone's Weekly.* It may include the entertaining social commentary of a columnist such as the late Joe Creason who wandered the length of Kentucky for the *Louisville Courier-Journal* for many years writing about the people he met and commenting about their problems or of a defender of the underdogs of urban society such as Jake McCarthy who writes a column entitled "A Personal Opinion" for the *St. Louis Post-Dispatch.* What these writers have in common is the freedom to be themselves, to establish an identity with members of their audience, to deal with their readers more personally. To the extent that they succeed, credibility is enhanced and persuasion is increased.

Many syndicated columnists also achieve a measure of the personal approach advantages. They do not suffer from the anonymity forced upon the newspaper editorialist. Their personality is often projected into their writing; the reader identifies with that personality. He may become a humorist, such as Art Buchwald; an essayist, such as Sydney Harris; a satirist, such as Russell Baker or Arthur Hoppe; a muckraker, such as Jack Anderson; a conservative, such as James Kilpatrick; or a liberal, such as Tom Wicker. As the mass media grows larger and more impersonal, efforts to personalize the opinion content of the media—at least some of it—adds a new dimension to the opinion function.

Summary and Conclusion

The opinion function of the mass media, one writer calls it "the ubiquitous ingredient,"[13] manifests itself in various forms: in newspaper and broadcast editorials, in essays and commentaries, in paragraphs and columns, in viewpoints, analyses, documentaries, letters from the editor, in a seemingly endless variety of forms. But in the last analysis, the opinion function of the mass media is an attempt to extend the news columns of newspapers and the news programs of the electronic media. Opinion writing goes beyond the objective news treatment. Editorial opinion is designed to make the news more understandable and to bring the news into focus, to put it into a better frame of reference to show its significance. It is not surprising that such a demanding effort by so many different media should take various forms. It should not be surprising that faced with such a demanding task the media editorialist may often fail. The focus of the remaining chapters of this book is an effort to better understand various elements of the problem facing the media editorialist as well as to explore methods of overcoming those shortcomings.

NOTES for Chapter 2

[1] For the complete editorial, see Hillier Krieghbaum, *Facts in Perspective* (Englewood Cliffs, N.J.: Prentice-Hall, 1956), pp. 20–21.

[2] Leon Flint, *The Editorial* (New York: D. Appleton, 1926), p. 1.

[3] M. Lyle Spencer, *Editorial Writing: Ethics, Policy, Practice* (Boston: Houghton Mifflin, 1924), p. 16.

[4] Jim Allee Hart, *Views on the News: 1500–1800* (Carbondale, Ill.: Southern Illinois University Press, 1970), p. 197.

[5] *Ibid.*, p. 197.

[6] See Warren G. Bovee, "The Mythology of Editorial Anonymity," *The Masthead* 24 (Fall 1972): 26–35.

[7] As quoted in Krieghbaum, *Facts in Perspective*, pp. 160–61.

[8] Walter H. Stewart, "The Editorial Paragraph: A Century and More of Development." An unpublished Ph.D. dissertation, Southern Illinois University, 1970.

[9] Rufus Terral, "Every Man a Paragrapher," *The Masthead* 19 (Summer 1967): 28–32.

[10] Report on Editorializing by Broadcast Licensees, 13 F.C.C. 1246 (1949).

[11] "The Public and Broadcasting—Procedural Manual," 37 Fed. Reg. 20509, 20512 (September 29, 1972.)

[12] For a discussion of these various categories of questions, see Harold F. Graves and Bernard S. Oldsey, *From Fact to Judgment*, 2d ed. (New York: Macmillan, 1963).

[13] Hulteng, *The Opinion Function*, pp. 1–4.

3

Choice of Subjects: *Determining What Needs Illuminated*

"If you have nothing to say, don't!"

That was the advice of Vermont C. Royster, editor of the *Wall Street Journal,* to members of the National Conference of Editorial Writers more than a decade ago. It's still good advice. The Pulitzer Prize winning editorialist had other ideas on how not to write an editorial. He asserted, for example, that editorial columns are not the place to put news, however important, or background articles, however informational, nor was a mere expression of opinion by the editor viewed as being of much value to the reader. By what standards, then, should the editorial be measured? Royster would establish one rigorous standard for all editorials:

> The editorial page of the paper should begin where the rest of the paper leaves off. It should be, first and foremost, the place where the reader comes knowing that he will find ideas about things that are being reported in the rest of the newspaper. "Ideas"—that is the key word.[1]

While it is true, he noted, that the reader may find information on the editorial page, sometimes amusement, and quite often opinions, the good editorial page must contain more. While the opinions often may be profound and deal with the great events of the day, they also may represent only a passing thought on those events, or they may present simple ideas about simple things, "for the simplest ideas are sometimes the most startling." Royster admitted, however, that his precept about ideas was easier stated than achieved. It's difficult with some issues to find the light switch for readers and help them see more clearly. It is difficult for even an editorialist to be profound every day.

It also may be difficult to express informed opinions about *all* the important daily news events which are relevant to readers or viewers. Nicholas von Hoffman, a *Washington Post* staffer and syndicated columnist, has noted:

> It's unnatural to have an opinion about everything and everybody. It's probably a species of insanity. Forty or 50 well-thought-out, studied opinions are all a sane and healthy person needs. Any more than that and he risks exhaustion and derangement. It's very tiring summoning up an opinion about everything one sees and hears, and it's crazy, too, for if man is made to inquire, probe, search, and question, he's not made to do so in regard to everything; sometimes he's better off accepting with a nod and a grunt, just flowing with it, not removing himself to size it up and pass judgment.[2]

While there is, without doubt, much truth in von Hoffman's tongue-in-cheek advice, one virtue of an editorial page is that it can extend the news columns, illuminating countless subjects and topics. Alexis de Tocqueville, for example, once observed:

> Nothing but a newspaper can drop the same thought into a thousand minds at the same moment. A newspaper is an adviser that does not require to be sought, but that comes of its own accord and talks to you briefly every day of the common weal, without distracting you from your private affairs.[3]

One of the most difficult tasks facing the mass media editorialist may be determining what to write about and how to develop editorial ideas. This is generally true despite the fact that the potential range for editorial subjects is as broad as human knowledge and experience. Guidelines for determining what needs to be illuminated are the subject of this chapter.

Editorialist as "Free Spirit"

When a mass media editorialist chooses a subject to illuminate, an issue to argue, a problem to solve, or a question to answer, he is assuming that the subject, the issue, the problem, or the question is relevant—or can be made relevant—to his readers or viewers. Editorial writers sometimes express the desire to be "free spirits," independent from newsroom pressures, free from the pleas of advertisers, free from political pressures from whatever source, even free from the perceived restraints of the latest electronic technology. This quest for independence can be an effective persuasive stance, up to a point. The credibility of both the news medium and the editorialist is determined partially by the perceived objectivity of the source—the editorialist's ability to tell it the way it is. But the editorialist must not lose sight of the self interest of members of his audience. As one journalism educator noted more than fifty years ago, "It is the taste of the fish, not the fisherman, that determines the bait to be used."[4] The editorialist is simply not free to ignore the interests of his readers or listeners; the prosperity and happiness which most people are interested in is their own.

Neither is the editorialist free to take whatever approach he pleases to a subject if he wishes to be effective. It has been noted, for example, that there are three general levels, or echelons, of conversation. They are, from lowest to highest (1) people talking about people, (2) people talking about things, and (3) people talking about ideas. These categories may be applied to editorials as well. Editorials which simply deal in personalities, that are concerned primarily with personal invective or innuendo, are usually low-level editorial concerns. Editorials which deal in things are usually more interesting, but such editorials still may not be particularly provocative or challenging. But the third level, editorials which deal with ideas, is at the top of the hierarchy. This is the type of editorial which the *Wall Street Journal* editor was boosting above. This isn't to say, of course, that editorials shouldn't sometimes deal with individuals, for occasionally an individual is the issue. But even an editorial which deals with people should focus upon the issue rather than upon the individual per se, and the editorial should be thought provoking, should provide the reader or listener with new ideas, with new concepts, with new insights into the issues and problems surrounding the individual's performance or lack of performance.

One Newspaper's Effort

The diversity possible in the choice of subject matter on editorial pages might best be demonstrated by examining the editorial content of a representative community newspaper for a week. The *Alton* (Ill.) *Telegraph,* a six-day evening paper, one of the oldest dailies of continuous publication in the Midwest, for example, has been responding to interests and needs of its readers for more than 140 years. The *Telegraph* is published in a city of 40,000 located 25 miles northeast of St. Louis with a circulation of 40,000. The newspaper's thousands of readers during the week of July 19 to July 25, 1977, had an opportunity to read a total of nineteen editorials, averaging three a day. Fourteen of the nineteen editorials dealt with local issues, two with state topics, and three with national problems or issues.

Telegraph readers also had the opportunity to read a number of syndicated columnists, either on the daily editorial page or the four op-ed pages published during the week. They included Jack Anderson, Clark Mollenhoff, Don Oakley, Victor Riesel, John Roche, Carl Rowan, Tom Tiede, Robert Walters and Martha Angle. The pages also carried these regular features: letters to the editor under a "What YOU Think" heading; a local historical feature, "Telegraph of Yesterday";

and two shorter features, "Barbs" and "Quote/Unquote." One issue of the op-ed page carried a Louis Harris poll and another an Associated Press feature, one of a series on "Power in Illinois" dealing with Alton's Phyllis Schlafly, a syndicated columnist and head of the national stop ERA campaign.

The local editorials, which dominated the page, dealt with a variety of subjects and issues. A number expressed concern about various aspects of local government: proposed changes in county tax assessments, measures to safeguard against the misuse of county and city taxes, crowded conditions at the local jail, even the problem of providing adequate punishment for youths caught "skinny dipping" at the country club lake. Other editorials dealt with the local implications of federal actions, for example, a proposal for assessment of fees from barge operators for use of the Alton lock and dam on the Mississippi River, the possibility of locating a new state prison at a former Nike Missile base, and changes in the succession procedure in appointing a local postmaster. Other editorials dealt with the possible impact of state actions on the Alton area: the establishment of a portion of Upper Alton as a special district by the Illinois Historic Sites Advisory Council and pending judicial action involving the enrollment of blacks in an Alton-based state dental school. Other local topics ranged from the death of an Alton centenarian whose bequest of one million dollars provided for continuing nursing education to the need for a Chamber of Commerce executive board and from the tragic electrocution of a young man in the illuminated city water fountain to the possibility of an "Alton Day" at the county fair.

While none of these local editorials dealt with issues of great national import, they were not unimportant to *Telegraph* readers. More importantly, a local newspaper, such as the *Telegraph,* is often the only medium which has an interest in such problems or is in a position to deal with such issues effectively. Hodding Carter, publisher of the *Delta Democrat-Times* of Greenville, Mississippi, observed after winning a Pulitzer Prize for editorial writing that most of the issues he had dealt with editorially in winning the award were trivial measured against the "cataclysmic events of the world," but they were not trivial to readers of his newspaper.[5] Local issues are important.

The discussion of national issues on the *Telegraph* editorial pages was left largely to the syndicated columnists, although the *Telegraph* did comment briefly on the proposed Concorde flights to the United States, the Alaska pipeline, and the South Korean influence scandal. Likewise, only two issues having largely state-wide interest were discussed: one editorial argued that Illinois' new governor was losing his "Mr. Clean" image while another warned that Amtrak's passenger service in Illinois needed closer scrutiny.

The *Alton Telegraph* may or may not be a typical community daily newspaper, but its editorial page serves as an excellent model of the diversity which a small daily can achieve. A careful reading of an editorial page such as that published by the *Telegraph* also demonstrates that an editorial page can be local without being parochial, it can be conservative (which the *Telegraph* is—and Republican) without being bland and uninteresting, and it can and must continue to be relevant to its readers despite the increasing cost and complexity of newspaper production during the 1970's. It must continue to be relevant if it is to survive, and the *Telegraph* has survived for more than 140 years.

The Importance of Reading

The editorialist not only has a great deal of freedom in his selection of subjects, he usually approaches his work much differently than his newsroom colleague—the reporter. Unlike the reporter, the editorialist is not restricted to events; he can discuss philosophy, ethics, historical events, or any number of topics. This freedom also allows him to order his sources of information differently. The newsman, for example, relies most heavily upon conversation with news sources for his stories; he observes some of what he writes about; his experience conditions what he sees and writes; he engages in some reflection, hopefully, as he writes his story and may even read from various sources for a better understanding of what he writes about. The editorialist, on the other hand, practically reverses this ordering process.

The mass media editorialist relies most heavily upon reading as his primary source of ideas and information: his own newspaper, the news magazines, topical books, and many of the reference materials discussed in Chapter 4. Next in importance to the editorialist is reflection; an editorial which deals in ideas is largely a product of thought. Experience, however, can be a valuable source for the interpretation of information for the editorialist as for the reporter. But the editorialist relies less heavily upon observation for his information, though he needs to travel and inspect conditions about which he writes. The editorialist generally places even less reliance upon conversation. Ideally the news staff has investigated the facts of a breaking news story before the editorialist deals with it. There are times, of course, when the editorialist must call on a news source personally to gain information which has not been included in the news story.[6]

Illuminating the News

One of the primary purposes of an editorial is to help the reader or listener to better understand the daily news reports. Most editorials, therefore, are tied to some "news peg." An event precipitates a question and the editorialist often feels compelled to comment upon it. A problem is discussed at a city council or school board meeting and the editorialist examines possible solutions to that problem. Some governmental action is reported in the news columns and the editorialist examines the possible consequences of that action. A public figure dies and the editorialist takes note of his passing. In all this there is an assumption that the editorial comment should be timely—as the news is timely. This compulsion to comment immediately upon the news may have certain persuasive advantages,[7] but being over-timely may also be perilous to the extent that it results in writing with too little background and thought.

A. Gayle Waldrop, in an editorial writing textbook used for many years in schools of journalism throughout the country, noted that while many current news topics are interesting on their own account, others tend to be "dry stuff" for the reader. Termed as the worst in the "dry stuff" category is the big-news editorial which comments at length on the exploits of some public official or public figures as reported on Page 1 when a brief editorial "hooray" might have been sufficient.[8] While choice of subjects is one of the deciding factors in determining whether editorials will be read and whether they are worth reading, hitting the reader "while the iron is hot" should not always be the primary concern of the editorialist. Walter Lippmann, while editor of the *New York World,* was asked how recent an idea should be for an editorial; he replied that it could be anywhere from two hours to 2,000 years.[9] A discussion of Julius Caesar's outlook on life, however, might be a difficult editorial topic with which to gain the attention of many modern-day readers and viewers. Timeliness and proximity are both important qualities of editorials just as they are important qualities of news. But some editorial topics, just as many feature stories, rely upon qualities other than timeliness for their appeal.

Dealing with Public Issues

To be worthy of the required newsprint consumption or broadcast time, one writer points out, an editorial must have something to offer the reader or listener beyond what the news reports offer. It must explain something, or must identify an issue, or make a case either for or against a cause or course of action. An editorial, in some instances, may do these all at the same time.[10] Not all news events, obviously, need to be explained, nor do all deal with issues or call for some course of action.

The broad category of political news, however, is one major source for editorial comment in the mass media. Political communication has likewise been of great interest to communications researchers. Whether or not the press plays a persuasive role in the dissemination of political information is questioned by some researchers, but the important role the press plays in making mass media audiences aware of the issues is generally supported. What the press covers, and what the editorialists comment upon, voters generally feel is important. Under this so-called agenda-setting function, it is asserted that the press not only makes the public aware of the issues of a campaign, but also sets the public's priorities.[11]

In dealing with political issues, as with all aspects of the news, the editorial writer may be performing one or more of the following functions: (1) he may merely attempt to explain the importance of the day's events, (2) he may fill in the background to give further significance to the event or issue, (3) he may predict the outcome of an issue or forecast the future developments as a result of the news event, or (4) he may pass moral judgment on the event, a long tradition of editorial writing.[12] Much political news lends itself to such editorial treatment, even to endorsing candidates, although less than one-third of the dailies in the United States endorsed a candidate for president in 1976. For example, only 411 daily newspapers endorsed President Ford while 80 endorsed candidate Carter.[13]

Public issues, however, may involve other than political officials and candidates for public office. Private individuals also become involved in a multitude of events of public or general concern and, as a result, become public figures and subject to editorial comment. Many of the issues public figures become involved in may be political in nature, but they need not be to qualify for "fair comment and criticism" by the editorialist. Such issues may be business oriented, or they may deal with entertainment, with athletics, with the fine arts, with environmental concerns, or with other topics of public concern. But not all issues should be subject to editorial comment. Condemnatory editorial comment about race or religion, for example, is usually on the restricted list. Other controversies not truly a matter of general public concern should also be ruled out. The growing awareness and demand for individual privacy must be of concern to the media editorialist.

Letters as Editorial Catalyst

An often overlooked source of editorial ideas is the letters-to-the-editor column. A letters column, conducted properly, should provide an open forum where readers are relatively free to express, in their own way, their views, opinions, and concerns. If there is nothing vital being published in the editorial columns, however, the letters may not be particularly vital either. In other words, there is usually a correlation between the quality of the editorials and the letters. But where the letters column is open and where readers respond, the letters column should provide a barometer of public opinion and a gauge of what's on readers' minds. The editorialist should respond to those problems and issues, if possible.

Gene Cervi, editor of the *Rocky Mountain Journal,* after chiding his competitor, the *Denver Post,* for the "prodigious effort in its July 6 edition," noted that the *Post*'s four editorials on that date got no closer to Denver than Pittsburgh. Cervi's editorial concluded:

> All of which leads to speculation on precisely why the Post troubles to devote an entire three columns to its own opinions at all. In theory, at least, editorial opinions serve the public purpose of interpreting the true meaning of the news, of opposing something or someone which ought in the public interest to be opposed; or praising praiseworthy actions or people otherwise likely to get short shrift. The Post is far from unique in failing to reflect before it opines, whether its editorial stand will have any impact on its subject matter—or even come to the attention of any person involved.

Although Cervi was dubious that conditions at the *Post* were likely to improve, he offered a suggestion:

> There is little prospect the Post will correct its myopia. Apparently its editorial writers are incapable of reading its own letters-to-the-editor columns, in which on the same day appeared at least three legitimate issues of local concern—and all of which merited thoughtful scrutiny.[14]

A few newspapers have experimented with tying the editorial column and the letters column even more closely on a once-a-week or once-a-month basis. The *Milwaukee Journal* and *Philadelphia Bulletin,* for example, posed periodic questions to which readers were asked to respond. In the *Bulletin,* a typical page of the "Saturday Forum" contained a dozen letters answering a question posed by the newspaper, with a related editorial in which the newspaper discussed the issue raised in the question. The same basic format was followed by the *Journal.*[15] Such tying of the letters column to the editorial column with a common editorial topic or idea has also been done in relation to procon editorial efforts, for example, in the *St. Petersburg* (Fla.) *Times* and *Cedar Rapids* (Iowa) *Gazette.* While the primary purpose of such projects is usually the promotion of access to the editorial page, it also provides ideas for editorial comment on topics of demonstrable interest to readers.

A more unusual link between editorial and letter commentary occurred during the 1976 election on the editorial page of the *New York Times.* A letter, headed "Moynihan Endorsement," dated September 10, 1976, stated simply:

> As the Editor of the Editorial Page of the Times, I must express disagreement with the endorsement in today's editorial columns of Mr. Moynihan over four other candidates in the New York Democratic primary contest for the United States Senate. John B. Oakes

The letter was apparently written at the invitation of the publisher of the *Times* upon Oakes' vigorous objections to his paper's endorsement of Moynihan. At least two things mark such a letter-from-the-editor as unusual: (1) that it expressed an open disagreement between the publisher and the editor and (2) that it placed the editorial page editor in the unusual position of writing a letter to himself since he was both the addressee and addressor.[16]

Problem-Solving Editorials

The choice of editorial subjects can be viewed as a searching out of problems to be solved. The editorialist chooses topics from the news reports which are most likely to pose problems for his readers and illuminates those topics or issues in an effort to offer solutions for the reader caught up in the changes. An assumption is that the editorialist seeks out those issues which present problems which have solutions, leaving unattended those about which little can be done. Not all news, of course, can be viewed as creating problems for readers, but a surprising amount of news is about change, and change often presents problems.

Several steps are involved in such a problem-solving editorial exercise: (1) the problem must be recognized, (2) the problem must be defined or classified, (3) various solutions must be suggested, (4) these solutions or premises must be tested, and (5) the best, most suitable solution or hypothesis must be offered.[17] In a sense, this is the process the editorial writer goes through in analyzing any event or situation in order to give it meaning. All thinkers proceed in much the same manner, one journalism educator has noted, because the thinking process consists "merely in arranging a set of data into a tentative pattern of thought (hypothesis), and then testing the soundness of the pattern by inquiring into the probabilities of the explanation."[18]

Editorials as Informal Essays

Not all editorial topics must deal with profound events or issues or with relevant problems arising from reports in the news columns. An editorial topic may be chosen primarily for the opportunity it affords the editorialist to "amuse and amaze" his readers. One writer has noted:

> If editorial writers dressed the way they write, many of them would wear blue serge or Oxford gray suits, white shirts, and black shoes. They would be those staff members who repeatedly were assigned the informative and argumentative editorials. Over in a corner telling jokes and enjoying themselves thoroughly would be a smaller group of jolly souls in sports clothes. In our comparison, they would be the successful change of pace editorial writers whose aim is either to amuse or to amaze their readers.[19]

In this category of topics which amuse and amaze may be the personal essay or personal column which takes a more informal approach, which allows the writer to chat personally with the reader, which relies upon sincerity and friendliness (not just amusement) for its appeal.

The informal essay, humorous or serious in nature, thrived during the nineteenth century and on into the early part of the twentieth. Such a form has fallen into disuse in recent years, one writer has observed, perhaps because the genre suffered from too many shoddy practitioners, too many "phony boob spellings and dialects," and too many "plain folks" homilies that infected so many newspapers in the first two decades of the twentieth century.[20] The writer goes on to note that while artful fun pieces and original, imaginative writing are not every editorial writer's forte, the potential for such writing may be greater than one would suspect if newspapers and broadcast stations were willing to commit the time and space required for developing such talent.

One doesn't have to have the talents of a Russell Baker, an Arthur Hoppe, or an Art Buchwald to write a provocative change-of-pace editorial or have the personal touch of an E. W. Howe, a Henry Beetle Hough, or a Harry Golden to write an effective informal essay. Many community editors engage in personal editorializing regularly. Take, for example, the opening paragraph from this prize-winning editorial essay written by a Canadian editorialist, Foster M. Russell, entitled simply, "The Cry":

> The seagull cries in the wake of Port of Cobourg; not the selfsame cry of yesterday or yesteryear but the funereal note in the new score of today; with time writing music in the wisp of the mind, the baton waving on in seconds, the black dots in the bar reaching high to the cry of the gull, and the grace notes echoing down in the wash of the soul.

The seagull's "piquant cry" reminded the writer of the voice of a friend "lost in the way of the wind" or of an old man tired in "the twilight of spun years." With this utter song of loneliness was joined intermittently "the full-joy of spirit in the sad-sweet orchestration of life."[21] The essay is an impressionistic, penetrating, poignant, perhaps sentimental piece of personal writing. It meets the standard that editorial expression should convey ideas, yet it isn't tied to the news in any direct way.

An attempt is being made by some larger newspapers to personalize the normally anonymous editorial writer through the publication of personal columns or institutional ads. The *Minneapolis Star,* for example, describes such an effort:

> We are trying in a limited way to personalize our editorial writers although we continue to use the unsigned editorial. Three of us write weekly columns in which we are free to use the personal pronoun. . . . our theory is that we think such a treatment makes us seem more

> real to the people who read our editorials. People, I think, are willing to argue with and listen to the guy next door or at the next desk, but can't quite handle a relationship with an institution.[22]

For the mass media editorialist who has the freedom to write more personally, the choice of topics for editorial comment is vastly expanded beyond the current events treated in the news columns.

Editorial Brainstorming

Decisions concerning which editorial topics or editorial issues to deal with, how those ideas should be developed, and how the ideas and issues fit into the editorial policy of the newspaper grows more complicated as the medium increases in size. For this, as well as other reasons, editorial staffs of three or more usually have periodic conferences—often daily—to discuss what is to be written about, what stance the newspaper will take, and to make assignments for the research and writing of the editorials. The overall function of such editorial conferences will be discussed in Chapter 13. There is an aspect of such conferences, however, which has to do with developing editorial ideas. The process is often called "brainstorming."

The theory underlying brainstorming is that the individual engaged in group participation is often more creative than he is as an individual. The technique calls for a kind of free-association verbal production with participants instructed to more or less suspend critical judgment and to suggest anything that occurs to them on a given problem or topic. Some social science researchers, however, question this theory.[23] The editorial conference, in any case, offers the opportunity for the brainstorming of potential editorial ideas.

Quite often editorial writers are instructed to come to the editorial conference with one or more topics or issues they are prepared to research and develop. The cartoonist, who usually takes part in such conferences, may also come with an idea or two for a cartoon for the next issue of the paper. Whether or not the process involves brainstorming in a free-association sense, these ideas are discussed, the stance to be taken on each is discussed, alternative answers or solutions may be discussed. Out of this discussion may come entirely new ideas on what should be studied and illuminated, on possible solutions to problems, on tentative answers to questions which should be checked out. Before a brainstorming topic can become an editorial, of course, critical judgment must be reapplied and the idea, first produced in a "kind of free-association," must be plugged into reality. Brainstorming procedures afford a means of thinking more creatively, of expanding editorial horizons, of producing better solutions to problems, or of producing a more effective editorial column or page. The problem, of course, is ultimately to separate the "brainstorms" from valid editorial ideas.

Avoiding Afghanistanism

Jenkin Lloyd Jones, editor of the *Tulsa* (Okla.) *Tribune,* in 1948 challenged members of the American Society of Newspaper Editors to "quit looking at Afghanistan and start looking at the county courthouse." Jones asked:

> Where else can the interested citizen get guidance and advice affecting his city and his state than in his local daily? . . . The tragic fact is that many an editorial writer can't hit a short-range target. He's hell on distance. And there's a lot that is comfortable about this distance. It takes guts to dig up dirt on the sheriff, or to expose a utility racket, or to tangle with the governor. They all bite back, and you had better know your stuff.[24]

For the past thirty years the tendency to write about far-away issues and problems has been referred to as "Afghanistanism," and the implication is that the editorialist is fearful of tackling problems closer home.

Editors of *The Masthead* asked a panel of editorialists more recently if the pendulum had swung too far toward treatment of local subjects to avoid the brand "Afghanistanism," termed a dirty word with more than four letters. "Have we been scared off from international editorials to the point of neglect?" the panelists were asked. "Are we so busy getting the downtown litter picked up that we're ignoring issues of universal concern?"[25]

One panelist, Francis P. Locke, editorial writer for the *Press* and *Daily Enterprise,* Riverside, California, found himself less critical than he had been twenty-five years earlier upon hearing the ASNE speech by Jones. Locke noted that concomitant changes had, through the years, progressively interlocked local, national, and international questions. He concluded:

> An informed and aggressive editorial page that reaches out to enlighten others, and occasionally to exhort them, can perform an indispensable service. Sometimes that service will be to stop unauthorized hometown trash burning or to nerve public officials to denial of an industry's request for a smog variance. But at least as often as before, the service will be to shine some light on the new stirrings in the Third World, the deployment of the MIRVS or the mysterious ups and downs of the dollar.

Other panelists noted that geography is not the problem, the problem is a lack of courage to write about things that matter; that Afghanistan is no longer a far away place, it is a close neighbor in a world shrinking each year through developing technology. A few panelists pointed out, however, that pure "Afghanistanism," writing innocuous editorials about far away places to avoid coming to grips with the tougher problems at home, is as objectionable today as it was when Jones coined the term in 1948.

Avoid "Canned" Editorials

An altogether too frequent source of editorial ideas, indeed a source of pre-packaged editorials ready to be spooned into the editorial column of the newspaper or to be broadcast, is the so-called "canned editorial" supplied by such firms as E. Hofer and Sons. For many years this firm's *Industrial News Review* and packet of prepared editorials was mailed monthly to thousands of newspapers throughout the United States with a note to the editor which said in part:

> The aim of the Industrial News Review is to advocate and encourage policies which it believes essential to the well-being of Our Country, the development of industry, the sound investment of savings, and steady employment of American workers. . . . Its findings are not copyrighted and are submitted for consideration or reproduction, with or without credit, in whole or in part, or for any commentary use of statistics, quotations or opinions contained.[26]

To publish editorials prepared by Hofer while crediting the editorial to *Industrial News Review,* of course, would not constitute publication of "canned" editorials. It is when newspapers publish editorials from such sources as their own views (and hundreds do) that an ethical problem arises. The reader of a "canned" editorial must assume that the editorial expresses the considered judgment of the newspaper; in fact, the views expressed are those of the private power companies and other businesses which support Hofer as its public relations agent.

Frank E. Smith, a former editorialist who had subsequently become a Tennessee Valley Authority director, told readers of *The Masthead* in 1971 that a random sample of editorials unfavorable to TVA over the past five years had showed that 60 percent appeared in more than one newspaper, but that there had been no indication on the editorial page that they were not the individual product and opinion of the paper which printed them. All of the editorials, Smith said, appeared to be a Hofer product. Smith went on to name a group of widely dispersed newspapers in which the same editorial critical of TVA was published, word for word, without attribution to *Industrial News Review.*[27]

Hofer, of course, is not the only public relations firm which attempts to borrow the good name of newspapers and broadcast media to air the opinions and views of its clients. Through the years, however, it has been among the most successful of many such operations. Unless such pre-packaged editorials actually express the editorial views of the newspaper or broadcast station, use of "canned" materials is perilous. The credibility of the editorialist is certainly involved. Serious ethical considerations are involved. The use of "canned" editorials, however, should be distinguished from publication of editorials from other sources, clearly marked as being from such a service as *Editorial Research Reports* or from the *New York Times,* or wherever. Reprinted editorials from other sources may indeed be regarded by readers as acknowledgment by the editorialist that he doesn't have a monopoly on all the valid editorial ideas. Here he is willing to reprint and share the views of others with his readers.

Other Hazards to Be Avoided

The editorialist as persuader is not only the target of the public relations man, he is often sought out by the chamber of commerce manager, or the local advertiser, or others with an axe to grind, seeking editorial comment in support of this or that project. Too often the editorialist may feel compelled to bestow his blessings on local bargain days, on the winner of the local beauty queen contest, or on the county fair. Such "duty" editorials are often irritating to the reader, according to a former editorial page editor turned consumer of editorials.[28]

Running a close second to the "duty" editorial may be the commentary which merely regurgitates the news story, an editorial which turns up with regularity in both print and broadcast commentary. Such an editorial is made even more bland by concluding with some such inanity as "It will be interesting to see how this situation turns out." Such an editorial, related to the over-timely comment on the news which only demonstrates to the reader that the writer is as confused about the issue as the reader, is better off left unwritten, shortening the editorial column, if necessary.

Another hazard to avoid is that of the editorialist, whether out of a sense of duty or because of an attempt to be timely, to expound on any issue in a fashion which betrays his lack of knowledge of the subject. In fact, an editorialist should never write on a topic unless he has some expertise or is sufficiently interested to research the topic before he sits down to write. It would be far better for the editorialist to fail to comment than to fall flat on his face in attempting to be an instant expert on every issue in the news.

The editorialist also should be cautious in making predictions or in passing judgment about matters pending in the courts. The Watergate investigation and the resurgence of investigative reporting on many fronts have led many young journalists to seek to imitate the role played by Woodward and Bernstein. But not every break-in will turn out to be a Watergate, and not every investigation will have as a protagonist the President of the United States. Such comment is fraught with ethical as well as legal considerations. The risks are usually not worth the hazards involved.

Summary and Conclusion

Selecting the topics and issues to be illuminated and coming up with editorial ideas about those topics and issues is one of the most important tasks facing the mass media editorialist. One writer has noted that the choice of editorial subjects may be one of the deciding factors in determining whether editorials will be read and whether or not they are worth reading. The quality of the thinking which goes into developing the ideas and the soundness of the reporting and writing, of course, are also important.[29] The editorialist needs to illuminate all the news and all the issues which need such comment. On the other hand, he must confine himself to those issues which he has the expertise to deal with and those issues which he has the interest and time to research and reflect upon. The mass media editorialist also needs to remember his audience, directing his comments to their self-interest, noting their concerns as reflected in the letters column or elsewhere. He needs to develop the readership of his page by writing, occasionally, to amuse and entertain as well as to explain or argue a point of view.

In developing editorial ideas the newspaper or broadcast editorialist needs the freedom necessary to choose, research, develop, and write objectively about any issue which is relevant to his readers or viewers. He needs to have the independence to write about pertinent local issues as well as relevant national and international issues. It is important, however, that he avoids letting others use the good name of his medium to disseminate "canned" editorial messages. He needs to avoid other such hazards which would damage his own credibility or that of his medium. The list of hazards facing the mass media editorialist and the challenges facing him daily are formidable.

Louis M. Lyons, retired curator of the Nieman Foundation, speaking to members of the National Conference of Editorial Writers in Boston in 1970, expressed sympathy for the editorialist faced with a "world of instantaneous reporting of everything," bringing a "confusing welter of facts" every day which often become both indigestible and unassimilable. Indeed, it is the facts that have become repellent to readers. While it may be a desperate time to try to offer wisdom in editorials, Lyons noted that "any thoughtful discussion of the irreconcilable and imponderable present is welcome."

Lyons expressed sympathy for the newspaper editorial writer for other reasons. He noted, for example:

> Not only is he confronted with the impossible task of translating or transmuting the irrational into meaning. But he is surrounded, if indeed not overwhelmed, by colleagues who are one up on him. At one side the columnists, free to express their individuality and opinionations with a fervor and dynamic that is denied the anonymous voice of

> institutional consensus. On the other side, the specialists of the staff, in increasing variety and competence, each of them more specifically informed in his field than the editorialist can be in all the fields he must cover. They intrude on and usurp his authority.[30]

Impossible though the task may be, that is the role of the mass media editorialist. He must begin his task by choosing daily from among "the confusing welter of facts" those which most need illuminating and which his own knowledge and the resources of his medium best allow him to undertake.

NOTES to Chapter 3

[1] Vermont C. Royster, "Parsley Is a Poor Diet," *The Masthead* 19 (Summer 1967): 12–15.

[2] Nicholas von Hoffman, "Species of Insanity," *The Masthead* 29 (Spring 1977): 39.

[3] Alexis de Tocqueville, "A Newspaper's Virtue," as quoted in *The Masthead* 28 (Winter 1976): 29.

[4] Matthew L. Spencer, *Editorial Writing: Ethics, Policy, Practice* (New York: Houghton Mifflin, 1924), p. 61.

[5] Hodding Carter, "On the Importance of Trivia," *The Masthead* 9 (Summer 1957): 43–44.

[6] For a discussion of the contrasting uses of different sources by the editorialist and reporter, see Leon N. Flint, *The Editorial* (New York: D. Appleton, 1928), pp. 42–58.

[7] See discussion of primacy effects in Chapter 9.

[8] See A. Gayle Waldrop, *Editor and Editorial Writer,* 3d ed. (Dubuque, Iowa: Wm. C. Brown, 1967), pp. 47–49.

[9] See Hillier Kreighbaum, *Facts in Perspective* (Englewood Cliffs, N.J.: Prentice-Hall, Inc., 1956), pp. 108–9.

[10] John L. Hulteng, *The Opinion Function: Editorial and Interpretive Writing for the News Media* (New York: Harper & Row, 1973), p. 51.

[11] See William Glavin, "Political Influence of the Press," ANPA *News Research Bulletin* 4 (November 10, 1976). For a fuller discussion of the agenda-setting function, see Chapter 1.

[12] William M. Pinkerton, "Who Should Interpret the News?" *Nieman Reports* 2 (January 1948), p. 13.

[13] For a report of endorsements in the 1976 campaign, see *Editor & Publisher,* (October 30, 1976), p. 5.

[14] Editorial, *Denver* (Colo.) *Rocky Mountain Journal,* July 8, 1971.

[15] See Robert T. Pittman, "10 Best Bets for Edit Pages," *The Masthead* 26 (Summer 1974): 30–38.

[16] For a discussion of Oakes' letter, see Stuart H. Loory, "The Editor as Letter-Writer," *The Masthead* 28 (Winter 1976): 21–22.

[17] For a discussion of problem-solving editorials, see Krieghbaum, *Facts in Perspective,* pp. 183–87.

[18] See Chilton R. Bush, *Editorial Thinking and Writing* (Westport, Conn.: Greenwood Press, 1932), p. 72.

[19] Krieghbaum, *Facts in Perspective,* p. 220.

[20] For a discussion of the informal essay, see James C. MacDonald, "Anyone for Ectoplasm on the Half Shell?" *The Masthead* 24 (Fall 1972): 44–46.

[21] Editorial, *The Cobourg* (Ontario, Canada) *Sentinel-Star,* September 24, 1969.

[22] See Robert T. Pittman, "10 Best Bets for Edit Pages," *The Masthead* 26 (Summer 1974): 30–38.

[23] See W. Edgar Vinacke, *The Psychology of Thinking,* 2d ed. (New York: McGraw-Hill Book Co., 1974), p. 309.

[24] As quoted in Waldrop, *Editor and Editorial Writer,* p. 51.

[25] See, Symposium: " 'Afghanistan' Revisited," *The Masthead* 24 (Summer 1972): 8–25.

[26] See *Industrial News Review* (Hillsboro, Ore.: E. Hofer & Sons, 1913–. Monthly). Since 1975 the service has been supplied on a subscription basis to newspapers desiring the materials. Various other organizations, for example, the National Association of Manufacturers, also supply materials for reproduction or copying by editors without credit to the organization.

[27] Frank E. Smith, "Still Too Many 'Canned' Editorials," *The Masthead* 23 (Summer 1971): 26–28.

[28] See Robert F. Campbell, "An Often Disappointed Reader," *The Masthead* 22 (Summer 1970): 12–13.

[29] See Waldrop, *Editor and Editorial Writer,* p. 47.

[30] Louis M. Lyons, "What Is Left for Editorial Writers?" *The Masthead* 22 (Winter 1970–71): 1–6.

4

Finding Facts: *Basic Reference and Source Materials*

ONCE THE EDITORIALIST has chosen his subject, or has been assigned a subject to analyze and comment upon, his next concern is the researching of that issue, problem, or question—in all directions, in all its important aspects. Digging for facts and information to document an editorial can be painstaking and difficult, but research pays off in persuasive writing as it does in most other scholarly efforts.[1] Good research may indeed be a continuous process for the full time editorialist. Stephen S. Rosenfeld, editorial writer for the *Washington Post,* for example, has noted:

> There is in a sense hardly a waking hour when I am not researching one editorial or preparing to write another, since everything I read, every conversation I have on anything, every fugitive thought on the bus going home, contributes to either the store of information or the framework of judgment which I bring to my work.[2]

The mass media editorialist, whether he writes for the *Washington Post* or the *Eugene* (Ore.) *Register-Guard,* must keep informed because he is expected to be able to comment upon and to illuminate the more complex news events and issues. He is expected to be informed about the arguments, both pro and con, on vital public questions and to take a stand on pertinent issues affecting his readers. In his evaluations he is expected to document his views and bolster his conclusions with factual information and supportive evidence. To effectively perform his persuasive role as an agenda setter and as an opinion leader, the mass media editorialist must somehow live up to these expectations. But how can the editorialist, particularly those employed on non-metropolitan newspapers in smaller communities, perform such a demanding role?

Many newspaper editorialists point out that a more adequate editorial staff might help alleviate the problem. On too many small dailies, for example, on 53 percent of those with circulations of less than 100,000, one person may be charged with the sole responsibility of the editorial page.[3] An estimated two hundred small dailies, according to another source, have no editorial pages to staff.[4] Scattered surveys indicate that as many as one-half of the weekly newspapers carry no regular editorial page. While the community editor who publishes editorials has only one page a week to contend with, his efforts are often spread so thin among dozens of other tasks that he has little time for writing editorials and still less time for research and reflection—both important aspects of effective opinion writing. Broadcast editorializing, as reported in Chapter 1, may be even more limited in scope.

A second concern, and one which tends to emphasize the problem faced by too small an editorial staff, is the absence of needed reference and source materials. This deficiency often makes it impossible for the editorialist to engage in the necessary research demanded to produce well documented, factually accurate editorials. This condition exists despite the fact that it has been demonstrated that the editorial reader often cares less about what the newspaper's opinion about an event or issue is than he does about the basis for that opinion. It is important, therefore, that the editorial show the factual basis of the problem and the reasons underlying the views expressed if it is to be persuasive.

It has also been shown repeatedly that many readers and viewers do not remember the essential facts of even continuing news stories. An Institute of Public Opinion survey, for example, found that half of the respondents could not identify their congressman by name, and two-thirds of a national sample polled by Gallup could not explain the function of the electoral college.[5] An editorial must provide the needed factual background for the forgetful reader. Other surveys provide even more startling findings concerning mass media audiences. A national survey of literacy completed in 1976, for example, found that one out of every five Americans was "functionally illiterate and unable to cope with life's basic demands."[6] Another survey found that 47 percent of the country's 17-year-olds had little knowledge about the U.S. government; for instance, they did not know that each state has two United States Senators.

Research in attitude formation and attitude change also has shown that the audience's perception of the credibility of the source—the trustworthiness, for example, of the editorialist or his medium—is an important aspect in determining the effectiveness of a persuasive communication. A misstatement of fact or the lack of a factual basis for the opinions expressed do little to enhance the audience's perception of that credibility.[7]

While the need for source and reference materials is well established, what constitutes an adequate reference shelf for the mass media editorialist may vary from one community to another, from one editorialist to another, and from one medium to another. The discussion below is meant to establish various categories and to set out examples of the most useful sources within those categories. Space limitations do not permit the detailed discussion of a long list of reference materials. Such guidelines, in any case, are available elsewhere.[8] And, while the discussion will be oriented toward the newspaper editorialist, the source and reference materials discussed are, in most cases, equally valuable to the broadcast editorialist.

The Newspaper as Source

One basic category of source material available to all editorialists, of course, is the content of the editorialist's own newspaper (or, in the case of the broadcast editorialist, his own station's scripts and tapes). The newspaper's morgue, if there is one, should also be of special service to the editorialist. It may be necessary, however, for the editorialist of a community newspaper to set up his own reference file containing clippings and other materials deemed to be of future use on topics which are of particular interest to him—and his readers. Editorials are often viewed as meaningful extensions of the news columns, as noted in Chapter 3. What better place exists for the editorial writer to begin his research than with his own newspaper? Exchange newspapers, of course, should supplement the editorialist's search. The news magazines can also provide the backgrounding needed for international, national, and sometimes state issues.

For the larger metropolitan newspapers, of course, the morgue will be a part of the newspaper library. The Chicago *Sun-Times* and *Daily News,* for example, have an editorial library which includes not only the morgue but most of the source and reference materials to be discussed in this chapter. The library not only serves the editorial staffs of the two Field newspapers; employees of other departments of the newspaper division, as well as affiliated companies of Field Enterprises, may use the library if they receive authorization from their department head. Use of the library by persons outside the newspaper organization, however, is discouraged. Some papers deny access to library and files to all outside persons. In addition to the clipping files, the *Sun-Times* and *Daily News* library contains other newspapers, magazines, books, photographs and negatives, bibliographic services including indexes and digests, with a professional librarian on duty most of the week.

A computer program has recently been developed which will allow newspaper librarians to index and store up to one million pages of written, printed, or pictorial data and retrieve it electronically by what is described as "a low cost and simple-to-use directory system." By using a video display terminal, an editorial writer, for example, can request a listing of all the stories in the computerized morgue pertaining to a particular subject. This listing may then serve as a reference to an existing clipping file, microfilm, filed copies of the daily newspaper, or some other storage medium. It is even possible for the editorialist to get photocopies of the information requested for his own use.[9]

The *New York Times* has been a pioneer in utilizing computer technology to convert its huge morgue, which contained an estimated twenty million clippings from the *Times* and other publications, into an information bank from which information is automatically retrievable by that newspaper's staffers. The system incorporates a complex indexing system, microfiche for communicating the actual page of the newspaper to the terminal screen and a "hard copy" facility which permits the newsman or the subscriber to the *Times* service to get a printout on paper of the index entry. In the fall of 1972 the *Times* was able to offer college and corporate users an automated three-year index with abstracts incorporating everything from 1970. The available base has expanded steadily in both directions since that period.

Editorialists from most newspapers, unfortunately, may be wrestling with newspaper clippings from the morgue or from their personal files for some time in retrieving stories which have been published in their own newspaper. For other than metropolitan newspapers, likewise, editorialists may be using the services of a local public or professional library for many other reference materials described below. For some of the governmental documents described, they will more likely be found in depository libraries which are furnished such material free of charge. The social studies department of Morris Library at Southern Illinois University, for example, receives about 25,000 documents each year from the Superintendent of Documents. These documents have been accumulated since 1932.

General Editorial References

The editorial writer should have ready access to the more basic references since they are usually available in the newsroom. First there may be an assortment of dictionaries, including, hopefully, an unabridged version (Webster's, Funk and Wagnalls or Random House) and one or more specialized dictionaries. These latter may include a thesaurus (such as Roget's) and a book of synonyms (such as *Webster's New Dictionary of Synonyms*), and a book on usage. Roy H. Copperud's *American Usage: The Consensus* is an excellent comparative study of American usage in which the author has collected and compared the judgments of six other language experts, including Rudolf Flesch, Theodore M. Bernstein, Wilson Follett, and H. W. Fowler. A dictionary of American slang may also be found in many newsrooms. A volume such as *Black's Law Dictionary* and a medical dictionary might also prove useful.

The newsroom might also be expected to have in use a one-volume encyclopedia (such as the Columbia *Viking Desk Encyclopedia*) and some type of almanac or factbook (such as *World Almanac* and *Book of Facts* or *Information Please Almanac*). Likewise, some type of biographical dictionary should be available in the newsroom. Two functional one-volume works are Webster's *Biographical Dictionary* and Scribner's *Concise Dictionary of American Biography.* Other standards in the newsroom may include a United States and world atlas, the *U.S. Postal Guide,* the state Blue Book dealing with state government, telephone and business directories, perhaps Bartlett's *Familiar Quotations* and the state's revised statutes. These and other standard references may be shared with the reporting staff, particularly on the smaller newspaper.

Biographical References

Often the standard one-volume biographical dictionaries will not include the one person an editorialist is interested in or, if it does, the information will be too sparse to fill his need. An excellent source dealing with living persons throughout the world who have come to the general public's attention because of their newsworthiness is *Current Biography.*[10] Each monthly issue contains about thirty brief article-length portraits with sources of information which point to other research. The monthly issues are cumulated in annual volumes which contain about 350 biographies a year.

Other multi-volume works include the *Dictionary of American Biography,*[11] which sketches every American who satisfied two requirements: he must have made a significant contribution, and he must be dead. The DAB is prepared under the auspices of the American Council of Learned Societies and is considered one of the most reliable of all American biographical dictionaries. The four volumes of *Who Was Who in America,* which may be found in some newsrooms, also contains brief sketches of the dead VIP's, while the current volume of *Who's Who in America* sketches the living VIP's.

The editorialist who has difficulty finding a biographical sketch of a person he is researching might want to turn to the *Biography Index,* located in most libraries, which indexes biographical material and articles in current books and in 1,500 periodicals.

Yearbooks and Almanacs

Sooner or later every professional journalist becomes familiar with the news reference services of *Facts on File.*[12] This weekly report averaging twenty pages surveys important news events in encyclopedic format, taking up on current events where the yearbooks and almanacs leave off. The looseleaf file is fully indexed twice monthly, and the index is made cumulative every month, every three months, and every year. The information in *Facts on File* is abstracted daily from leading news sources by a staff of research editors who edit and classify the information covering the gamut of news events both in the United States and abroad. Though carefully indexed, sources of the information are not given. The same publishers also provide *Editorials on File,* a twice a month looseleaf editorial survey with cumulative index. Editorials drawn from 115 selected U.S. newspapers on important issues of the day are reprinted, providing full texts during the year of more than 4,000 of what the *Editorials on File* publishers consider to be the most significant editorials.

Other yearbooks which might be useful to the mass media editorial writer include the *Statesman's Year-Book,*[13] a comprehensive international fact book; *Yearbook of the United Nations,*[14] which provides a continuing historical account of the activities of the United Nations and its thirteen specialized agencies; the *Book of the States,*[15] providing statistical charts and information on important aspects of state government; and the *Municipal Year Book,*[16] which provides a detailed account, sometimes in essays, sometimes in the form of statistical tables, of the "current activities and practices of cities throughout the United States."

Other fact books—and the list expands each year—include, besides the *World Almanac* and *Information Please Almanac* mentioned above, the *Official Associated Press Almanac, CBS News Almanac, Reader's Digest Almanac, The People's Almanac, Congressional Quarterly Almanac,* as well as yearbooks dealing with such specialized subjects as *Editor & Publisher International Yearbook* and *Broadcasting Yearbook.*

Indexes, Digests, and Abstracts

Finding what one wants in a library is often made much easier through the use of such search tools as indexes, digests, and abstracts. Most college students, for example, soon become familiar with the *Readers' Guide to Periodical Literature,* which indexes the content of more than 100 general and popular magazines. Other useful search tools include *Index to Legal Periodicals,* which indexes about 300 legal journals and law reviews; the *Book Review Index,* which indexes reviews from nearly two hundred journals; as well as a number of newspaper indexes. These latter include the *New York Times Index,* the *Wall Street Journal Index,* the *Christian Science Monitor Index,* the *London Times Index,* and a monthly *Newspaper Index* which deals with the *Chicago Tribune, Los Angeles Times, New Orleans Times Picayune,* and the *Washington Post.* Without these indexes research in the periodical literature would be next to impossible.

Digests and abstracts also serve as search tools into the literature in various areas. The *Book Review Digest,* for example, condenses critical opinion about books from about seventy-five English and American general periodicals. The *Digest of Education Statistics* covers the whole field of American education, presenting information from governmental and private sources in statistical tables. Seven Decennial Digests provide a massive search tool which indexes points of law in every reported case litigated in the American courts, cumulating the digests during ten-year periods. A monthly publication, *Psychological Abstracts,* is an indispensable search tool in psychology which summarizes, without evaluation, the content of articles in scholarly journals as well as books related to that field. Without the *Psychological Abstracts,* for example, research of Chapters 8, 9, and 10 of this book would have been exceedingly difficult. The editorialist using a library for research in these or other areas needs to become familiar with the search tools available to him in the area or discipline into which his topic falls.

Statistical, Geographical References

There are two other special categories of information the editorialist must often seek out because it is important that such information be correct: one deals with numbers and statistics of all types, the other with place names. The most reliable source of national statistics, without doubt, is the *Statistical Abstract of the United States,*[17] a digest of the statistical data collected by all agencies of the U.S. government and some private agencies. This standard reference contains statistical tables on population; vital statistics such as births, deaths, marriage, divorce, etc.; immigration and naturalization; and detailed breakdowns on education, law enforcement, federal courts, prisons, welfare service, prices, elections, etc. Another Government Printing Office publication, *Historical Statistics of the United States, Colonial Times to 1957,* is helpful for early records. Another historical reference which might be of interest to many editorialists is a *Statistical History of the American Presidential Elections,*[18] which includes 133 tables that report the votes and percentages for each election in each state for both major political parties as well as the minor parties.

The definitive and authoritative reference on place names in this country is an unpretentious volume found in most newsrooms, the *United States Official Postal Guide,* published by the Postal Service, which lists every post office in the nation. In addition, some type of world atlas with its compilation of maps, or gazetteer, a geographical dictionary listing places and giving statistics about them, is needed for reference. *Rand McNally Commercial Atlas and Marketing Guide,* which gives detailed treatment of the states and the outlying possessions of the United States, would fill the need for an atlas. A remarkable geographical dictionary is *Columbia Lippincott Gazetteer of the World,* which lists some 130,000 names of places and geographical features as well as supplying information regarding population, location, altitudes, trade, industry, natural resources, history and cultural institutions. There are, of course, dozens of other suitable atlases and gazetteers available to the editorialist.

Editorial Research Reports

One of the best sources of information focusing upon current issues and problems available to the mass media editorialist is *Editorial Research Reports.*[19] The backbone of ERR is the "Printed Report," issued four times a month, which selects a major issue currently receiving public attention and objectively assembles the full basic facts in about 6,000 words. A typical report starts with a recital of upcoming or recent developments, followed by an exposition of the main elements of controversy, the arguments on both sides, and the influences at work. The next section goes further into the background, historical development, and earlier controversies. The last section looks to the future and considers proposals for solution of a problem, or the action in prospect, thus completing the circular pattern which characterizes the structure of most reports. A 500-word digest suitable for publication on the editorial page, or elsewhere, accompanies each report. ERR also furnishes a five-day-a-week "Daily Service," a succinct background on a single spot news development of about 550 words.

In one sense *Editorial Research Reports* performs the editorialist's research for him, at least on the specific topics which ERR chooses to pursue. It is not surprising that the *Editorial Research Reports* byline is seen frequently on the editorial pages, as well as elsewhere in the nation's newspapers. Even if the digests or the daily service is not used, however, the longer printed reports provide an excellent reference file for future use.

Legislative References

No other topic receives as much attention from the mass media editorialists as do political and governmental issues. This is not surprising since government is so pervasive and such a powerful influence in almost every aspect of one's livelihood. To keep abreast of what's going on in government is, therefore, a real challenge for the editorialist. One of the best sources which digests congressional and political activity each week, making it easier to follow the news, is *Congressional Quarterly Weekly Report,*[20] a privately published report mailed to subscribers every Wednesday night. The report provides a continuing record of the action on bills, the votes of members of Congress, the full text of presidential press conferences, as well as major statements, messages and speeches. Congressional Quarterly, Inc. also publishes *Editorial Research Reports* and an annual almanac, as noted above, plus a series of topical books.

One of the important documents published by the Government Printing Office is the *Congressional Record,* a more or less verbatim report of what is said and done on the House and Senate floors. Congressmen have the opportunity to edit their remarks, however, if they do it quickly, and they have a privilege of extending their remarks in the record. There is no way, unfortunately, to distinguish between what was said on the floor and what was written into the daily *Record.* A useful auxiliary reference book about the composition and operation of Congress is the *Congressional Directory,*[21] one of the best sources for biographical information about members of Congress and their committee assignments. The directory also provides information about individuals and organizations, either governmental or private, who are associated with Congress.

The legislation coming out of a session of Congress is first issued by the U.S. Government Printing Office in slip law form. Slip laws are available in most law libraries as well as in a monthly pamphlet, *U.S. Code Congressional and Administrative News Service.* Most states have similar reference reporting the passage of new state laws which is available in the law libraries of that state. In Illinois, for example, the Illinois Government Association publishes the *Legislative Synopsis and Digest.* Other useful legislative sources include the *Illinois Legislative Council Bulletin* and the *Legislative Information Bulletin.* The editorialist might also have use for a copy of the revised statutes of his state.

Executive, Administrative References

A far more challenging problem for the editorialist than keeping up with the Congress may be keeping abreast with the goings-on in the executive branch of the government. This is partially true because of the thousands of administrative rules and regulations issued by regulatory agencies which have the force of law. The volume of the quasi-legislative output of the federal agencies, for example, far exceeds the volume of the legislative output of Congress. The best key to the numerous new administrative rules and regulations is the *Federal Register,*[22] which must publish all such administrative rules and regulations having the force of law. Issued daily except Saturday, Sunday, Monday, and the days following holidays, the *Register* is indexed quarterly and annually to simplify research. Besides publishing the new regulations from the various bureaus and agencies, the *Register* is perhaps the best source for all presidential proclamations and executive orders. These administrative rules and regulations are eventually codified under fifty titles similar to the arrangement of United States statutes in a set of volumes known as the *Code of Federal Regulations* which is available in most law libraries. It is interesting that the mass of federal regulations requires considerable more library shelf space than do the federal statutes.

The Office of the Federal Register also publishes every Monday a *Weekly Compilation of Presidential Documents,* available in most law libraries, containing statements, messages, and other presidential materials released by the White House. Similar materials eventually are published in annual volumes entitled the *Public Papers of the Presidents.*

Judicial References

While legal research is perhaps more systematized than most scholarly disciplines, it often appears foreboding and unnecessarily complex for the non-lawyer. It is not impossible, however, for a journalist to become a proficient legal researcher. James J. Kilpatrick, for example, turns out excellent syndicated columns from time to time analyzing various actions being taken by the courts. So does Anthony Lewis of the New York *Times* who also has written a classic book-length study of a landmark U.S. Supreme Court opinion entitled *Gideon's Trumpet.* Editorialists, particularly, should at least have a working knowledge of the legal system, how it operates, and an idea of how to find the law on a given topic.

Two invaluable sources reporting current court operations which every editorialist should be familiar with are *United States Law Week* and *Media Law Reporter,* available in most law libraries. *Law Week* is a two-volume, loose-leaf service, one volume dealing with general law which is supplemented weekly, the other containing the complete texts of Supreme Court decisions generally published within twenty-four hours after they are rendered. This timely private service, however, is unofficial, but it is used by lawyers as well as other legal researchers until the official Court decisions are eventually published in the *United States Reports.* A related service which discusses the merits of pending cases under consideration by the Court before the decisions are rendered is the *Preview of United States Supreme Court Cases.* The Bureau of National Affairs, Inc., publishers of *Law Week,* began publishing a similar report for the field of communications law in 1976. Entitled *Media Law Reporter,* it is a weekly, loose-leaf report containing the full texts of all pertinent federal and state court decisions affecting newspapers, magazines, radio, and television.

Two other organizations which attempt to keep journalists and others informed about government censorship are the Freedom of Information Center, located on the campus of the University of Missouri, and the Reporters Committee for Freedom of the Press, which has headquarters in Washington. The reports of both organizations are supplied through subscription and are available in most university libraries where journalism law is taught. Each *Freedom of Information Center Report* deals with a pertinent censorship problem facing the print or electronic media. The Reporters Committee issued ten *Press Censorship Newsletters* from November 1973 through October 1976. The *Newsletter* was converted to a magazine format in 1977 with the first issue of the new periodical, *The News Media and the Law,* issued in October 1977.

Guides to Governmental Documents, Agencies

The United States Government, as the largest publisher in the world, turns out thousands of reports, pamphlets, books, etc., every year. Even government workers are often frustrated by the sheer volume of publications and have trouble locating some of the requested materials which bear the imprimatur: Washington, D.C.: Government Printing Office. An indispensable index which gives a bibliography of publications issued by every department and bureau of the federal government from 1895 to the present is the *Monthly Catalog of United States Government Publications,* a publication prepared by the U.S. Superintendent of Documents.[23] Each monthly issue has instructions for ordering the publications as well as listing the identity of the author, the title, and a brief description of the publication, the price, the date, the number of pages, and often the Library of Congress catalog number. This monthly index will be found in libraries which have been designated as depository libraries. An abbreviated version of the monthly catalogue, entitled "Selected U.S. Government Publications," is available to anyone requesting it.

Information about the various agencies of the federal government is published in an annual directory entitled *U.S. Government Organization Manual.*[24] The manual describes the functions and authority of each department and agency of the executive branch and the regulatory agencies, names and lists the functions of major officials, gives a chart of the organizational structure, and includes a bibliography of major publications issued by the agency. It is, without doubt, one of the most important one-volume reference books for administrative law research. An appendix in volume 1 of the *Code of Federal Regulations* also serves as a guide to all the publications by governmental agencies with lists where information on a specific topic may be found in the various publications of federal administrative materials.

Avoiding Blandness

A frequently heard criticism of newspaper editorials is that they are bland and uninteresting. A bland, "say-nothing" editorial can often be turned into informative, interesting editorial comment through better research and documentation. Roger Bourne Linscott, former *New York Herald Tribune* book section columnist and editorial Pulitzer Prize winner in 1973, should never be charged with blandness. His editorials in the *Berkshire Eagle*, Pittsfield, Massachusetts, have, through the years, been instrumental in bringing about changes in Berkshire County. The following editorial, one of the 1973 Pulitzer winners, helped to head off a $213 million highway project. It is a good example of a well researched and documented editorial.

OUR $213 MILLION GIFT HORSE

When liberal academic types complain that this nation is suffering from a badly distorted sense of political priorities, the complaint is often cast in such abstract terms that it doesn't really register.

But we now have a concrete locally-oriented example of what they're talking about in the form of the state's proposal to allocate $213 million of interstate highway funds to a revamping of Routes 7 and 8 here in Berkshire County.

Nobody in these parts, of course, is likely to object very strenuously to such an outpouring of federal largesse. It would be nice to have a super-road to hustle transients through the area and to give all parts of the county speedier access to the Massachusetts Turnpike. And there is always the rationalization that if the Berkshires don't get the money some other area will.

Nonetheless, $213 million is a staggering sum of money. And at the risk of seeming to look a gift horse in the mouth, it is tempting to consider some of the other things that such a sum could buy.

For instance, with $213 million you could clean up the Housatonic River from its tributaries in Windsor to the Connecticut border, with probably enough left over to create recreational ponds and parks along its course.

Or you could build and equip enough schools to take care of all of the county's public educational needs for the next decade.

Or, if you wanted to dole out the $213 million to the cities and towns of the Berkshires as a revenue sharing device, it would be sufficient to permit a total moratorium on all local real estate taxes, throughout the county, for a period of about 10 years.

Or, to carry it from the sublime to the ridiculous, as a direct per capita hand-out it would be enough to provide a cash payment of nearly $3,000 apiece to every one of the county's 70,000-odd adult inhabitants.

But none of these purposes, worthy or otherwise, can have any claim on the federal money. The highway lobby has long since seen to that. The $213 million (more precisely, 90 percent of it) would come from the federal Highway Trust Fund, which is lavishly nourished by the federal gas tax and is earmarked by law exclusively for highway purposes.

Indeed, as things now stand the Highway Trust Fund's multibillion-dollar cornucopia can't even be applied to alternative forms of public transportation, despite the fact that a decent mass transit system in this country would serve to lighten the burden on our highways and save our cities from strangulation at the hands of the motor car. Just this week, Transportation Secretary John Volpe asked Congress for permission to spend a portion of the fund on mass transit in the coming fiscal year—and the best bet on Capitol Hill is that the answer will be no.

In the case of the Berkshires, the plan is to make available for Routes 7 and 8 most of the money the federal authorities had allocated to the Boston area but which isn't being spent there because of the governor's moratorium on new highway construction within the Route 128 circle. Because of the lower land-taking costs in the hinterlands, the state highway planners figure they can build 66 miles of super-road in the Berkshires for what a mere 4 miles would cost in the congested Boston area. This, they point out, is quite a bargain.

No doubt it is, if measured solely in miles of concrete. And no doubt, if the money has to be spent somewhere and can be spent on highway construction only, we should welcome it. But there's no law against wishing for a system in which urgent social needs might be able to take fiscal priority over the inexhaustible demands of the automobile.

Berkshire Eagle, Pittsfield, Mass., March 17, 1972
Reprinted by permission.

Framed and hanging on the wall of Editor Linscott's office in Pittsfield are a couple of editorials from another newspaper, which shall remain anonymous, which he notes are so "marvelously fatuous" that he is "proud NOT to have written" them. "Whenever I have a particularly bad day at the typewriter I re-read them and feel a lot better," he says. Here is one of those editorials as it appeared at the top of the editorial column:

GREAT STATESMEN

There never was a time when the world had more need of great statesmen than it has today.

Yet the globe is certainly not crowded with them.

Statesmen, of course, are political leaders with keen vision, high ideals, knowledge of public and international affairs and the ability to get constructive results.

During World War II, Winston Churchill attracted universal attention.

He was a man of much ability and rallied his nation for the great military conflict.

He also won the support of the United States with his historic oratory and his skillful diplomacy.

Yet, during his long career, Mr. Churchill made many mistakes and they were usually big ones.

Most diplomats make mistakes.

Perhaps the world is too complicated for any one individual to comprehend.

Some diplomats get started on the wrong path and are too stubborn to let the hard facts interfere with their theories.

Men of this sort are dangerous to the nation which they are helping to guide.

America, by common consent, is the most powerful nation in the world today.

How can she most effectively use that power to help keep the world at peace?

Our diplomats, regardless of which political party is in power, make their share of mistakes.

We cannot afford to go on making mistakes.

When and how are we going to find and keep the road to world cooperation?

That is one of the most important questions of our time.

The question which the editorial raises may be important, but its superficial treatment can hardly be said to illuminate the question. More research and documentation are needed. More reflection and creative thinking are needed. More and better ideas are needed.

Summary and Conclusion

One general conclusion which may be drawn from the brief examination above of source and reference material available to the mass media editorialist is that most of the information the editorialist seeks is somewhere available. It may be another matter to acquire and have on hand the more basic, most-often-used references and to locate the more costly, multi-volume indexes, services, references in a nearby library—and to take the effort necessary to become familiar with all of them. If familiarity breeds comfort, as one social psychologist contends, then the key to the development of better researched editorials may be a greater familiarity with the multitude of basic sources where factual information about current events and issues which affect the public interest may be obtained and/or verified.

Several years ago a panel of editorialists were asked in a symposium a basic question: "Whom do you trust?" The panelists were encouraged to talk about their sources of information and inspiration, how they organized information, what they felt was essential and what wasn't, which sources were suspect and/or indispensable. The answers ranged from "don't trust anyone" to the use of "everything except scissors and paste." One editor, after discussing many of the references listed above, expressed a frustration felt by many editorialists faced with the daily glut of information. He said:

> Ever try to get a drink of water from a fire hydrant? The sensation is about the same as seeking inspiration and information from the spate of material that flows across the editorial desk: You get soaked but not satisfied.[25]

The point is, of course, that the editorialist must ultimately trust somebody for the facts in his editorial. Even the information in some of the standard sources discussed above, of course, is at times inaccurate, but reliance upon memory or word of mouth is generally far less reliable.

The compiler of any basic source and reference list, of course, should proceed with caution. Newspapers serve different communities, their editorial pages pursue different policies and view the world differently. Radio and television stations are even more diverse. In addition to these variables, the editorialists are different; they have different goals and different needs. A newspaper editorialist, trying to compile a list of references more than a decade ago which he called "the editorial elbow," noted:

> It is somewhat presumptuous of one editor to tell another what he ought to have on his shelf. It's something like telling a person which flowers he ought to have in his garden. So much depends upon the editor himself, his background and interests, and the sort of thing he is likely to write about. The most useful reference books are the books the user knows best. They are the books he turns to because he knows they contain the information he wants. He has lived with them.[26]

While the "complete listing" which this editorialist proposed a decade ago would no longer be sufficient today, it is true that any useful reference shelf is personal, and the references need to be familiar and to be trusted by the editorialist—else they are not likely to be used.

NOTES for Chapter 4

[1] See, e.g., Robert E. Webb, "Research Pays Off," part of a symposium on "What Kind of Writing Pays Off?" *The Masthead* 11 (Fall 1959): 20–21.

[2] Stephen S. Rosenfeld, "Researching and Writing," in *The Editorial Page,* ed.: Laura Longley Babb (Boston: Houghton Mifflin, 1977), p. 43.

[3] For a discussion of the staffing of editorial pages, see Laurence J. Paul, "Many Pages Wretchedly Understaffed," *The Masthead* 14 (Spring 1972): 1–4.

[4] Kenneth R. Byerly, *Community Journalism* (New York: Chilton Co., 1961), p. 281.

[5] See, e.g., Chilton R. Bush, ed., *News Research for Better Newspapers,* vol. 3, p. 51; vol. 5, p. 22.

[6] Associated Press report in *St. Louis Post-Dispatch,* Janury 26, 1976, p. 6A.

[7] Bradley S. Greenberg and Michael E. Roloff, "Mass Media Credibility: Research Results and Critical Issues," ANPA *News Research Bulletin* 6 (November 4, 1975).

[8] See, e.g., Mona McCormick, *Who-What-When-Where-How-Why Made Easy* (New York: Quadrangle Books, 1971); Saul Galin and Peter Spielberg, *Reference Books: How to Select & Use Them* (New York: Vintage Books, 1969); Eleanor Blum, *Reference Books in the Mass Media* (Urbana: University of Illinois Press, 1972).

[9] *ANPA Research Institute Bulletin* 1253 (January 25, 1977); and "Morgue Retrieval System Has Million Page Capacity," *Editor & Publisher,* June 15, 1974, p. 22.

[10] *Current Biography* (New York: H. W. Wilson Co., 1940–. Published monthly, except August).

[11] *Dictionary of American Biography* (New York: Scribner's 1928–1973, 20 vols., index, and Supplements I, II, and III).

[12] *Facts on File* (New York: Facts on File, Inc., 1940–. Weekly).

[13] *Statesman's Year-Book* (New York: St. Martin's Press, 1864–. Annual)

[14] *Yearbook of the United Nations* (New York: United Nations and Columbia University Press, 1946–. Annual).

[15] *Book of the States* (Chicago: Council of State Governments, 1935–. Biennial).

[16] *Municipal Year Book* (Chicago: International City Managers Association, 1934–. Annual).

[17] *Statistical Abstract of the United States* (Washington, D.C.: Government Printing Office, 1878–. Annual).

[18] Svend Petersen, *Statistical History of the American Presidential Elections* (New York: Ungar, 1968).

[19] *Editorial Research Reports* (Washington: Congressional Quarterly, Inc., 1923–).

[20] *Congressional Quarterly Weekly Report* (Washington, D.C.: Congressional Quarterly, Inc., 1945–. Weekly).

[21] *Congressional Directory* (Washington, D.C.: Government Printing Office, 1809–. Annual).

[22] *Federal Register* (Washington, D.C.: Government Printing Office, 1936–).

[23] *Monthly Catalogue of United States Government Publications* (Washington, D.C.: Government Printing Office, 1895–. Monthly, with annual cumulations).

[24] *U.S. Government Organization Manual* (Washington, D.C.: Government Printing Office, 1935–. Annual).

[25] "A Symposium: Whom Do You Trust?" *The Masthead* 22 (Fall 1970: 30–41.

[26] Robert B. Frazier, "The Editorial Elbow," *The Masthead* 15 (Summer 1963): 5–16.

5

Reflection:
An Important Ingredient in Persuasion

EDITORIAL THINKING AND reflection should precede editorial writing. This is true primarily because the act or process of editorial thinking should result in better editorial ideas, in the formulation of new and more perceptive insights, in a more thorough testing of assumptions and hypotheses, in a more systematic rationalization of alternative solutions to problems and better answers to troublesome questions. But reflective thinking is hard work; indeed, thinking may be the most difficult undertaking of man, Ralph Waldo Emerson once noted. At least reflective thinking is difficult. During every awakening hour, sometimes even when one is asleep, something is usually going through one's head—daydreams, reveries, castles built in the air, or mental streams of consciousness, which may be even more idle and chaotic. Reflective thinking, however, involves more concentration, more effort, less randomness. John Dewey, the American philosopher and educator, pointed out many years ago:

> Reflection involves not simply a sequence of ideas, but a *con*-sequence—a consecutive ordering in such a way that each determines the next as its proper outcome, while each outcome in turn leans back on, or refers to, its predecessors. The successive portions of a reflective thought grow out of one another and support one another; they do not come and go in a medley. Each phase is a step from something to something—technically speaking, it is a *term* of thought. Each term leaves a deposit that is utilized in the next term. The stream or flow becomes a train or chain. There are in any reflective thought definite units that are linked together so that there is a sustained movement to a common end.[1]

James H. Robinson, author of *The Mind in the Making,* identifies not two, but four kinds of thinking. The first he labeled "reverie," which he viewed as spontaneous and a favorite kind of thinking. A second involved decision-making which often demands a good deal of careful pondering and recollection of pertinent facts. A third type, rationalization, may be stimulated when one's beliefs or opinions are questioned. The reasons given in support of one's preconceptions or routine beliefs, however, may have little value in promoting honest enlightenment because they often are the result of personal preference or prejudice and not an honest desire to seek or accept new knowledge. The fourth type Robinson labeled "creative thinking," thought which goes beyond the other three categories and which may lead one to change his mind. Noting that in the past creative thinking was called "reason," Robinson argued that his label was more appropriate:

> For this kind of meditation [creative thinking] begets knowledge, and knowledge is really creative inasmuch as it makes things look different from what they seemed before and may indeed work for their reconstruction.[2]

Reflection, particularly in the creative sense, allows the mass media editorialist to make decisions, to draw inferences, to arrive at conclusions through the judicious use of his mental powers. As pointed out in Chapter 3, the most important ingredient in opinion writing, either in the print or electronic media, is ideas, and ideas are the product of thought and reflection. The editorialist has the responsibility to sit back and reflect. He needs to take the time to define his community's continuing role in the total, massive effort to solve society's growing problems. In reference to those goals he needs to make sense out of the glut of information which is being communicated daily to his readers or listeners.

An often heard criticism of the media's opinion function is that not enough thought goes into such writing. One author has noted that editorialists have "too many thoughts and too little thought." Too often, it is pointed out, an editorialist must choose his subjects from two to twenty-four hours before his copy must go to press or his commentary goes on the air. Even though the mass media opinion writer theoretically has been disciplined to respond to these daily deadlines, the product of his thought often suffers as he spends the time needed for reflection hurriedly seeking, assessing, and sorting out the basic facts surrounding the issue he is attempting to illuminate. The result may be superficial treatment of often complex and important public issues.[3]

Thinking versus Logic

Making sense out of the glut of information which is being communicated daily by the mass media may require, as Dewey has noted, a careful ordering of ideas, a logical reasoning process, and a careful comparing and balancing of evidence by the editorialist. While these logical steps may flow from the reflective process, there are important differences between formal reasoning (logic) and thinking as it might be engaged in by the editorialist. A favorite form of the logician is the syllogism: "All men are mortal; Socrates is a man; therefore, Socrates is mortal." Thinking, it has been noted, might better be illustrated by examining the state of mind of Socrates' disciples when they were considering, at the time of his trial, the prospects of his death. Logical forms generally do not pretend to tell how one thinks or how he should think, nor are such forms necessarily helpful in reaching conclusions or in arriving at beliefs and knowledge. Logical forms, however, may provide an effective way in which to set forth what has already been concluded, so as to convince others of the soundness of the results.[4]

Actual thinking, of course, is usually not without its own logic; for example, it is orderly, it is reasonable, it is reflective. Dewey has noted:

> When we say a person is *thoughtful,* we mean something more than that he merely indulges in thoughts. To be really thoughtful is to be logical. Thoughtful persons are heedful, not rash; they look about, are circumspect instead of going ahead blindly. They weigh, ponder, deliberate—terms that imply a careful comparing and balancing of evidence and suggestions, a process of evaluating what occurs to them in order to decide upon its force and weight for their problem. Moreover, the thoughtful person looks into matters; he scrutinizes, inspects, examines. He does not, in other words, take observations at their face value, but probes them to see whether they are what they seem to be.[5]

Logic viewed from such a perspective avoids the criticism of formal logic that it is "an unnatural way of thinking" and "a contrived technique of going from unwarranted assumptions to foregone conclusions."[6]

The editorialist also needs to be aware of two approaches in the reasoning process arising from logic: inductive and deductive reasoning. They represent two sides of the same street. Inductive reasoning is a case approach in which individual examples are examined to arrive at some valid generalization about all cases. Deduction is the opposite—deductive reasoning goes from the general to the particular. The syllogism involving Socrates above is an example of deductive reasoning. "All men are mortal," the major premise, is a generalization—hopefully a valid generalization. "Socrates is a man" is the minor premise—hopefully a valid assumption. "Socrates is mortal" is a conclusion deducted from the three-step syllogistic process. The conclusion, of course, in such a formalized logical process, is no more truthful than are the major and minor premises. If the major premise is based upon an unwarranted, unproven assumption, the conclusion will likewise be invalid. (For a further discussion of logical fallacies, see Chapter 7.)

The editorialist will be reasoning from the specific to the general as well as from the general to the specific. In most actual thinking the two processes march hand in hand. The editorialist might find it helpful to review the basic rules of logic as set out in some standard textbook.[7] He might find there useful guidelines for measuring the "logic" of his editorial conclusions, once formed.

Thinking as a Scientist

There are two basic ways of making a decision: arriving at a conclusion or reaching a solution to a problem. One is to make observations, weigh the alternatives, and decide what to do or not to do, what solution to implement or not to implement. Such an approach would be the more rational, the more logical, the more scientific way. Or, one may decide without conscious thinking, as one does about many little things which one faces each day. An individual might be in continual turmoil if he had to think consciously about every little thing he did during the day. One would lose a great deal in spontaneity, and it would be difficult to accomplish very much if one had to stop repeatedly to reflect. But for the mass media editorial writer, seeking to inform a mass audience as to the proper interpretation of some political action, arguing for some course of action, or offering some solution to a problem of great relevance to readers or listeners, his approach needs to be more rational, more scientific. He needs to engage in straight thinking. He needs to think more as a scientist thinks. Here, for example, are suggestions, as adopted from "The Six Tools for Thinking" by Kenneth S. Keyes, Jr.,[8] which might assist the editorialist in thinking more scientifically:

1. The editorialist needs to approach his research and writing with an open mind, willing to search for all the facts from reliable sources, observing first hand when possible. Keyes notes that it sometimes takes but one new fact to bring an entirely different conclusion about an issue or different solution to a problem. Scientific thinking demands approaching one's research with a willingness to entertain new ideas, to consider new problems, to listen to more than one side of an issue. Such open-mindedness, Dewey observes, may be more active and positive than the word suggests:

> It is very different from empty-mindedness. While it *is* hospitality to new themes, facts, ideas, questions, it is not the kind of hospitality that would be indicated by hanging out a sign: "Come right in; there is nobody at home." It includes an active desire to listen to more sides than one; to give heed to facts from whatever source they come; to give full attention to alternative possibilities; to recognize the possibility of error even in the beliefs that are dearest to us.[9]

2. The editorialist, even more than an individual engaging in reflective thinking in some other area, needs to recognize that the subtle

world in which he lives is not painted in a bold black on white. Indeed, the editorialist's color is usually grey, not an unrelieved black or white. If all the arguments are either for or against a given issue, the chances are that the need for editorial illumination or for interpretation is not that great. It is the controversial topic where good arguments exist on either side of the question—for example, capital punishment, abortion, the equal rights amendment—in which the editorialist is most often engaged. Even the dichotomy of good and bad when applied to thinking needs to give way to thinking in terms of degree. The Likert-type scales often used in measuring opinion, for example, aren't simply measurements of "agree" or "disagree" to a given statement or assertion. The scales may run from "agree completely" on one end of the continuum to "disagree completely" on the other end. The intermediate points—"almost completely agree," "agree somewhat," "neither agree nor disagree," "disagree somewhat," "almost completely disagree"—afford the respondent an array of scale points upon which to make his choice. This concept, when applied to reflection about important editorial issues, should result in a better balanced, more realistic evaluation than would the black/white, good/bad, either/or approach. At least that is the theory.

3. The editorialist, if he is to think as a scientist, must also take care to discount his own prejudices and predilections. William James, the great American philosopher, once noted that one can only see through his own eyes. Others have demonstrated that one's experience tends to condition what he observes or what he fails to observe. Indeed, it has been argued that an eyewitness is not necessarily a good witness merely because of the fact that he was present when an event occurred. His experience tends to determine both how much and what he observes, just as the three blind men described the elephant differently, depending upon the portion of the animal's anatomy each was exploring. The editorialist needs to be aware, therefore, of his biases, his personal interests, his feelings about certain issues, about certain public figures, about certain likes and dislikes, and he should attempt to discount his prejudices if he is to think scientifically.

4. The editorialist in his thinking and reflection needs to remember that things which look to be the same, or which are labeled the same, are often different—and that such differences may make a difference. In the latter case, language often tends to suggest similarity, providing a semantic problem if such verbal maps are assumed to be accurate maps of the territory—to use a familiar analogy of the general semanticist. The group word "Congressmen," for example, reminds one of the similarities of the 535 persons serving in the United States Congress. While every editorialist knows that each member of Congress is different in ways which make a difference, he may tend to react to and evaluate Congressmen he does not know on the basis of the attri-

butes of those he does know, assuming similarity. The general semanticist would argue that the editorialist should engage in "indexing"—suggesting that the label "Congressman" be used with a subscript, for example, "$Congressman_1$" is different from "$Congressman_2$" is different from "$Congressman_3$." The subscript is used to remind one that there is a difference; reflective thinking may indicate that the difference makes a real difference in the event or issue being illuminated or analyzed. This same caution needs to be exercised by the editorialist in his on-the-spot observations—things which on first glance may appear to be the same may, upon more careful examination, be found to be different. And that difference, if introduced into the reflective thinking process, may make a difference in the solution, conclusion, or answer proposed.

5. The editorialist, if he is to remain a scientific thinker, must never forget that the things occurring around him are constantly changing—that the world about him is in constant process. This step goes beyond the matter of indexing to note the differences in things which are labeled or at first glance appear to be the same. It argues that no one thing is ever twice the same. Heraclitus the Greek had an illuminating metaphor for the concept though he expressed the view more than 2,000 years ago. He contended that one can never step in the same river twice. Wendell Johnson, elaborating upon the metaphor in *People in Quandaries,* noted that:

> No other fact so unrelentingly shapes and reshapes our lives as this: that reality, in the broadest sense, continually changes, like the river of Heraclitus—and in recent years the river of Heraclitus appears to have been rising. The currents are faster, the eddies more turbulent, and the stream is overflowing its banks more and more each day. What we once thought of as safe ground has been abandoned to the flood. The dikes of civilization are watched with anxious eyes.[10]

That statement was made more than thirty years ago. The modern-day editorialist also needs to remain aware that the world about him is not only constantly changing, as the river, but the eddies grow more turbulent from time to time and the river periodically floods and must be watched with anxious eyes. He needs to keep watch if he is to remain a scientific thinker.

6. The mass media editorialist also needs to consider where things take place, who said what, where, under what conditions, and with what effect. Keyes called this process the "where index," though he used it more in the sense of an environmental index. In a more modern context, it would involve concerns which the sociologists call role playing, with interaction, and with acting out one's social role in terms of one's perception of the expectations of others as well as his own expectations of the social role he now occupies. The pronouncements of

the local mayor, for example, should be viewed in the light of the role played by a mayor and should be evaluated in light of the circumstances (the where) under which they were said. The "where index" suggests that a critical evaluation of the facts, once gathered, should become a part of creative, reflective thinking. Maybe the mayor's pronouncement was nothing more than an expression of what he perceived (being a good politician) was expected of him—under the circumstances. Any editorial conclusion anticipating a change of policy on the part of the city administration based upon the utterance, therefore, might be wholly unwarranted.

Thinking About Thinking

Reflective, creative thinking, as distinguished from reveries and daydreams, requires a degree of concentration, some guidance, some systematic approach—some thinking about one's thinking. Reflection may require, for example, a decision as to what aspect of the problem or question to focus upon first. It's difficult to think productively about the whole of a complex situation all at once. The problem needs to be pulled apart for analysis to discover the key question from the dozens of possible questions which could be raised about such a complex problem. Such an approach might be analogous to the rule of the American Boy Scouts for finding a lost object. The Scout determines where the article supposedly was lost, then starts walking in ever-widening circles until he finds the lost object. While the object will seldom be precisely in the center, the system usually produces better results than casting far and wide unsystematically in erratic criss-crossing paths. Deciding upon one key question may provide that focus from which the editorialist can launch his thinking and his research.

Not only does the mass media editorialist need to focus and concentrate upon some pertinent aspect of the problem he is analyzing, he needs to select a location for reflection most conducive to such concentration. Walter Lippmann, who liked to approach an issue from a detached point of view, withdrawing from the hubbub of the marketplace, wrote in *Public Opinion* more than fifty years ago:

> Every man whose business it is to think knows that he must for part of the day create about himself a pool of silence. . . . So long as he is physically imprisoned in crowds by day and even by night his attention will flicker and relax. . . . How capricious, how superfluous and clamorous is the ordinary urban life of our time. We learn to understand why our addled minds seize so little with precision, why they are caught up and tossed about in a kind of tarantella by headlines and catch-words, why so often they cannot tell things apart or discern identity in apparent differences.[11]

Lippmann has often been categorized as the "ivory tower" philosopher. But every editorialist from time to time needs his ivory tower where he can withdraw from the confusing marketplace though he must by necessity spend a part of his time there. He needs somewhere to withdraw for a "pool of silence" where reflection and creative thinking are likely to be fostered. Marquis Childs of the *St. Louis Post-Dispatch,* as a syndicated columnist, liked to reflect and write in the Bahamas, cut off from the hubbub of the communications world. William Allen White, editor of the *Emporia* (Kan.) *Gazette,* liked to do his more extensive writing from his cabin in Colorado. Other creative writers have their favorite spots for reflection and writing. But the average work schedule for the newspaper or broadcast editorialist will often not allow for such a total withdrawal from the workaday world.

The editorialist, however, can seek an environment where he will be less disturbed to allow time for reflection and where he can concentrate upon his creative effort. The middle of the newsroom with all its confusion and ringing of telephones may not be the best place to attempt such a feat. Even an open door to a private office may be invitation enough for an intrusion into one's "pool of silence." Perhaps the door should be shut, one's feet placed on the desk, the telephone taken from the cradle, and concentration and reflection nurtured in any other way possible. Other editorialists, of course, may be able to reflect and engage in straight thinking in the middle of the newsroom, or on a subway, or on a stool in a crowded bar—if they have enough power of concentration to shut out the hubbub of the workaday world. Nor is straight thinking always aided by isolation. It is often beneficial, for example, to share one's thoughts with a colleague. What is essential is the avoidance of the unwarranted stress and turmoil of the marketplace.

Not only does the editorialist need to focus and concentrate on the problem he is attempting to analyze from a location in which he will not be unduly disturbed, he needs to develop the habit of writing down his editorial thoughts because they may be fleeting. Not only does the writing prevent the thought from escaping, such ideas and conceptions, which may appear chaotic when bouncing around inside one's head, become clearer when sketched on paper. One author has noted:

> There is nothing so clarifying as writing things down. One may go so far as to say that a man does not know what he thinks until he writes it down. Then, when he reads it over, he finds out for the first time what his own thoughts really are.[12]

Not only does writing things down bring one face to face with factual information, it also gives one the opportunity to check the correctness of his thinking and to sort out the reverie and wishful thinking.

Indeed, Graham Wallas, a British psychologist, suggested more than fifty years ago that there are four stages in the natural thought process during which time the thinker, such as an editorialist, might bring his art to bear: (1) the preparation stage, (2) the incubation stage,

(3) the illumination stage, and (4) the verification stage.[13] These so-called stages of thought control will form the basis for the discussion which follows.

Preparation: Reasoning from Facts

The first stage in which the editorialist can bring a conscious effort to bear upon the process of reflection is in the accumulation of knowledge related to the problem being studied. Facts and other related information are essential to thinking scientifically about any problem. The editorialist may, of course, rely upon the thinking and reflection of others about those facts, but reliance upon the reflection of others dooms an editorialist to a role as follower rather than that of an opinion leader. Furthermore, the editorialist will never be comfortable or will never be confident in the editorial positions he advocates if he does not begin his thinking by looking at the facts for himself. Such facts, one writer notes, may be garnered from four principal sources: from direct observation, from one's memories, from reports provided by other persons, and from self-evident truths. Once gathered, however, the facts will remain dead as far as reflection is concerned unless they are put to use to suggest and test some idea, to search for the way out of a difficulty, or to help provide a valid solution or conclusion to a pending editorial problem.

Formal education may also provide an excellent entry to the preparation stage of thought control. Education, for example, should help one see things more clearly, should help one to distinguish between the essential and the trivial, and should help provide a meaningful frame of reference or an effective system of thought to assist in making the valid judgments necessary in editorial reflection and writing. The very process of education, likewise, provides, through the effort of observation and memorization, a body of remembered facts and concepts which gives the educated person both a wider range of vision to deal with complex problems and perhaps a more developed system of thought. But even for the more educated, better prepared editorialist, the problem being studied must first be stated, the subject delineated, the focus determined, the tentative hypothesis formulated, and the subject investigated in all directions. If the first step isn't taken, the following steps may not occur, Wallas has noted, because:

> Our minds are not likely to give us a clear answer to any particular problem unless we set it a clear question, and we are more likely to notice the significance of any new piece of evidence, or new association of ideas, if we have formed a definite conception of a case to be proved or disproved.[14]

Of course the preparation process for a specific problem is not an isolated event. The editorialist often does not have the luxury of investigating one problem at a time; he is usually working to prepare himself on many problems at once. Robert M. White II, editor and publisher of the *Mexico* (Mo.) *Ledger,* has observed:

> Good editorials, I believe, are the product of what Arthur Hays Sulzberger has called the well-stocked mind. I think good editorials are the result of steeping yourself, day after day, every waking hour, not only with facts that go into editorials but also with that most basic factor of all—the human factor.[15]

That well-stocked mind is the purpose of the preparation stage of the thinking process. Preparation, like education, spurs reflection and critical thinking which in turn produces good, or at least better, editorials.

Incubation: Editorialist as "Man Thinking"

The incubation stage of thought control, according to Wallas, follows preparation and is a period during which the individual voluntarily abstains from conscious thought. During the incubation stage, however, a series of unconscious and involuntary (or fore-conscious and fore-voluntary) mental events occur. It is important, therefore, that the preparation be done early enough so that there is sufficient time for incubation. Wallas quotes a well-known academic psychologist and minister as saying that he had found by experience that his Sunday sermon was much better if he posed the problem on Monday than if he did so later in the week. This was found to be true though he might give the same number of hours of conscious work to it in each case.

The mass media editorialist likewise needs to research and reflect about his assigned topic sufficiently early so that he may have the incubation period required for mulling over the problem, to allow an interval free from conscious thought on the particular problem during which time, however, nothing is allowed to interfere with the free working of the unconscious or partially conscious processes of the mind. Louis D. Brandeis, a brilliant legal scholar and an associate justice of the Supreme Court of the United States, once wrote a friend about the need to "keep his mind fresh":

> The bow must be strung and unstrung; work must be measured not merely by time but also by its intensity. There must be time for that unconscious thinking which comes to the busy man in his play.[16]

Brandeis, no doubt, was referring to the incubation process of fore-voluntary, fore-conscious thought.

Mark Twain, who served a literary apprenticeship as a journalist, had difficulty on occasion in completing his literary works because, as one critic put it, "his tank ran dry." In the writing of *Huckleberry Finn,* for example, this drain occurred about the time Twain got Jim and Huck down the Mississippi as far as Cairo. Twain, in fact, was forced to lay aside the book for several years. Finally he visited his boyhood home in Hannibal, Missouri, once again and rode a riverboat on the Mississippi to restock "his tank." In the terms of the four stages of thought control, Twain's preparation and his facts became too removed, his thought process in the incubation stage had nothing to feed upon, and his mind ran dry. Or, as many creative writers might put it, his inspiration ran out.

John Dewey had a more scientific explanation for this common experience among creative thinkers when, after prolonged preoccupation with an intellectual topic, the mind ceases to function readily, new suggestions and ideas cease to occur. Dewey said:

> This condition is a warning to turn, as far as conscious attention and reflection are concerned, to something else. Then after the mind has ceased to be intent on the problem, and consciousness has relaxed its strain, a period of incubation sets in. Material rearranges itself; facts and principles fall into place; what was confused becomes bright and clear; the mixed-up becomes orderly, often to such an extent that the problem is essentially solved.[17]

Illumination: Finding the Happy Idea

The most complex of Wallas' four stages of thought control is the illumination stage when the instantaneous flash or click of inspiration occurs, producing the "happy idea." The problem is that most efforts to control the thought process at this point are unlikely to improve one's thinking. It is at this point also that the editorialist most needs that "pool of silence" referred to by Walter Lippmann. Not only should one guard against interruptions by the telephone, or the entrance of someone into the office or room, or questions from others which may disrupt the illumination, he should also realize any effort to write before the illumination comes may also destroy the thought process expected to produce the happy idea. One writer notes that such thoughts "are so elusive that to attempt to articulate them is to scare them away, as a fish is scared by the slightest ripple."[18]

Compulsive reading, sometimes necessary in the first stage of thought control—preparation—may work to the detriment of the editorialist in the illumination stage. Wallas suggests that the "habit of industrious passive reading" may be harmful to the thought process, particularly when there is a rising consciousness which indicates that the fully conscious flash of success is coming. He notes that Carlyle once told Anthony Trollope that a man, when traveling, "should not read, but sit still and label his thoughts." But what can the editorialist do when he feels an illumination coming on, or as Wallas puts it, what can he do when he feels in his fringe-consciousness an association-train, a state of rising consciousness which indicates a flash of success is coming? Apparently, not much. He can lay aside his reading and maintain a "pool of silence," but he can't do much toward controlling his thought-process at this point. Wallas notes:

> A schoolboy sitting down to do an algebra sum, a civil servant composing a minute [a report], Shakespeare re-writing a speech in a play, will . . . gain no more by interfering with the ideas whose coming is vaguely indicated to them, before they come, than would a child by digging up a sprouting bean, or a hungry man in front of a good meal, by bringing his will to bear on the intimations of activity in his stomach or his salivary glands.[19]

For the editorialist the primary danger of spoiling the illumination whose coming is near at hand is being forced to begin his writing before he feels prepared. Like all writers, however, the editorialist must sooner or later make that conscious effort to capture his thoughts on paper. The success of his effort may well have been predetermined by the success of his reflection, for as Editor White of the *Mexico* (Mo.) *Ledger* has noted:

> Good editorials are written those last few minutes before you go to sleep at night. Good editorials are written when you're shaving in the morning, or at the wheel of your car driving to work. Good editorials are written while you are shoveling snow off the walk, or cutting grass. They're even written while your two-year-old daughter is sitting on your lap happily trying to put bobby-pins in your crew-cut.[20]

It is possible, of course, for the illumination to come as one writes, seemingly flowing through one's fingertips. One authority suggests that the concentration needed in writing may bring forth thoughts and ideas which may come in no other way.[21] But it is also true that a blank sheet of paper in a typewriter or the emptiness of a blinking video display screen before one's eyes may offer a formidable barrier to creative thinking, particularly where no preparation, no incubation, or no illumination has preceded the writing effort.

Verification: Does the Idea "Plug In?"

During this fourth stage of thought control, the validity of the idea produced must be verified and tested and it must be reduced to writing in a precise editorial statement. The editorialist, for example, must be sure that the illumination is not merely a reverie or daydream. He needs to be sure that the answer being proposed is indeed an answer to the question presented in the editorial. He needs to be sure that the solution being offered solves the problem. He needs to be sure that his conclusion plugs into the issue being discussed. Without such verification, the editorialist may be writing the non sequitur—the conclusion which does not follow. Such verification is important because, as Wallas notes, the fruit of such unconscious reflection occurring during the incubation and illumination stages rarely emerges ready-made for use. At times these thoughts may be little more than inspirations, the results of which must be verified and the consequences deduced.

The economy of the four-stage concept, however, is that the editorialist may be in the preparation stage of thought control on one topic while, at the same time, he may be incubating two others. In the meantime he may receive an illumination about a third topic while he is in the process of verifying and writing on a fourth topic. The various processes of thought are not too different from the experience of a student involved in three or four courses during a given semester. While he is preparing and ordering the vast amounts of information received in one course, he may be incubating and reflecting—perhaps unconsciously—about another, and he may be undergoing tests calling for verification of the content of a third course. Theoretically, if he does the preparation in each course sufficiently early, the incubation stage will allow for the unconscious reflection which will produce the illumination needed to answer the questions posed by the instructor—the examination being the verification stage.

Enemies of Effective Thinking

The hurried, cluttered, noisy atmosphere of the newsroom or editorial offices of the typical newspaper or broadcast station is admittedly not alway conducive to reflective thinking. It is often difficult for the editorialist, as noted above, to concentrate and reflect without more tranquillity or more isolation than the typical newsroom provides. It may be difficult to achieve the "pool of silence" Lippmann finds useful for effective reflection. The problem, however, may be greater than this. The hurried deadline pressures of the newroom may discourage even taking the time for reflection. If it is important that editorial thinking precede editorial writing, then it is fallacious to assume that one does not have time for meditative thinking. Without sufficient time to reflect, the product of the editorialist's effort—the editorial itself—will often lack the illumination, the insights, even the ideas needed to make the offering either useful or persuasive.

There are, of course, numerous other enemies of constructive thinking. Purposeless reverie and daydreaming, for example, usually lead to nothing. There must be concentration, direction, and purpose to the reflection. For the daydream to become a useful editorial idea it must survive the verification stage of thought control, as noted above.

What one writer calls "wishful thinking" can also be detrimental to effective thinking to the extent the thinker tends to champion too strongly a theory he has created. For example, if he clings to the theory as true because he hopes it is, he may remain ignorant of the real facts of the case. The theory, therefore, may be only a picture furnished by his imagination. Since imagination is one of the elements in "sagacity," the writer notes, it is only natural that, in problem solving, some of the suggestions furnished by the imagination may emanate from the realm of the fanciful.[22] This isn't to say, however, that wishful thinking may not often lead to creative, problem-solving ideas. But the facts, the reality of the problem, cannot be ignored.

Prejudice, likewise, is a formidable enemy of constructive, scientific thinking to the extent that it closes the door to truth and knowledge. It has often been observed that one mark of the educated person is his open-mindedness. The editorialist also needs to approach his task with an open mind. His initial approach to a research problem should be with questions, not answers. Questions are more conducive to reflective thinking. Answers based upon prejudices rather than fact are not.

If the editorialist is to function as an effective interpreter and illuminator of the day's intelligence, he needs, above all, to be open-minded. Indeed, he needs to approach his work as a scholar might. Ralph Waldo Emerson told students at Cambridge in his famous lecture more than 140 years ago that a scholar, in his "right state," should be "man thinking."[23] The mass media editorialist as "man thinking" will produce better researched, better focused, more persuasive editorials. They will be more persuasive—and provocative—because they are more likely to be filled with the product of reflective thinking—ideas.

NOTES for Chapter 5

[1] John Dewey, *How We Think* (Boston: D. C. Heath, 1933), pp. 4–5.

[2] James R. Robinson, *The Mind in the Making* (New York: Harper & Brothers, 1921), pp. 33–62.

[3] For a discussion of "Thinking as a Scientist," see A. Gayle Waldrop, *Editor and Editorial Writer,* 3rd ed. (Dubuque, Iowa: Wm. C. Brown, 1967), pp. 118–20.

[4] Dewey, *How We Think,* pp. 71–78.

[5] *Ibid.,* p. 76.

[6] Rudolf Flesch, *The Art of Clear Thinking* (New York: Harper & Row, 1951), p. 63.

[7] See, e.g., Raymond J. McCall, *Basic Logic* (New York: Barnes & Noble, 1952).

[8] Kenneth S. Keyes, Jr. *How to Develop Your Thinking Ability* (New York: McGraw-Hill, 1950).

[9] Dewey, *How We Think,* p. 30.

[10] Wendell Johnson, *People in Quandaries* (New York: Harper & Row, 1946), p. 24.

[11] Walter Lippmann, *Public Opinion* (New York: Macmillan, 1922), p. 47.

[12] A. Gordon Melvin, *Thinking for Every Man* (New York: John Day, 1942), p. 114.

[13] For a discussion of the four stages of thought control, see Graham Wallas, *The Art of Thought* (London: Jonathan Cape, 1931), pp. 79–106.

[14] Wallas, *The Art of Thought,* p. 84.

[15] Robert M. White II, "Good Editorials Are Only Typed at a Desk—They're Written by Experience," *The Quill* (March 1953), p. 7.

[16] Alpheus Thomas Mason, *Brandeis: A Free Man's Life* (New York: Viking Press, 1956), p. 78.

[17] Dewey, *How We Think,* p. 284.

[18] Henry Hazlitt, *Thinking as a Science* (New York: E. P. Dutton, 1916), p. 82.

[19] Wallas, *The Art of Thought,* pp. 99–100.

[20] White, "Good Editorials," p. 7.

[21] Hazlitt, *Thinking as a Science,* p. 191.

[22] Chilton R. Bush, *Editorial Thinking and Writing* (Westport, Conn.: Greenwood Press, 1970), p. 214.

[23] "The American Scholar," in *Ralph Waldo Emerson: Selected Prose and Poetry,* ed: Reginald L. Cook (New York: Holt, Rinehart and Winston, 1950), p. 49.

6

A Few Persuasive Techniques: *A Matter of Craftsmanship*

IT IS IMPORTANT that the mass media editorialist display a reasonable degree of courage and common sense in choosing issues and problems to write about. It is important that he do the research necessary to fully understand the complexity of the issue or problem. It is important that he take the time for reflection and creative thinking about the alternatives open to his readers or listeners in dealing with the issues and problems and the consequences of those alternatives. It is important, in other words, to have something worthwhile to say on a topic or issue of relevance to members of the audience. How the editorial message is written is also important. If it is too flat, too colorless, too pedestrian, the fruits of the editorialist's research and thinking may go for naught simply because the message isn't read or listened to or otherwise heeded. If the arguments presented are imprecise or if the meaning is obscure, the editorial may be rendered ineffective even if it is read or heard because the message has not been understood.

Desmond Stone, editorial page editor of the *Rochester* (N.Y.) *Democrat* and *Chronicle,* speaking at a critique session in writing at the 1976 convention of the National Conference of Editorial Writers, concluded that, "There's nothing so wrong with editorials that good writing can't fix." One of the problems, Stone said, is in thinking that editorial writing has to do something vastly different from any other kind of newspaper writing. He noted:

> On the contrary, except for the fact that an editorial expresses opinion and marshals arguments, it ought to pass the same acid tests as the best of column or investigative or feature writing. It ought to

> have the same high readability, the same tight organization, the same vivid phrase-making, the same scene-setting.[1]

Stone suggested various guidelines for editorial writing designed to put more "zing" into opinion writing, for example: the editorialist should "worry about words," make the writing "march," make the writing vivid, make it pithy, make it original, make it clear, make it nostalgic, make it "literarily allusive," make it "irresistible," make it "sharp pointed," make it "colorful."

There is, of course, no formula or model for opinion writing comparable to the inverted pyramid and its traditional trappings which has guided newsmen—for better or for worse—ever since the telegraph came into use in news transmission. There are, however, numerous techniques, principles, suggestions—call them what you wish—which should be helpful to the opinion writer striving to write more effectively and more persuasively. This chapter will deal with a few of the more pertinent of these techniques.

Keep the Writing Simple

To communicate one must write understandably. Robert Gunning, who formulated his "Ten Principles of Clear Writing" more than twenty-five years ago, was primarily concerned with keeping one's writing simple. At least seven of his ten principles, for example, dealt with a preference for the simple: keep sentences short, prefer the simple to the complex, prefer the familiar word, avoid unnecessary words, write like you talk, use terms your readers can picture, write to express not to impress.[2] To follow such rules is admittedly often easier for the reporter than for the editorialist who must deal with more complex issues and problems.

Simplicity in writing, however, is but the outward sign of reflection and depth of thought. If the editorialist has researched and thoroughly understands the issue or problem he is writing about, he should be able to keep his editorial explanation simple. Simplicity in writing is, after all, knowing what to leave out. Simplicity first requires understanding on the part of the editorialist. Simplicity also requires that the editorialist be attuned to the knowledge and understanding of his readers and listeners. If he doesn't have an understanding on both of these levels, he will not know what to leave out.

Horance G. Davis, Jr., editorial writer for the *Gainesville* (Fla.) *Sun* and professor of journalism at the University of Florida, won a Pulitzer Prize in 1971 for a series of thirty-one editorials on school desegregation ordered by the Supreme Court in Alachua County, Florida. The following editorial from that series provides an excellent example of a persuasive message cast in language simple and direct enough to be understood by all members of the audience to whom it is directed.

FOR HOODLUMS ONLY

This one is for young hoodlums.

Well, not exactly hoodlums. But if your household has a young rebel with little respect for his fellows and a disregard for property rights, who likes to make people squirm, has been known to twist arms, plays the big shot role and generally likes to raise hell . . . if you have a youngster like that in your household . . .

Clip this out and put it beside his supper plate.

Generally, we aim to communicate with readers and not speak for them. But, today at least, we're convinced we speak for 99 per cent of all Alachua Countians—including the moms and pops, the cops and the judges, the teachers and the principals, the blacks and the whites.

The message: We will not condone hoodlumism in the public schools.

We had a touch of it last year. Some of it had a racial connotation after integration on February 1. But it boiled down to outright violent conduct—petty robbery in restrooms, beatings on the parking lot, robbery on a school bus, even a minor riot or two.

Tragic as it was, one lad of 17 years drew a 15-year-prison sentence. He took $6 at knifepoint.

His name was Izell Tyrone Booth. We do not think young Mr. Booth should be an "example" of justice in Alachua County. Appropriately stiff punishment should prevail in any future incident where the evidence merits conviction—and it should fall equally upon white or black, old or young.

And there is the matter called verbal violence—those little words which make the blood run hot. And those nutty demonstrations, like shouting down speakers and obscene salutes.

They cause trouble also.

Just so we understand each other, let's lay it on the table.

For those of you slightly rebellious and finding it hard to adjust, there's Mountain Top School out at the juvenile shelter. A nice fellow out there, Russell Ramsey, will keep you up on schoolwork and try to help iron things out.

For those who persist, there is suspension and expulsion from school. And for those who make that bad, bad mistake, the result is even more unpleasant. Try these for size:

—Inciting or encouraging to riot, two years in prison and a $500 fine.

—Assault, five years imprisonment and $3,000 fine.

—Possession, use or concealment of a deadly weapon, up to five years imprisonment and $10,000 fine.

—Arson, up to 20 years imprisonment.

Please conclude from this that Alachua County WILL have peace in its schools this year. We WILL make safety havens of the campus. We WILL guarantee the welfare of our youngsters.

School opens next Monday.

So if you plan to make it a hot time on the old campus this year, take a piece of advice.

Don't.

Gainesville (Fla.) *Sun,* September 11, 1970
Reprinted by permission.

Keeping language simple, of course, affects writing style. One may write elegantly, for example, and still write accurately and understandably despite the flourishes. But elegant writing also may bring imprecision and make understanding more difficult. Overwriting of any type can be unproductive and self defeating. One writer has noted that style in writing needs to be as simple as possible within the requirements of the occasion. The admonition to keep it simple requires that everything be eliminated that does not concern the issue or problem or add to its interest or intelligibility. A work of art, a great thought, an editorial paragraph, even a sentence, can be obscured by too much light as well as a lack of illumination. A profusion of words doesn't necessarily enhance a reader's understanding. Keep it simple.

Say What You Mean

Keeping one's writing simple may help say precisely what one means to say, but communicating one's understanding of an event or issue requires more than mere simplicity of style. It requires, for example, that the words (as language symbols) be understood by the reader, listener, or viewer in the same way as they were meant by the editorialist. It requires, in the language of the general semanticist, that the map drawn through language symbols fits the territory—the real world as experienced by the message recipient. If language isn't used with such precision, then one may not be communicating to an audience what one means.

It has been suggested that the mass media communicator needs to imagine the reader or listener sitting across the desk while he is writing. The editorial message should then be written as one might talk directly to this individual member of the audience. One's words, for example, need to be chosen carefully in order that the person across the desk will understand immediately. If a word or a concept is used in a different sense or in an unusual context, the word needs to be explained. If an abstraction is used to convey an idea because such an idea is difficult to capture accurately by more concrete words, the abstraction needs to be defined. Gunning calls this mental process of remembering one's reader "tying in with the reader's experience." He observes:

> Words can be empty of meaning or they can mean the opposite of what they are intended to, when considered in relation to a background. And the background a reader brings to your words comes solely from his own experience. You can effect it only indirectly.[3]

Writing more understandably, of course, is also a facet of "saying it simply" to the degree that short, familiar words and short sentences are more readable. In fact, Gunning labels his readability formula as a "fog index." If an editorial is sufficiently "foggy," it isn't likely to convey to its audience, with any precision, what the editorialist has on his mind. Short words are often more understandable than long words because they are more concrete—they stand for things one can see and touch. The problem with many long words is that so many are abstract—they are symbols for ideas rather than things which may be observed. Abstractions tend to hinder communications. Gunning tells the story of Arthur Brisbane, as an editor for Hearst, providing an object lesson for a new writer who brought him an editorial with the headline: "Hygienics and Dietetics in Ancient Times." Noting that the editorial made a highly interesting comparison between modern and ancient health and living standards, Brisbane crossed out the headline and wrote in the words: "Pity Poor Moses—He Had No Bathtub." The point is, Gunning noted, that if the editorialist wants to be read—and understood—he must shy away from abstract terms and use terms the reader can picture.

First Impressions: The Opening

In Chapter 3 the statement was made that most editorials have three parts: (1) the statement of the subject, issue, or problem to be dealt with, (2) comment about the subject, issue, or problem, and (3) a conclusion or solution drawn from the comment. The three editorial parts, however, are not necessarily ordered in that way. The lead paragraph of the editorial may be based upon a news peg or be a summary statement of an issue or problem. Or, the editorialist may offer his reactions first and then in the body of the editorial give the basis for the opinion. The lead paragraph of a change-of-pace editorial or column, of course, can be as varied as that of a feature story, drawing from a variety of appeals to attract the reader or listener. It is important, however, that the opening of an editorial message be sufficiently provocative to catch the attention of the reader or listener. If a summary statement of the subject, issue, or problem will do that, there are certain persuasive advantages to developing the editorial arguments from fact to judgment, as discussed in Chapter 9. There are occasions, however, when the thesis, the editorial judgment, or the conclusion may best be used to open the editorial.

Phil Kerby of the *Los Angeles Times*, winner of the 1976 Pulitzer

Prize for distinguished editorial writing for his eloquent pleas in support of a free press, individual privacy, and open government, frequently uses a statement of the editorial conclusion in beginning his editorials. The following four conclusion leads are from editorials in his Pulitzer Prize series:

> Decision by decision, the courts are narrowing the First Amendment rights of the American people. What would be forbidden under the Constitution if attempted by statute is being accomplished by judicial fiat.
>
> * * *
>
> The decision of a three-judge panel in the case of the abducted newspaper editor is simply absurd. But absurd as it is, the ruling is a logical extension of a 10-year trend toward judicial censorship.
>
> * * *
>
> This country may be moving toward secret trials. U.S. Supreme Court Justice Harry A. Blackmun's ruling in a Nebraska mass murder case points in that direction.
>
> * * *
>
> Legislation now pending in Congress to revise the federal criminal code should be junked.
>
> Senate Bill 1, a massive and complicated measure 753 pages long, is so pervasively and fatally flawed that it lies beyond the scope of any rational amending process.

Such a direct approach may be too abrupt in dealing with many editorial issues. A hint of the conclusion, for example, may be included in the opening, but the conclusion isn't allowed to dominate the paragraph. One or more of the following elements, however, are usually found in the opening lines of most persuasive messages: (1) an *exordium,* to arouse sympathy and interest in the subject or issue being dealt with, (2) a *narrative,* to give the pertinent background of the subject or issue, and (3) a *partition,* stating the thesis or giving a hint of the conclusion or an indication of how the editorial arguments will be developed.[4]

All three of these elements—exordium, narrative, and partition—are apparent in the long opening paragraph of the following Pulitzer Prize winning editorial written by Philip L. Geyelin, editorial page editor of the *Washington Post.* The editorial, titled "Dean Rusk, the Stalwart at State," written in 1969 upon the retirement of Rusk as Secretary of State, opens with this carefully written, analytical paragraph:

> Sometime around the middle of his awesome eight-year term as Secretary of State, Dean Rusk took a sighting on a distant objective in the Vietnam War, lowered his head, and charged. It is written by some that he did not look up again and by others that he did look up from time to time to check his bearings and study the alternatives, and, finding them wanting, pressed on. In any case the effect was the same, for his determination was always dogged, his concept of the problem clear, his conviction unshakable. When he left office after his last working day, there was no hint that he wanted from our Vietnam ef-

> fort anything other than what he had always wanted: for the North Vietnamese to be compelled, with our help, to leave their neighbors alone. That was his litany and, of course, not everybody agreed that this was something reasonable to want, or feasible to achieve, or that even if it was, we were going about it the right way. But that is not the point here for it is easy to second-guess and the returns are not all in. The point here is that Dean Rusk was a remarkable man, possessing in large measure just about all the virtues one would wish to find in a public servant with a heavy public trust: courage in the face of critics; steadfastness in adversity; loyalty, integrity, discretion, a brilliant intellect and the strength and energy to go at it full tilt seven days a week for eight long years.

The reader's interest is caught immediately by the suggested metaphor of the Secretary of State, his head lowered, charging forward like a bull (the exordium). Editor Geyelin then amplifies the opening statement and offers the reader Rusk's "litany" and goals as Secretary of State (the narrative). Finally, the thesis of the editorial is presented: that despite the view of critics, Rusk was a remarkable man with "just about all the virtues one would wish to find in a public servant" (the partition).

It is also possible to combine two or more of these three elements into a much shorter editorial lead. It is even possible to present the narrative element in such a striking manner that the requirement of the exordium (the attention compeller) is also satisfied. Here is such a use of the narrative element by Warren Lerude, Pulitzer Prize winning editorialist of the *Nevada State Journal* and *Reno Evening Gazette:*

> Fair comment and criticism is being directed at the news media for its coverage of Joe Conforte, his whorehouse, and the tragic slaying there last week of a world famous boxer.
>
> It's natural that the media be subjected to such critical analysis. There is no question that coverage of such activities does, in fact, spread Joe Conforte's name around more.
>
> The coverage, however, is necessary if the people are to be informed of the problems the whorehouse is creating for the community.

Note that the first paragraph merely sets forth the news (the narrative backgrounding), but the need to discuss the issue is clearly implied and the reader's interest is aroused (the exordium), even in the first paragraph. The lead is expanded in the second paragraph; the thesis (partition) follows in the third paragraph.

The exordium lead, of course, can take various approaches in an effort to gain the attention of readers. Change-of-pace methods, however, need to be used with restraint and be in good taste if the editorial is to be effective. Horance G. Davis of the *Gainesville Sun* often employs feature approaches. In this Pulitzer Prize winning editorial entitled "Fearing Fear Itself," for example, Davis relies upon a historical analogy to begin one of the editorials in the series boosting school desegregation of Florida schools:

> "Wanted: Young, skinny, wiry fellows not over 18. Must be expert riders, willing to risk death daily. Orphans preferred."
>
> That's how the Pony Express advertised for mail carriers back in 1860. It was a cliff-hanging occupation defying Indians, weather and renegades.
>
> But the advertisement also pretty much describes the hazards of the Alachua County school system, as sketched by the Rev. Carl George. . . .

Another of the *Sun*'s desegregation editorials, this one entitled "Blight on the Bloom," opened with a narrative lead setting a scene which contrasted sharply with the events discussed in the editorial:

> A brisk warm breeze swept the Gainesville High School campus late Thursday morning and the dogwood petals fell to the ground and were swept along like rollicking children in search of Easter eggs.
>
> Here and there a maintenance worker crossed from one building to another on some nameless task but there was a disturbing incompleteness, an odd desolation unexplained until we realized the parking lot was vacant.
>
> Where were the boys and girls?

The boys and girls were either roaming the streets of Gainesville or loitering outside the police station. A few, Davis noted, were bleeding in the emergency room at the general hospital. The "incomprehensible had happened"; racial strife had visited Gainesville.

In still another editorial in the series entitled "Goodbye, Willie Loman," Davis used Arthur Miller's "Death of a Salesman" to fashion this effective lead:

> Willie Loman was a beer-and-undershirt sort of guy who really wanted to be something better, especially in the eyes of his son Biff, but he couldn't quite make it. He wasn't humble about it, and he turned into a loud-mouthed bore, trying to egg Biff on, until Biff said one day:
>
> "Pop! I'm a dime a dozen and so are you."
>
> And Willie's wife saw Willie's eyes film over and she cried in desperation, "He's a human being and a terrible thing is happening to him. Attention, attention must be paid to such a person."
>
> But it was too late, and Willie Loman left the house and committed suicide.

This editorial, which discussed the Supreme Court's decision ordering desegregation of the Gainesville schools, used Willie Loman again in its conclusion:

> The world is going to change for us all next February 1. We can greet the new challenge with hope and enthusiasm. Or we can look

> into the eyes of our children and see our failure mirrored there as Willie Loman saw his failure reflected in the eyes of his son Biff.
>
> "He's a human being and a terrible thing is happening to him," cried out Willie Loman's wife as Willie left the house.
>
> That is one heritage we will not leave.

The feature approach is used regularly, of course, by such change-of-pace writers as Russell Baker of the *New York Times*. In a 1977 syndicated column which playfully dealt with a modern addition to the language of government gobbledygook, Baker began:

> Utile.
>
> That was how Carruthers felt. Naturally he worked for the Government. It is the nation's biggest employer of the utile. This is because one of its biggest jobs is utilizing. If you have a lot of utilizing to do, it is vital to have utile people on the payroll.

Whatever approach is taken by the mass media opinion writer, it is important that the opening words of an editorial or opinion column catch the attention of the reader, listener, or viewer. It may make a difference whether the rest of the message is attended to or not. If communications is halted with the opening paragraph, not much interpretation, not much illumination, not much persuasion is likely to occur.

Arguing in a Straight Line

If the opening of the editorial has identified the event, issue, or problem (and perhaps given a clue to the stance the editorialist will take or a hint of the conclusion or solution to be offered), the body of the editorial should present the arguments and the documentation necessary for the conclusion to properly follow. Arguing in a straight line calls for a logical progression of the strands of the argument which will come together in the summary and conclusion. Following this process means avoidance of such verbal fallacies as setting up the so-called "straw man" only to knock the premise down, reasoning in a circle or "begging the question" (assuming what is to be proved), asking the "complex question"—the double barrelled approach that incriminates a person no matter how one replies. Such verbal fallacies will be discussed in Chapter 7.

Arguing in a straight line also implies a unity of organization and careful attention to detail which will produce what one writer describes as "all in a piece" writing. This title implies that an editorial should consist of sentences and paragraphs which are so linked to one another that the ideas and arguments flow in a seemingly endless line from opening to conclusion. Because so many journalists use short sentences and short paragraphs and rely heavily on the subject-verb-object approach, they are often accused of being "choppy" writers. In instances where there is no apparent connection between sentences or paragraphs, critics may be justified in referring to a journalistic offering as "hack writing." Clifton Lawhorne, a former Texas newsman turned journalism professor, discussed techniques which should help assure smooth flowing sentences and paragraphs during a seminar on editorial writing conducted by the International Society of Weekly Newspaper Editors in 1970. Among his suggestions were these:

1. Even though a new paragraph may begin a new line of thought, some connective may be needed between the new thought and that of the paragraph just ended. The connective does not have to be a long phrase. Indeed, it may be only one or two words, for example, furthermore, again, in short, meanwhile, later, in brief, of course, finally.

2. Word bridges can connect sentences without the bother of formal connectives. A word bridge is often no more than repetition of a single word or a word in the second sentence which points to the word used in the first. For example, "The decision of a three-judge federal panel in the case of the abducted newspaper editor is simply *absurd.* But *absurd* as it is . . ."

3. The devices of consistency (normal action sequence) and contrast may be used as action connectives. For example: "He walked to his apartment. He took out his key and opened the door. As if in a trance, he sat in the overly large chair . . ." (consistency); "Most people like to travel by automobile. A few, however, prefer airplanes" (contrast).

4. Closely connected with contrast is the thesis-antithesis statement which may be used to help focus a thought. For example, "Government officials say they are truthfully reporting gas and oil reserves, but the majority of U.S. citizens in a recent poll indicate they feel officials are lying."

5. Parallel construction also helps to provide a useful thinking in a straight line approach as well as creating repetition which boosts clarity, emphasis, and improves persuasion. For example, "The News admires the Senator *not for* his political cunning, *but for* his integrity; *not for* his considerable ability on the political stump, *but for* his careful attention to the needs of constituents."

6. The idea at the end of the sentence is the most important because it is this idea that logically leads to the next sentence or paragraph. For example, if one wrote that "President Carter is being compared to President Kennedy by some analysts, but there are many differences," it might be expected that the next paragraph would discuss the differences. If the sentence read, "Although there are many differences between President Carter and President Kennedy, the two men have marked similarities," it might be expected that the discussion which follows would focus upon the similarities.

Careful organization, tight editing, skillful use of transitions, and avoidance of the common fallacies of logic—all these steps are necessary if the editorialist is to argue persuasively. But the most important prerequisite to arguing in a straight line is for the editorialist to have formulated his ideas into one central concept and to know what he wants to say before he sits down to the typewriter or video display terminal to write.

Phil Kerby of the *Los Angeles Times,* winner of the 1976 Pulitzer Prize for distinguished editorial writing, is a master craftsman at arguing in a straight line with carefully positioned word bridges, connectives, and transitional phrases to help guide the reader through the editorial arguments. Kerby's prize-winning editorial series makes an eloquent plea in support of a free press, individual privacy, and open government. In the privacy editorial below, note the use of transitional devices for example, "Naked a child enters . . . and naked he may live out his life"; "It happens by decree in authoritarian regimes . . . it happens by degree in democracies." One transition denotes time: "Last April the U.S. Supreme Court upheld . . . Now the Supreme Court has ruled." A Supreme Court opinion is cited; in the next paragraph the "decision" is discussed, followed by a paragraph beginning, "The tax case arose . . ." In the conclusion a contrast is set up: "Tax dodgers should be caught . . . But the price is high." Numerous other word bridges provide repetition: "privacy," "reasonable," "without," "used." Note how these devices help tie the arguments together into a unified editorial expression.

RUMMAGING IN OUR PRIVACY

Naked a child enters the modern, technological state, and naked he may live out his life under the unblinking eye of omnipresent government, if the process continues of stripping away, piece by piece, all the protections of individual privacy that once was thought to be the most essential requisite of civilized existence.

It happens by decree in authoritarian regimes, where the citizen has no shelter from government; it happens by degree in democracies, where intrusions, one after another, into privacy are reasonably rationalized by reasonable proponents of reasonable goals—most frequently the apprehension of wrongdoers.

Last April the U.S. Supreme Court upheld the Bank Secrecy Act of 1970, which opens the bank accounts of all Americans to inspection by the secretary of the Treasury. Banks are required to report in detail to the Treasury Department vast categories of transactions, and, moreover, any other federal department may obtain the Treasury information on request. And all this can be done without notification to the person under investigation, and without judicial review, for the high purpose of curbing white-collar crime.

And now the Supreme Court has ruled that the Internal Revenue Service may compel banks to disclose records of large numbers of depositors, without identifying any person by name, on suspicion that the records may disclose tax evasion.

Chief Justice Warren E. Burger, writing for the majority, said the "investigative authority" of the IRS "is not limited to situations in which there is probable cause . . . to believe that a violation of the tax laws exists."

The decision, the chief justice said, does not sanction any "fishing expeditions," and he advised trial judges to limit the power carefully by making the IRS justify every summons. But the power is there to be used, and it will be used; the history of powerful government departments seeking court approval for investigations is a history of almost unbroken success.

The tax case arose when a Kentucky bank forwarded to the Federal Reserve System $40,000 in worn $100 bills that the bank had received in two deposits; the Federal Reserve routinely reported the information to the IRS, which suspected that the money might have been hidden to avoid taxes. The bank resisted a summons for the records that would identify the depositor.

Now, in pursuit of tax dodgers, the IRS has the authority to rummage through the bank deposits of Americans on the basis, as one dissenting justice said, of "shot-in-the-dark" speculation.

Tax dodgers should be caught, and perhaps more will be trapped in the large net that has now been given to the IRS. But the price is high. It is the expanding reach of government into the shrinking area of individual privacy.

Proof Structure: A Case for Documentation

If the editorialist writes in such a manner that the reader or listener cannot follow his line of argument, or worse, if he has no line of argument, then he has little hope of writing persuasively. If the argument offers opinion only with no supporting information, no illustrations, no amplification of the reasons for the stated opinions or conclusion, the editorialist may also find his arguments going unheeded. To state it another way, the editorialist's opinion is no better than his knowledge. Information likely led the editorialist to his idea in the first place; the idea led to research and reflection and, finally, to the editorial opinion or conclusion. That opinion, when presented in a mass media editorial or commentary, likewise, needs to be carefully documented if it is to convince the reader or listener of the rightness of the opinion.

The weaving of such supporting information, illustrations, or amplification into opinion writing has been referred to as "proof structure" by some writers. The fundamental unit of proof structure is the paragraph with a topic sentence stating what is to be proved and additional sentences providing the proof. In an editorial, however, the topic sentence may be the thesis set out in the opening paragraph to be documented or proved in the various paragraphs preceding the conclusion. The topic sentences and the documentation are often woven together so skillfully that the reader may hardly distinguish the two. Indeed, one rule of thumb for the improvement of opinion writing is to use as few sentences as possible that are either entirely factual or entirely opinion. Fact and opinion should be meshed together in every sentence when possible.[5]

Paul Greenberg, editorial page editor of the *Pine Bluff* (Ark.) *Commercial* and a Pulitzer Prize winning editorialist in 1969, is a convincing case-maker for the conservative point of view on the editorial page of the *Commercial* as well as in his syndicated opinion column, "Right Angle." He makes his case, as in the following editorial calling for the resignation of Bert Lance, Director of the Office of Management and Budget, through careful attention to an array of arguments which question the fitness of Lance for the budget director's position. The "proof structure" in this editorial takes the form of a memo to Lance. Note how the editorial, after setting out the opinion that Lance should resign, enumerates and amplifies the many reasons for such a conclusion.

MEMO TO BERT LANCE: RESIGN!

The latest revelations of the way Bubba Bert conducts his banking business make the case conclusive: Bert Lance should resign as director of the federal Office of Management and Budget forthwith.

First there were those personal loans from big banks that came coincidentally with the establishment of correspondent accounts from the little bank he dominated. Now the New York Times has unearthed an agreement by which Mr. Lance formally agreed to correct some embarrassing management at his Calhoun, Georgia, bank. The agreement was coincidentally rescinded by the government one day before Jimmy Carter announced that he had chosen buddy Bert as director of management and budget for the entire federal government. Such coincidences just seem to follow Bubba Bert around.

The rescinded (and until last weekend suppressed) agreement between Mr. Lance's bank and the comptroller of the currency indicates that Mr. Lance had his foibles as a management expert. The crackerjack banker whom Jimmy Carter chose for one of the highest fiscal offices in his administration turns out to have been cited for several serious deficiencies in judgment and control, some of which were not technically in accord with the law.

Mr. Lance was the immediate superior of a vice president at the Calhoun bank who managed to embezzle a million dollars over the course of four years through a series of bogus loans. All right, it happens in the best of banks. But Mr. Lance acknowledged in court records that he was aware that his aide was in financial difficulty. And although warned as early as 1971 that the suspect appeared to be making irregular loans, no effort was made to discipline or remove the felonious vice president until four years later in 1975, the year in which the embezzler was convicted and sent up for eight years.

This is not a propitious record to bring to the federal Office of Management and Budget. Nor is it assuring to see by this just revealed agreement that Mr. Lance's bank allowed its officers, and Mrs. Lance, too, to make overdrafts on their accounts. The embezzling vice president on Mr. Lance's staff had run up $190,000 in overdrafts. But not to worry, he was able to pay some of it off—with money he borrowed from the bank.

To quote Jeffrey Bogart, the assistant United States attorney at Atlanta who prosecuted the embezzler, Mr. Lance's bank at Calhoun was "run like a piggy bank."

The Justice Department was investigating Bert Lance himself because of his overdrafts at the bank—until, again coincidentally, this investigation was dropped two days before his nomination as director of management and budget was announced.

It doesn't take a banking expert to see that Mr. Lance should turn in his resignation at once. He could then devote more attention to his own affairs, which would seem enough of a challenge right now without taking on the federal government's. Simultaneously, an investigation should be launched to determine how these intriguing details of his career were kept from Congress and the American people while Mr. Lance's appointment was whizzed past Congress. How come, within 48 hours of his appointment, both the Justice Department's criminal investigation and the comptroller of the currency's agreement are dropped? And never heard of until last weekend? Was that another of the remarkable coincidences that have doggedly followed Mr. Lance's career?

The curious history of Bubba Bert's finances seem a far cry from the pure, open, why-not-the-best, trust-me line Jimmy Carter was handing out on his way to the White House. The American people not only deserve a prompt resignation from Mr. Lance but a full explanation from the Carter Administration. One can imagine the war whoops in a Democratic Congress if one of Gerald Ford's top appointees turned out to have such a record. The silence from Capitol Hill and the White House just now is deafening in its partisanship.

Let us now praise William Proxmire, the only senator to vote against Mr. Lance at his cuddly confirmation hearings. In the future, more deference should be paid Senator Proxmire's judgment. Perhaps by asking him to take on the investigation into the highly coincidental circumstances surrounding Mr. Lance's appointment.

Pine Bluff (Ark.) *Commercial,* August 17, 1977
Reprinted by permission.

Case making by an editorialist may be viewed as assisting as well as opposing the operation of government. F. Gilman Spencer, editor of the *Trentonian,* Trenton, New Jersey, won a Pulitzer Prize in 1974 for his editorials which helped to focus public attention on the scandals in New Jersey state government which resulted in federal prosecutions. In fact, the nomination for the Pulitzer Prize was made by the acting United States Attorney for the District of New Jersey who noted that those in government have "an obligation to praise the press and to give recognition to a member of the journalism profession who has not only distinguished himself by his courageous and well-written editorials but who has also served the public interest as well." Spencer's effectiveness in case making, even against politicians in high places, is demonstrated by this editorial from that prize-winning series.

UNANSWERED QUESTIONS

Former Democratic Governor Richard Hughes will be the next Chief Justice of the New Jersey Supreme Court. All that remains between him and the highest judicial post in this state is the ceremonial rite of installation. His nomination by outgoing Republican Governor Cahill was accepted without question by just about everybody. Just about everybody, that is, but this newspaper. Prior to the State Senate's unanimous confirmation of the Hughes' nomination, we questioned, once again, Mr. Hughes' failure to vigorously pursue the corruption that plagued this state during his eight years as New Jersey Governor—corruption which subsequently led to the federal conviction of scores of public officials, including both the former secretary of state and the state treasurer in his own administration.

Despite Mr. Hughes' tremendous accomplishments in virtually every other area of the public sector, we felt his record on the corruption issue—an issue that had all but shattered the image of the state he served—required at least a cursory inquiry by those passing upon his qualifications to head the highest court we have.

Earlier this week, Mr. Hughes said it would be grossly improper for him to comment on the extortion convictions of his former Secretary of State Robert Burkhardt and his former State Treasurer Robert Kervick. He said it was improper because both cases are still pending in the courts. He termed a Trentonian reporter's request for such a comment "outrageous" and he accused the newspaper of conducting a "vendetta" against him.

We believe that no request for a former governor's comment on the criminal behavior of convicted cabinet officers can be fairly termed outrageous.

We also believe that Mr. Hughes' views on official corruption, both as it specifically affected this state during his two terms and as it has generally affected this state and the nation, are indisputably germane to any comprehensive examination of his qualifications for Chief Justice.

As for the charge that we are conducting a vendetta, we have no defense . . . if a proper definition of vendetta is asking hard-to-ask questions which we consider to be wholly in the public interest.

We seek to imply nothing, Mr. Hughes. We simply believe it is the duty of the State Senate to ask questions, which in your case weren't asked . . . or, certainly, weren't asked publicly. We must wonder why the U.S. Senate feels compelled to put such questions to Supreme Court nominees in open confirmation hearings and why the New Jersey Senate does not.

And we must hope that someday someone will understand that such hearings here could remove as much doubt as they could create.

The Trentonian, Trenton, N.J., November 23, 1973
Reprinted by permission.

Without being exposed to the other editorials in the series, as *Trentonian* readers were, one reads "Unanswered Questions" with a clear feeling that the New Jersey State Senate did not do its job properly. The proof structure is there; Editor Spencer makes his case.

Repetition, Parallelism, Enumeration

Three effective stylistic devices which may often be used by the mass media editorialist to emphasize a point or to clarify a complex argument are (1) repetition of a key word or phrase, (2) parallelism of expression similar in content and function, and (3) enumeration of three or more elements in a series of factual statements or editorial assertions for easier comprehension by the reader or listener. All three devices are associated with repetition, an important persuasive technique discussed in Chapter 9. Parallelism is the repetition of some element in the sentence. Balancing of various elements is involved: noun balances with noun, phrase with phrase, clause with clause, idea with idea. A parallelism does not say the same thing in different words; the repetition is a repetition of structure. Various words or phrases, however, may be repeated in the process. The Beatitudes, for example, use both repetition and parallelism effectively:

> Blessed are the poor in spirit: for theirs is the kingdom of heaven.
> Blessed are they that mourn: for they shall be comforted.
> Blessed are the meek: for they shall inherit the earth.
> Blessed are they which do hunger and thirst after righteousness: for they shall be filled.

The repetition and parallel construction continues through four more verses.

The enumeration of three or more elements in a series of statements or assertions in an editorial, such as the enumeration at the opening of this section, will not only assist the reader in grasping the relationship of the elements, it will also afford the writer the opportunity to cast the enumerated items in a parallel structure. It will allow the repetition of key words or phrases, further enhancing persuasion. Lucile Vaughan Payne, author of *The Lively Art of Writing,* observed that:

> Parallel structure, fully understood and put to use, can bring about such a startling change in composition that student writers sometimes refer to it as "instant style." It can add new interest, new tone, new and unexpected grace to even the most pedestrian piece of writing.[6]

Parallelism for the grammarian is an important element of coherence. It is, as E. L. Callihan, author of *Grammar for Journalists,* has noted, simply the principle of placing ideas which are parallel (alike) in thought or meaning into grammatical forms or constructions that are alike (parallel).[7]

While parallelism and enumeration may both be used by the editorialist to enhance repetition as a persuasive technique, there is a point beyond which repetition, without variation, may be detrimental in argumentation. The variation in repetition, however, needs to come in constructions other than those requiring parallelism. Here are a few paragraphs from an award-winning editorial, one of the "Golden Dozen" chosen in 1970 by the International Conference of Weekly Newspaper Editors, which uses repetition effectively. The editorial, entitled "Pick a Label," written by Mrs. M. J. Schneider of the *Boyertown* (Pa.) *Times,* begins:

> There seems to be a deadly new game going round our country these days: "Pick a Label." It's as if we all have in our possession giant label-making machines and are convinced in the present crisis that each person needs a tag: radical, reactionary, establishment, hippie, square, pig, super-patriot, you name it.
>
> Pick a label.

The exclamatory phrase, "pick a label," is used four more times as a transition between paragraphs before the writer varies the repetition with, "So easy to pick a label." Then follows these concluding paragraphs:

> I appeal to all of us in these times of stress: Let us throw away our label-makers. They can be as deadly as guns.
>
> For, having everyone carefully labeled, we can no longer see the persons behind the labels, the sons and neighbors we once knew. If their labels differ from ours they become the enemy. The tragedy of Kent showed us that.
>
> It is much easier to throw rocks or to shoot at labels than at people. Labels don't have fears or joys, hopes or needs. Only people have those.
>
> Labels don't bleed when they die. Only people do that.

Use of Literary Devices

While the editorialist perhaps should be held to the same standards of writing as the newsman in terms of high readability, tight organization, and careful scene setting, as proclaimed by Desmond Stone in the opening of this chapter, the editorialist still has far more freedom to employ literary devices and literary allusions in his writing than do his mass media peers. Editorials should appeal to the senses and the imagination as well as to the intellect. The editorialist needs to take advantage of every opportunity to use appropriate figures of speech, for example, or to enhance the message he is communicating by literary allusion for at least two reasons: (1) such devices allow him to avoid what Lucile Vaughan Payne calls "solemn vapors"—a writer's disease brought on by the excessive use of abstractions such as equality, patriotism, democracy, and happiness—striving instead for more concrete, more graphic language, and (2) such devices afford a freshness of expression and originality, if used wisely, encouraging readers and listeners to participate in the communications process.

One of the most effective ways of making an editorial abstraction concrete, for example, is through the use of metaphor—a single vivid image that illustrates an idea—or through the use of simile—a slowed-down metaphor which uses an "as" or "as if" or "like" to get to its image. Metaphor and simile both make a comparison, either explicit or implied, between two things—one literal, the other figurative, for example, "Happiness is a warm puppy." One test of a good metaphor or simile is that it should never require explaining. A good metaphor creates an image, and the image should explain itself. Metaphors and similes, however, when too frequently repeated soon become trite through overuse. The editorialist, as any writer, needs to bring his experience to his writing in employing fresh metaphorical language. He also needs to test such figurative language for its appropriateness. If care isn't taken in writing figuratively, the editorialist may develop what Jacques Barzun, nationally known educator and author, calls "the woolly metaphorical style."[8] Care needs to be taken also to avoid mixing metaphors, for example, a "crying over spilt milk" and a "have your cake and eat it too" in the same editorial would undoubtedly violate both the rule of triteness and coherence.

Another figurative approach which may sometimes be useful to the editorialist is personification, the representation of a thing, quality, or idea as a person. Personification is useful when thinking of human qualities helps one to better describe whatever it is he is illuminating. A Yonkers, N.Y., editorialist, for example, who identified inflation as the "pickpocket in our midst," wrote:

> He stalks the streets and fears no man. And so far he has proved invincible.

> He is congenitally cruel. For he selects as his choicest victims those who are most helpless against him, widows and orphans and retired pensioners and those too ill or aged to resist, all who may be on fixed incomes . . .[9]

Alliteration, likewise, may be useful to the editorialist to the extent that the repetition of an initial sound, usually of a consonant or cluster in two or more words of a phrase, helps to convey a thought to readers or listeners more effectively. William Safire, columnist for the *New York Times* and author of *The New Language of Politics,* has noted that many politicians make wide use of alliteration. Former Vice President Spiro T. Agnew, however, may have outdone them all with his "pusillanimous pussyfooting," "vicars of vacillation," "nattering nabobs of negativism," "hopeless hysterical hypochondriacs of history," as well as countless other phrases of soaring rhetoric. A reporter covering Agnew is said to have dubbed him "a functional alliterate."[10] Alliteration, however, may still serve a useful purpose in editorial writing to the extent that such repetition enhances comprehension and persuasion.

Editorial writers, it has been observed, should enrich their writing occasionally with literary references and allusions. Syndicated columnist James J. Kilpatrick, former editor of the *Richmond* (Va.) *News,* views editorial writing as a "lean and muscular business of putting words together so that, first of all, they convey clear and explicit meaning; and secondly, so that ideas are expressed with some grace and tempo." There should be more sentences, however, which "ripple, or soothe, or smash, or do anything but lie in the columns and flop their limp participles on a beach of type." And, Kilpatrick asks:

> Why do we flee from a literary allusion or a classical metaphor as if these devices harbored streptococci? They can add so much! . . . The Bible abounds with parallels and parables, but we rarely use them: Look at Elijah . . . And Shakespeare bulges with magnificent lines for paraphrase, yet if we borrow from his treasury we tend to use the same overworked images, the rose that smells as sweet, the Colossus that doth bestride some narrow world.[11]

Another Southern editorialist, Jonathan Daniels, editor emeritus of the *Raleigh* (N.C.) *News and Observer,* noting that editorialists have instructors who far ante-date Rudyard Kipling and his "six honest serving men," told an NCEW special critique session on writing at the 1976 convention:

> I hope I don't sound pretentious when I count as our teachers Jesus with his parables, Aesop with his fables, and Shakespeare with his dialogues. Certainly there was never a better pattern for a pontificating editor in this age of juvenile, as well as adult, delinquency than Polonius. I wonder how many editorials have been the equivalent of "I come to bury Caesar not to praise him," and how many more have been "to be or not to be" products. He is a poor editorial flatterer who has not

> learned to begin his editorial praise with a flaw in his subject or his denunciation by flinging a preliminary bone to the damned. The packing of the profundities of parables into a few simple lines is more difficult to emulate.[12]

Literary references, of course, can often be used in an even more substantive way in editorial writing. Owen McNamara, editor of the *Brookline* (Mass.) *Chronicle-Citizen,* for example, found that Thoreau's transcendental views held something in common with the youthful dissent of the late 1960's. McNamara's "Golden Dozen" award-winning editorial began:

> The hip recluse of Concord, Henry David Thoreau, used to cluck sadly because "The mass of men lead lives of quiet desperation." He was right, of course, in his time, and for many years after. But we perceive today that most men don't even feel that they are leading their lives to begin with. They are led, instead, by events, the feelings of the time and the decisions of other men. All that is left for many is the desperation.

After advising his readers on the wisdom of Thoreau's views on civil disobedience, the editorial concluded:

> We go to Thoreau for the last word of this desperate—but optimistic—essay:
>
> "The fate of the country . . . does not depend on what kind of paper you drop into the ballot-box once a year, but on what kind of man you drop from your chamber into the street every morning."
>
> —*Slavery in Massachusetts* (1854)

Appeal, Approach, Tone, Style

There are two basic rules in argument which the mass media editorialist needs to apply: (1) he must consider the interests, attitudes, knowledge, and feelings of his audience, and (2) he must consider his use of language, attempting to write in a manner that will convince his readers or listeners to accept his arguments. Effective argumentation, therefore, must first be empathetic argumentation. The editorialist must empathize—must have the ability to share in his reader's or listener's emotions or feelings—before he can take the second step—effectively consider what appeal, what approach, what tone, what stylistic devices to adopt in formulating his persuasive message.

Should the appeal of the editorial be to the intellect of the audience, for example, or should it be an appeal to the emotions? Should it be a straightforward, serious approach laying out all the arguments both pro and con, or should it be a change-of-pace piece employing satire, hyperbole, even irony? What attitude or tone should the editorialist adopt toward his subject: should it be sophisticated and technical or should it be colloquial, nostalgic, informal? Which stylistic devices—

techniques involving the "manner" of writing—should be employed? These are all proper concerns of the mass media editorialist. The answer to such questions should be arrived at, as indicated above, in terms of the interests of the audience most likely to expose themselves to that particular message. The appropriateness of the appeal or approach in terms of the subject matter being discussed should also be of concern to the editorialist. Some topics, for example, simply do not lend themselves to a humorous approach. The question which the editorialist must ultimately ask when writing a change-of-pace piece is: Will this approach be more effective than a more straightforward, serious, sophisticated editorial? If the answer is yes, and the editorialist has the extra time which the humorous or feature approach is likely to take, he should proceed. The variety which a change-of-pace approach brings to the editorialist's usual output may often be justification enough for trying something different. The change-of-pace, however, is by definition a departure from the norm; a too frequent use of the change-of-pace would tend to lessen its impact.

John Strohmeyer, editor of the *Bethlehem* (Pa.) *Globe-Times,* won the Pulitzer Prize in 1972 for editorial writing. One of the themes he dealt with was the need to reduce racial tensions in that steel town. But in the prize-winner editorial packet was the following editorial which takes an unusual approach in attempting to show that the Post Office's modern mechanized system wasn't infallible. The change-of-pace approach taken by the editorial is effective for at least two reasons: (1) it seems particularly appropriate that such comment taking the Post Office to task be cast in the form of a letter, and (2) the editorial is documented by empirical evidence contributed unknowingly by the Post Office itself: ten envelopes delivered, though two were stamped with only Christmas seals and the others with cancelled stamps pasted on from old envelopes. While the argumentation in the editorial is serious and straightforward, such an editorial, standing at the top of an editorial column, is sure to attract the attention of readers because of its unusual approach to the issue.

TO THE POSTMASTER

Mr. Merrill A. Hayden
Acting Postmaster General
U.S. Postal Service
Washington, D.C.

Dear Mr. Hayden:

We are sending along 80 cents to pay you for 10 envelopes without legal postage which the Globe-Times mailed the other day. The Lehigh Valley post office delivered all 10 as usual, even though one was stamped with only a TB seal, another with a Bethlehem Christmas City seal, and the others with canceled stamps pasted on from old envelopes.

It was eye-opening that not even one of these illegally-stamped letters was rejected by our post office's modern mechanized system. Particularly so, since your post office employes describe it as "infallible." However, the results of the tests were no more surprising than the reaction of Mr. Ron Powell, the information officer who speaks for you in Washington. His chief concern seemed to be that the Globe-Times "broke the law" in conducting the test.

We did break the law and we regret it was necessary. But we believe the culpability of the post office in all this is far more serious than our 80-cent defalcation. You, sir, have betrayed public confidence in your promises that the Postal Reorganization Act would increase the efficiency of the post office. What are we to make of your claims that a new structure with more authority and a 33 per cent increase in postage rates would permit you to operate on a business-like basis?

We do not think a business could long survive the practices that we observe from here. The Bethlehem area is served by a modern facility, the Lehigh Valley post office complex built only several years ago at a cost of $2 million. More mechanized equipment has been added this year as part of the $24 million catch-up program authorized for key post offices. Your men assure us that ours is about as modern an operation as you'll find in the nation.

And what has postal reform and heavy investment done for us so far? Months of observation of mails coming into our office show that nearly every mail brings letters where canceling machines have missed the stamps entirely. We can only guess how many unmarked stamps are recycled by alert office clerks all over the country. In view of our tests, we can only guess how soon it will be before members of this "ripoff society" discover that your modern machines are defenseless against re-used stamps, whether they have cancel marks or not. Or how soon it will be general knowledge that your automated systems do not reject letters stamped even with commemorative seals?

Your Mr. Powell suggests that the post office relies on an element of trust. Incredible. The days of trust and innocence are gone. No business today can survive the leakage of what amounts to an honor system and it is unfair to make the trusting citizens pay for such inefficiency. American know-how has solved far more difficult problems. Then why should the post office persist in installing costly machinery so lacking in technology that it does not have the capacity to reject a phony stamp?

We broke a regulation in conducting our test and we submit our reparations. What do you intend to do, Mr. Hayden, about your broken promise to bring efficiency to the U.S. Postal Service?

The Bethlehem (Pa.) *Globe-Times,* November 26, 1971
Reprinted by permission.

Not every editorial, of course, requires serious argumentation leading to a profound conclusion stated in an explicit manner. Nor does every editorial need to cast the editorialist as a Jeremiah predicting dire consequences if some advocated action is not taken immediately or expressing pessimism about future conditions. Not every editorial requires that the editorialist open a frontal attack on a public issue with a broadaxe. Indeed, the editorial rapier of satire may often be both more persuasive as well as more interesting because of its change-of-pace approach. The use of satire in literature, or in editorial writing, however, poses several problems for the writer.

One problem in using satire is the demand placed on the ability of the writer to control tone—the predominant attitude or mood of the editorial. The problem is made more complex because satire itself may take many forms. The satiric approach, for example, may range from direct attacks on the subject through sarcasm or invective to the use of irony, a kind of satire which expresses itself indirectly. Direct editorial attacks, however, may generate sympathy for the victim. And irony, the inverted statement in which the editorialist says the opposite from what he means, may be misread because of its indirectness.[13] Jonathan Swift's "A Modest Proposal" or Benjamin Franklin's "The Sale of the Hessians," however, are but two examples from literature which demonstrate that ironic satire can be effective. The key seems to be to make the proposals outrageous enough that the average reader will know that the writer does not mean literally what he is saying.

Satire, to be effective as an editorial weapon, needs to be less a direct attack on its subject than a witty, clever, inventive use of controlled language in which the editorialist, while perhaps expressing a strong personal feeling, avoids the direct abuse of invective, the poisoned dart of innuendo, or the broadaxe of sarcasm. Satire, one writer notes, should be the editorial rapier which, if used with skill, can be effective in throwing light on the evils and weaknesses of institutions, conventions, and customs. Parody, likewise, may be an acceptable form of editorial satire since it usually avoids the bluntness of sarcasm and invective.[14]

A second problem with the use of a satiric approach in editorial writing has to do with its effectiveness. Such an approach, if handled with skill, without doubt boosts readership. What is gained in attention, however, may be lost in comprehension. An experimental study, for example, using selections from Art Buchwald's syndicated columns found that Buchwald's approach, because of its indirectness, led to the misreading or misunderstanding of the message.[15]

Writing style, the manner in which the editorialist expresses his thought in language, is also involved with concerns about the appeal and approach taken by the editorialist, as it is in all phases of writing. Style, after all, involves the choice of words and expressions, the arrangement of words within sentences, the variety in the patterns of sentences, and, in a sense, every writing technique which tends to reveal the editorialist's unique way of seeing and thinking. Writing which lacks style—laborious, ponderous prose filled with clutter words and needless repetition—soon bores the reader or listener. Writing which is emphatic and affective, which tends to create tension in the mind of the reader, which allows the unique intellect of the writer to be revealed, is more interesting and more persuasive. The editorialist, who usually has the freedom to develop a more personal style, needs to be concerned with matters of style as well as with the use of persuasive techniques. It is important, of course, to muster one's persuasive arguments, but it is also important how the arguments are presented.[16]

Closing the Appeal

The marshaling of editorial arguments based upon reflection and research, the documentation of such arguments with great care and precision, the enhancement of such argumentation through repetition, through the use of figurative language, even through the skillful use of satire and humor, all these may fail if the editorialist doesn't close his editorial with some explicit resolution. One writer calls the conclusion an editorial knot, the tying together of the various strands of argument for the benefit of the reader or listener. In an editorial whose purpose is to illuminate, the conclusion may be a summary highlighting the significance of the issue being explained. In an editorial arguing a point of view, the conclusion should be an explicit statement of the medium's stance on the issue. In an editorial examining a problem, the conclusion should offer a feasible solution. In an editorial examining a question, the conclusion should provide an explicit answer which follows from the editorial investigation of the question.

If an explicit conclusion is more persuasive than allowing the reader or listener to arrive at his own conclusion based upon the editorial arguments—and the research literature indicates that this is true (See Chapter 9)—then the editorial should take a stance. In choosing the question or problem or topic or issue, the editorialist, in effect, is saying to his readers or listeners that the subject of the editorial is relevant. Most readers and listeners, it is argued, then expect the editorialist to take a stance, answering the question, offering a solution to the problem, telling the significance of the topic or issue. The conclusion, however, needs to follow from the arguments presented in the body of the editorial; else it becomes a non sequitur.

Conclusion drawing for the editorialist is, after all, only a special form of decision making. It is often a case of examining the alternatives, none of which are entirely satisfactory or without some risk or possible unpleasant consequences. One or more of the alternatives, however, may be both feasible and positive. If the situation entails a choice between two equally distasteful alternatives, then the editorialist is faced with a dilemma. More often than not, the solution of a problem, the settlement of an argument, the determination of a course of action is found in what one writer has called the "golden mean," the happy medium. The editorial conclusion, whatever it is, needs to be based upon logical reasoning and the reader or listener needs to be exposed to the reasons for the ideas and opinions expressed in the editorial conclusions. Such a conclusion provides the editorial with both the unity and thrust needed to make it persuasive.

Summary and Conclusion

Once the mass media editorialist has chosen his subject, once he has properly researched the issues involved, once he has reflected upon the dimensions of the various questions arising from the problem or the various alternatives and their consequences, then comes the most demanding task of his editorial role—exerting the craftsmanship necessary to formulate a compelling editorial message. A mastery of words is needed to say precisely what one means, to keep the language simple and readable, to employ an interesting style which provides "zing" to one's writing (using figurative language, literary allusions, and interesting analogies when appropriate), to present one's arguments in an orderly straightline fashion with convincing documentation leading to explicit conclusions acceptable to the reader or listener.

This mastery of words, this editorial writing style required for effective opinion writing goes well beyond the "carpentry of the craft" taught by the classroom teacher or the city editor, according to Jonathan Daniels, editor emeritus of the *Raleigh* (N.C.) *News and Observer.* A master writer may help one understand the architecture of style, but it takes each writer alone to "make the music which the best writing requires." Daniels, demonstrating his "mastery of words," offered this formula for editorial writing to his fellow journalists:

> Here, finally, is my formula for editorial writing: Ink, adrenalin, enough arrogance to put your opinions against the world or the dogcatcher's, enough exhibitionism to show itself through any patterns of anonymity, bullheadedness, occasional flashes of Bombastes or pastoral poetry in equal measure, a few drops of pity, and, above all, enough humor to appreciate the folly of the world and to provide a sneaking suspicion that the writer himself may be part of the joke.[17]

NOTES for Chapter 6

[1] Desmond Stone, "Put Some Zing in Your Writing," *The Masthead* 29 (Spring 1977): 24–27.

[2] Robert Gunning, *The Technique of Clear Writing,* rev. ed. (New York: McGraw-Hill, 1968).

[3] *Ibid.,* p. 148.

[4] See Steward La Casce and Terry Belanger, *The Art of Persuasion* (New York: Scribner's 1972), pp. 21–30.

[5] For a discussion of the concept "proof structure," see Casce and Belanger, *The Art of Persuasion,* pp. 1–20.

[6] Lucile Vaughan Payne, *The Lively Art of Writing* (New York: Mentor Book, 1965), p. 123.

[7] For examples of various forms of parallel structure, see E. L. Callihan, *Grammar for Journalists,* rev. ed. (New York: Chilton Book Co., 1969), pp. 222–25.

[8] For a discussion of the problems with metaphorical language, see Jacques Barzun, *Simple and Direct* (New York: Harper and Row, 1975), pp. 253–58.

[9] *Yonkers* (N.Y.) *Herald Statesman,* November 10, 1958.

[10] For a discussion of campaign rhetoric, see William Safire, *The New Language of Politics* (New York: Random House, 1968).

[11] James J. Kilpatrick, " 'Manifestly,' They Begin . . . ," *The Masthead* 19 (Summer 1967): 8–11.

[12] Jonathan Daniels, "Writer's Everest: Mastery of Words," *The Masthead* 28 (Winter 1976): 10–13.

[13] For a discussion of the importance of tone in using satire, see James Howe, *The Making of Style* (New York: Chilton Book, 1972), pp. 110–19.

[14] A. Gayle Waldrop, *Editor and Editorial Writer,* 3rd ed. (Dubuque, Iowa: Wm. C. Brown, 1967), pp. 190–91.

[15] Charles R. Gruner, "An Experimental Study of Satire as Persuasion," *Speech Monographs* 32 (1965): 149–53. For a further discussion of the effect of humor on persuasion, see Chapter 9.

[16] For a further study of writing style, see, e.g., "An Approach to Style," in *The Elements of Style,* 2d ed. eds: William Strunk, Jr., and E. B. White (New York: Macmillan, 1972), pp. 59–78; James Howe, *The Making of Style* (New York: Chilton Book, 1972); William Zinsser, *On Writing Well* (New York: Harper & Row, 1976).

[17] Daniels, "Writer's Everest: Mastery of Words," p. 13.

7

Verbal & Statistical Fallacies: *The Need for Precision*

THE EDITORIALIST, in seeking out truth, needs to think as a scientist, researching his facts from reliable sources, discounting his own prejudices, weighing both pro- and con-arguments in arriving at valid conclusions. He also needs to be aware of any verbal or statistical fallacies employed by others, including the sources relied upon for his own factual information as well as the efforts of opponents to refute his editorial arguments. Such deceptive practices, whether intentional or coincidental, need to be sought out if the editorialist is to maintain his posture as a scientific thinker, a trustworthy investigator, and a credible editorialist. The mass media editorialist also needs to be aware of the various verbal and statistical fallacies which often creep into persuasive messages in order to avoid them in his own writing.

The editorialist, as an objective, scientific investigator and trustworthy evaluator, seeks to marshal his evidence in a way which will allow him to appeal to reason. Such rational arguments, editorial or otherwise, as noted in Chapter 5, are based upon two kinds of logic. The first is *inductive,* the process of gathering and judging specific evidence to arrive at a general conclusion. To demonstrate that the mayor is inefficient, for example, the editorialist might enumerate a number of instances of fiscal mismanagement by the mayor. The second kind of logic is *deductive,* the process of deriving a specific conclusion from general premises. The classic syllogism involving Socrates is based upon deductive reasoning. "All men are mortal" is a generalized major premise. Since "Socrates is a man"—the minor premise—it can be deducted, therefore, that "Socrates is mortal." Or, to adapt the Mayor analogy: "All politicians are inefficient. The Mayor is a politician. Therefore, the Mayor is inefficient." The conclusion reached through the deductive process, of course, is no more valid than the generalization contained in the major premise from which it flows.

An error in deductive reasoning is called a *fallacy* by logicians. In this context, a fallacy arises when the three propositions of a syllogism are, in some manner, not logically related. Such a fallacy may occur when there is an illogically stated relationship between the premises or terms or when there is ambiguity in the statement of the propositions. Unwarranted assumptions and ambiguity characterize too many persuasive appeals appearing in the news media.

The fallacy problem, however, goes beyond the concerns of the formal logicians and treatment of the syllogism. The problem includes fallacies at both the verbal and statistical level. It may include fallacies in the examination of questions one poses. Some editorial queries, for example, pursue questions of fact; others may pursue questions of meaning, probability, value, or policy. It is important to recognize the type of question one is pursuing. Closely related to verbal fallacies are various *faults* which should be avoided, for example, Afghanistanism, chauvinism, dogma, bigotry, even dullness. Various of these verbal and statistical fallacies, plus various faults which should be avoided by the editorialist, is the subject of this chapter.

Unwarranted Assumptions

One important category of verbal fallacy is based upon what logicians call "unwarranted assumptions." Such a fallacy might result in editorial writing should the editorialist assume something in presenting his arguments which he has no right to assume. Or, in terms of formal logic, some fourth premise, probably suppressed and unstated, has crept into the reasoning, upsetting traditional Aristotelian logic. The editorialist need not be concerned with the various terms used by logicians, for example, *argumentum ad hominem* (directing the argument against the character of one's opponent), but he can benefit from an understanding of the bases which formal logic provides for identifying arguments. One writer points out, for example:

> In offering an argument one tries to convince or persuade others of a position or belief. The belief one wants others to accept is the *conclusion* of the argument. By definition, each argument has one and only one conclusion. The reasons or evidence which one offers for the conclusion are called *premises.* An argument may have any number of premises. In addition, in order to prove one's conclusion one may offer a series of interlocking arguments in which some conclusions are premises to other arguments so that the final conclusion follows from the whole series.[1]

Premises are sometimes identified by such key words as *since, for,* or *because;* conclusions may be marked with words such as *therefore, hence,* or *consequently.* In the mass media, however, key words may be missing; indeed, the major premise may be suppressed in the interest of brevity. The editorialist may write, for example, that "Mayor Smith cannot vote in the general election because he did not register." The minor premise is keyed with *because:* "He (Mayor Smith) did not register (to vote)." The conclusion then becomes: "Mayor Smith cannot vote in the general election." But the major premise is unstated: "Only those who are registered can vote." There is no fallacy problem here; the major premise is simply unstated.

Such reasoning may become fallacious, however, when it takes an unstated fourth premise to establish a logical relationship between the terms of the syllogism. This syllogism, derived from an often stated historical argument, for example, poses such a logical problem:

> Entangling alliances are things George Washington told us to avoid.
>
> The League of Nations is an entangling alliance.
>
> Therefore, the League of Nations is something we ought not to join.

Before this conclusion logically follows, a fourth, unstated premise must be assumed: "We ought to do nothing that Washington told us to avoid doing." Such an assumption, however, appears unwarranted.[2]

There are at least five unwarranted assumptions which the editorial writer needs to be aware of in order to detect such fallacies in the arguments of others as well as to avoid them in his own writing: (1) asking the complex question, (2) ignoring the question, (3) presenting irrational evidence, (4) begging the question, and (5) writing the non sequitur.

Asking the *complex question* is fallacious because the question is posed in such a way that an opponent cannot answer categorically without admitting the truth of the assumption, for example, "Have you stopped beating your wife?" Or, the complex question may be viewed as loaded or double-barreled because it really asks not one but two questions, for example, "Are you still a member of the Communist party?" In answering the explicit question of present membership, the respondent must answer another question concerning his past membership. The complex question, however, may be less incriminating but still conceal an unjustified assumption, for example, "Mayor Smith, why won't you consider a compromise?" Has the Mayor refused to consider a compromise?

The fallacy of *ignoring the question* (or, drawing the irrelevant conclusion, as it is sometimes called) occurs when something different than the point at issue is proven thereby ignoring the question posed in the argument. The proof presented in an editorial, for example, may be valid as far as the point being addressed is concerned, but the conclusion is irrelevant if the proof or the refutation ignores the essential question. If the refutation purposely focuses upon a side issue to divert the audience's attention from the primary question which is being ignored because it cannot effectively be addressed, the fallacy is sometimes referred to as a "Red Herring." In apologizing for President Carter's failure to keep a campaign promise, for example, it would be a false issue, one designed to draw attention away from the real issue, should the editorialist argue that politicians rarely keep such campaign promises.[3] A special form of irrelevant conclusion is the device of assuming an unwarranted assumption—setting up a "straw man"—which can be knocked down easily in the editorial. An assumption, for example, that joint-operating agreements between newspapers are formed for the primary purpose of producing better newspapers might easily be knocked down by showing that the primary motivation is for the purpose of increasing profits—a worthy motivation for any business. To the degree that such a "straw man" assumption is unwarranted, it tends to ignore a conclusion focused upon a more relevant question. Such propagandistic devices as "transfer," "name calling," "bandwagon," "testimonial," and "plain folks," to be discussed below, are common fallacies which are sometimes placed under the heading of ignoring the question.

The fallacy of *irrational evidence,* while closely related to irrelevant conclusions, is usually considered separately. It includes several forms of erroneous argumentation which should be rejected by an intelligent audience but often are not. An argument, for example, may be directed against the character of those holding opposing views rather than the issue in dispute. Such personal recrimination, which the logicians call an *ad hominem* attack, sometimes turns to name calling, is irrational and usually unproductive. One writer notes that newspapers sometimes fall into this error when they oppose a proposal that is in the public interest on the ground that the sponsors of the proposal are of bad or untrustworthy character or that they have ulterior motives.[4]

An appeal to the reverence which readers may have for a public official or public figure, such as the syllogism based upon President Washington's views concerning "entangling alliances" quoted above, rather than an appeal to the intellect of the reader, is another example of irrational evidence. Appeals to the prejudices and emotions of audience members rather than to their intellect is a special category of irrational evidence which the logicians call *argumentum ad populum.* Such an appeal is often used by the propagandist, both those in and out of politics. It was the forte, for example, of Sen. Joseph McCarthy of Wisconsin in the role he played during the Red baiting years following World War II. All types of irrational evidence, especially appeals to the ignorance and prejudice of members of the audience, should be avoided by the editorialist who expects to have any long-term effect as a persuader.

The fallacy of *begging the question,* assuming a conclusion that has not been established, is a form of unwarranted assumption often engaged in by the mass media editorialist. Begging the question may involve the failure to keep the phrasing of the question impartial, for example, "Should the State Legislature repeal the *inequitable* sales tax?" If the sales tax is already admitted to be inequitable, no problem remains since the truth of the called for conclusion has been assumed in the question. The common fallacy of begging the question can be found on every hand. Chilton R. Bush, former journalism educator and author, notes that John Marshall, Chief Justice of the Supreme Court of the United States, begged the question in his opinion in the landmark *Marbury v. Madison* decision in which the doctrine of judicial supremacy was established.[5]

Another form of begging the question has been labeled "reasoning in a circle." It consists of taking two propositions and using them in turn to prove the other. The conclusion that God exists because the Bible says that God exists, and the Bible is the word of God, is an example of circular argumentation. If one did not already believe in God, one would hardly accept as evidence the definition that the Bible is the word of God.[6]

The *non sequitur* fallacy involves writing an inference or conclusion which does not follow from the premises. A logician might argue, for example, that any sentence offered as a consequence of any other is a *non sequitur* unless it is a consequence.[7] Or, more generally, a *non sequitur* is a statement or remark which has no bearing on what has just been said. For the logician the fallacy lies in the fact that the terms of the syllogism are so illogically related that no valid conclusion can be deduced from them. For the editorialist, the conclusion which doesn't follow logically from the premises of the argument or from the evidence presented in the body of the editorial isn't likely to be effective or persuasive. The editorial conclusion, for example, that families who do not own their homes should not be allowed to vote on a special bond issue to expand the local school since local schools are financed largely from property taxes is a *non sequitur.* The conclusion does not follow because the unstated premise that non-property owners do not contribute toward property taxes is unfounded. It must be assumed that the landlord of the rental property is intelligent enough and business manager enough to set the rental of the property at a level that a portion of the rent can go to cover the annual property tax.

Fallacies of Ambiguity

The editorialist, however, may engage in unsound deduction and fallacious reasoning despite care in dealing with the logical relationship of the premises of his arguments. Such fallacies may be the result of ambiguity in the terms of the propositions or equivocation in the definition of his terms. Fallacies of ambiguity or equivocation may be of two types: (1) those involving quantity in which there is a confusion of the relation of the whole and its parts, and (2) those involving the qualitative meaning of terms. They result not so much from the use of equivocal or ambiguous terms as from the equivocal use of terms which result in fallacious reasoning. If a word, for example, "democracy," is employed in two widely different senses, there is equivocation but no one is likely to be fooled by it because the fallacy will be immediately recognized. It is the subtler ambiguities and variations in meaning which may cause one to fall victim to the fallacy of "weasel-wording." One writer notes:

> When we are told, for example, that a certain piece of legislation would restrict individual *liberty* and is therefore *undemocratic,* we must ask *in what sense* it would restrict liberty, and whether restriction of liberty *in this same sense* is undemocratic, and we must ask as well the precise meaning of "undemocratic" in this context. If there is the faintest variation in the meaning of either of these terms, the argument is entirely invalid.[8]

Popular thinking on political and other controversial issues may complicate matters for the editorialist by attaching to various terms a "hallowed" ambiguity. Such loaded words, for example, as "democracy," "science," "psychology," "practical," "academic," "socialism," "liberty," "Marxism," "fascism," "bureaucracy," "totalitarianism," "theoretical," "equality" are seldom precisely defined or univocally employed in argument. It is difficult, of course, to define such loaded words. They are "loaded" in the sense that they are emotionally charged, arousing visceral rather than cerebral reactions. When such words are used in argumentation, they need to be defined as precisely as possible to avoid the emotional implications. Then such words should be used as defined throughout the argument. One writer cautions:

> "Stretching" the meaning of a term in order to identify its connotation and associations with those of another term, thereby attaching to one term the emotional charge of the other—as in the attempt to identify "democracy" with "complete absence of government regulation," or "racial equality" with "intermarriage between whites and Negroes," or in the advertisers' frantic effort to label their products with the talismanic associations of such terms as "scientific proof" and "medical recommendations"—is a tempting rhetorical trick against which the student of logic should be always on guard. Ample exercise in exposing this fallacy can be had by anyone who takes the time carefully to read advertising copy, political speeches, or partisan editorials.[9]

Fallacies involving *quantity,* confusing the relation of the whole and its parts, generally arise from generalizations derived from too few specimens of a class. It may be a matter of what logicians call *division* when one assumes that what is true of the whole is also true of the parts taken separately. One cannot assume, for example, that because the Catholic Church condemns birth control that John Doe, a Catholic, does not practice it. Such a fallacy is usually easy to detect. The fallacy may be just the reverse, however, one based upon composition in which one assumes, based upon one or more of the parts, considered separately, that something is also true of the whole. Isolated statements from the writing of Thomas Jefferson, for example, have often been used to show his strong libertarian views concerning freedom of the press. An examination of all Jefferson's writings about the press, however, would force one to condition such a conclusion. Likewise, an editorial which makes a sweeping generalization about all state governmental workers on the basis of an examination of the efficiency of state workers in only one or two departments falls into the same error of ambiguity.

Equivocation and ambiguity may also involve *quality,* a fallacy due to a confusion in the qualitative meaning of terms. The logician might identify the fallacy as ambiguity of the middle term of the syllogism. One writer notes that:

> The fallacy . . . is the result of a substitution—usually an inadvertent one—of meaning in the terms, the substitution being due to the failure of the thinker to distinguish as to the *kinds* of members within a class. This fallacy, in the last analysis, is the result of an inability to classify things, that is, an inability to perceive the essential *quality* in things which makes them alike in one respect but which differentiates them in another respect.[10]

It would be erroneous, for example, to reason that a regional university should offer a curriculum in law because Harvard University has a law curriculum. Both may be universities, but they are in different classes; they are qualitatively different. Such a comparison would be analogous to comparing apples to oranges. Editorialists need to be aware of the errors of reasoning caused by equivocation and ambiguity.

Statistical Fallacies

Ambiguity and equivocation can cause problems in using statistics or in counting just as they can create verbal fallacies, as discussed above. The use of figures, in argumentation, for example, without placing them in some meaningful frame of reference, affords nothing more than a reflection of their own "dumb" images. Philip Meyer, national correspondent of Knight Newspapers and author of a book introducing reporters to social science research methods entitled *Precision Journalism,* stresses that journalists need to be able to communicate with figures as well as with words—they need to learn to count. Meyer points out:

> The new methods in the social sciences are, by and large, quantitative methods. They use numbers to count, measure, and evaluate. To the layman, as well as to the old-fashioned sociologist, it sometimes seems unlikely that so slippery a thing as human behavior can be reduced to elements that will yield to counting and measuring. We are used to counting things that hold still. But, with the use of probability theory, it is possible to deal with uncertainty in quantification, and numbers can be applied to such things as human behavior and human decision making.[11]

Precision journalism, however, can become imprecise if the editorialist or other mass media writer does not have an understanding of the limitations of research findings.

The editorialist, for example, must be aware of what Darrell Huff, author of *How to Lie with Statistics,* has called "statisticulation," the misinforming of people through statistical manipulation—"lying with statistics." Such statistical "lying," however, is not always intentional; it often occurs through the incompetence of the writer. And, Huff notes,

> the distortion of statistical data and its manipulation to an end are not always the work of professional statisticians. What comes full of virtue from the statistician's desk may find itself twisted, exaggerated, oversimplified, and distorted-through-selection by salesman, public-relations expert, journalist, or advertising copywriter.[12]

Huff's little book, which has gone through more than twenty printings, traces various ways which statistics may be twisted, exaggerated, oversimplified, and distorted. Both the Huff and Meyer book should have a place on every editorialist's bookshelf.[13]

On even the most basic level confusion often exists in reporting statistical matters, for example, in the ambiguity which often surrounds use of the term "average." The question immediately arises: Which measure of central tendency is being used to compute the average? Is it the mean, the arithmetical average; or is it the median, the middle figure of the distribution being described; or is it the mode, the figure which occurs most frequently? If the distribution approximates the so-called "normal curve," of course, it makes little difference which measure of central tendency is used. In normal distributions the mean, median, and mode all fall at the center of the curve. But in skewed distributions, where the scores or measurements are distributed disproportionately toward one end or the other of the curve, it may make a vast difference which measure of central tendency is used.

To use a simplistic example, suppose that five persons earned daily salaries of $20, $30, $40, $80, and $80 respectively. The mean average would be $50, the median $40, and the mode $80. Which would be the best measure to describe the "average" salary of members of the group? The mean of $50, it should be noted, is higher than the salary reported for three-fifths of the group. Likewise, $80 is a misleading average, even though more of the group make this figure than any other. The median figure of $40 is the best measure for such a skewed distribution, as salary distributions usually are. The point is, which measure of central tendency is used to report the average in this case makes a difference. Ambiguity results if that information is not reported.

In another sense, it should be remembered that average is, at best, merely a statistical measure for describing a distribution of scores or measurements. It is seldom an accurate measure of an individual. Indeed, the average man may exist only on the statistician's graphs.

When the editorialist ventures beyond simple descriptive statistics to statistical estimations and inferences, he needs to proceed with even more caution. He needs to remember, for example, that when significant differences are reported between two candidates in an opinion poll or between the views people hold about a concept or issue that such differences are always based upon probabilities. At the .05 alpha level, for example, the differences found would not occur by chance alone in 95 of 100 cases.

The editorialist also needs to remember that there is a standard error in such statistical reports; if the standard error is .03, for example, and the difference in voter preference between President Carter and Candidate X was .51 and .48, a margin of .03, then there may actually be no significant difference—or it could be twice the .03 reported. He needs to remember that the findings of an opinion poll are no better than the sample used and is no more reliable than the instrument devised and the methods used by the interviewers. The *Literary Digest*'s fiasco in 1936, for example, based upon telephone interviews, led editors to predict that Landon would defeat Roosevelt by a 370–161 electoral vote margin. The random sample from among only telephone users was not a representative sample.

Eight pieces of information, it has been suggested, should be reported (or known) about an opinion poll in order to properly interpret the results: (1) the size of sample and response, (2) definition of the population sampled, (3) identity of the sponsor, (4) exact wording of the questions, (5) allowance for sampling error, (6) findings based on the total sample, (7) the method of interviewing, and (8) the timing of interviewing. With such information the reliability can be better judged by the editorialist—and the reader.[14]

Cause and effect relationships are sometimes erroneously assumed in statistics, for example, in correlation. The measure of the extent to which two things vary together might serve as a working definition of correlation. Studies have shown that the grade point average of high school students is positively correlated with the grade point average earned in college, that is, the higher the high school g.p.a., the higher the college g.p.a. The statistical relationship in itself, however, doesn't necessarily mean the one causes the other. Cause and effect must be established outside the statistical correlation for such a claim to be valid.

For example, the incidence of the sale of ice cream and the number of persons engaged in sailboating might well be found to be positively correlated, but this relationship doesn't necessarily mean that the one causes the other. The cause may be a third variable such as the temperature.

Dave Hume, the British philosopher, held that for a cause and effect relationship to be established three conditions must be met: (1) the cause must precede or be simultaneous with the effect, (2) there must be some more or less clear connection in time and space between the two events being causally connected, and (3) there must be what Hume called a "history of regularity" in the first two conditions.[15] It would be fallacious to assume, therefore, that a high incidence of statistical correlation establishes a cause and effect relationship in the absence of these three conditions. For example, the rapid increase of college enrollments during the decade of the 1920s was positively correlated with the rapid increase in the number of inmates in institutions for the mentally ill. Can a cause and effect relationship be assumed? No, because there is no indication of which event preceded which, there is no connection seen or imaginable between these events spatially, and there is no history of regularity prior to the decade of the 1920s. Statistical correlation between lung cancer and cigarette smoking, however, is acceptable as an instance of causal reasoning because it does satisfy Hume's three conditions. Cigarette smoking does precede lung cancer, independent research on the effects of nicotine on the skin of mice makes a spatial connection imaginable, and there is now a long history of such correlation.

Editorialists need to be skeptical of statistics, both those they plan to use as well as statistics used by others. Politicians and governmental propagandists, for example, often use statistics in a way which helps them prove whatever it is they are trying to prove. With a little prodding, one critic notes, such statistics often are less convincing than at first glance. The Cost of Living Index, for example, is simply a market basket of items, some of which are not checked for two or three months at a time. The revered and often cited Gross National Product is less reliable, some say, than the less frequently used Federal Reserve Board's Index of Industrial Production. And the famed Dow-Jones average, it has been noted, doesn't even average the stock market, much less the whole economy. Edwin Diamond, in a commentary on WTOP-TV, Washington, D.C., also was critical of government unemployment figures. He noted:

> The latest and most potent numbers game involves the Labor Department's monthly unemployment figures. The department says 5.4 million Americans were out of work in February [1972], but when the figures are "seasonally adjusted," the rate of unemployment goes down. The reasons more people are supposed to be looking for jobs in

> February are only one of the statistical variables in job figures. The figures are based on sampling techniques and they involve calculations of "discouraged persons" people who have not looked for work recently and therefore aren't counted as unemployed when in fact they are.

The only solution to such abuses, Diamond concluded, may be for the journalist to be on his guard and to explain to his audience how such a numbers game is being played.

On Posing Questions

The type of question asked by the mass media editorialist provides another perspective to the problem of logical reasoning. To the extent that the editorialist goes "from fact to judgment" in problem solving, he first strives to seek out the right question. The question needs to be relevant to his audience and one for which he can hopefully provide an answer. Such a question may fall into one or more of five categories. It may be (1) a question of fact, (2) a question of meaning, (3) a question of probability, (4) a question of value, or (5) a question of policy. The first two types shouldn't pose any great difficulty for the editorialist in terms of avoiding either verbal or statistical error or fallacy. The other three often do pose problems.

An editorial might deal with a simple question of fact, for example, "Who started the melee at the City Council meeting which resulted in a black eye for the Mayor?" Such a question may be of more importance in a court of law than on the editorial page, but such a fact might be determined by the newsman or the editorialist through personal observation, through a reliable news report, or through a credible witness. If the question becomes one of meaning, a different problem may arise. If it were determined, for example, that Councilman Tunney threw the first punch after the mayor made a reference to "blackmailing," then the question posed might be, "What did the mayor mean by 'blackmailing' in his discussion at the City Council meeting?" Definitions, of course, are mere classifications that men devise. Such labels are made up of words; they are not things. Some words, however, are capable of more than one meaning, which causes problems. Such a problem often results from a failure to define terms in the process of logical thinking as well as in the political process evolving at a City Council meeting.

Editorial questions, however, usually go beyond questions of fact or of definition. They may deal with questions of probability, for example, "Is exposure of marijuana injurious to one's health?" Such an approach may pose questions of both fact and definition, but the answer must go beyond either. Or an editorial may pose a question of value, for example, "Is the use of marijuana an undesirable habit?" The editorialist is now dealing with the merits or effects, the excellence or mediocrity, the good or bad of a problem. Or an editorial may pose a question of policy: "Should the use of marijuana be legally sanctioned?" The editorialist is now asking an even more complex question involving change or advocating an action: "What should be done?"

Questions of probability, value, or policy all require inferences beyond the facts. They require care in defining terms to avoid the various fallacies of ambiguity discussed earlier in this chapter. They require care in arriving at conclusions through either deductive or inductive reasoning, or a combination of the two. They require care in examining the premises underlying the reasoning process to avoid unwarranted assumptions and the various fallacies which may arise from such logical reasoning.[16]

Other Faults to Be Avoided

There are additional precautions which the mass media editorialist needs to take if he is to be an effective persuader. Though they may not fit the various categories of fallacy as discussed above, they do constitute errors, faults, propaganda devices, call them what you will, and should be recognized by the editorialist for what they are and should generally be avoided.

One such fault is sometimes referred to as use of the "glittering generality," in which an issue or argument being espoused is associated or identified with such accepted ideals or "virtue words" as the "American way of life" or the "public interest." The idea of the propagandist is that, even though the term may mean different things to different people, it is assumed that most would approve of whatever connotation the phrase implies. Another spin-off benefit may occur when such generalizations include symbols of authority or prestige which may be "transferred" to the issue or argument being offered. The term "freedom of the press," for example, is sometimes used in connection with arguments in which the activity being discussed is only peripherally related to that First Amendment guarantee. It is hoped that the authority and prestige of that concept will be transferred to the situation or activity being discussed.

The "testimonial," a favorite device with advertisers, and the "band wagon" approach, the "everybody is doing it" appeal of the propagandist, may be more appropriate for the advertiser and propagandist than the editorialist, but that isn't to say they can't be used by the editorialist. The use of authoritative sources to give validity to an idea being espoused or to argue that numerous other cities have taken an action being advocated to the city council may both be valid approaches if the arguments are indeed based upon fact. The fallacy comes in the unwarranted assumption which too often underlies such allegations.

Another fault which may mar the effectiveness of an editorial is the inability or unwillingness of the editorialist to take a stance on an issue. One writer calls such a fault "straddling" in which the editorialist plays hide-and-seek with his readers from paragraph to paragraph, taking a position on first one side of the issue then the other. Another critic refers to this approach as the "Sir Roger de Coverley" in which the editorialist becomes a mere essayist who proceeds in a scholarly fashion to tell the reader that there is much to be said on the one side, but, again, there is also much to be said on the other. The essay editorial may end with such moronic remarks as "it remains to be seen," or "only time will tell" or "this is as it should be" which ignores the question being discussed.

Plain dullness is a fault which may kill readership of an editorial faster than any other shortcoming. Dullness may result from vagueness or imprecision in writing. It may result from what one writer called "droning," the needless repetition of the point being espoused, or "pneumaticism," being too wordy or taking too much space to say what one means. Another writer noted:

> A reader becomes bored when he begins to realize that some of the words he's reading aren't necessary. Or that they're not precise. Or that sentence structure is repetitious or in some other way only vaguely related to the logic of the ideas. In other words, a reader tires when he is encouraged not to pay attention because the language is imprecise enough not to be saying much anyway.[17]

The editorialist may also bore his readers if he becomes too chauvinistic in his approach or if he engages in dogma or bigotry. As noted in Chapter 3, he may also turn readers off if he engages in Afghanistanism, choosing far away subjects to write about, or if he displays ignorance by failing to research his subject.[18] The editorialist, to be effective, needs to strive to avoid all such fallacies, errors, faults, or other shortcomings.

Creel C. Black, editor of the *Philadelphia Inquirer,* patiently constructed the following editorial from sentences culled from editorials he had been asked to judge in 1972.[19] Note the Roger de Coverley approach, the abstractions and inanities, the platitudes and fence straddling, the lack of vigor and clarity in this "say-nothing" editorial, which, of course, completely ignores any logical progression of thought.

MAYBE TOO LITTLE, TOO LATE

What's to be done?

The world wonders with bated breath.

In answering this question, it is essential that the city and the educators and legislators involved look beyond tomorrow. We've been holding back for too long.

The more substantial issue is how long the present pattern will continue before the social and economic changes necessary to reverse it are demanded.

It is vital to get as much clarification on these points as possible before April 1.

This clearly is no simple task, but municipal commitment now would, perhaps, prove the decisive affirmation.

The people seem to understand what is needed. Do the politicians? That's the size of it. It's appalling.

The trend of putting things in broad categories has marked our social and political questions in recent times. Everything is oversimplified, and therefore distorted.

If we could find any politician—Democrat or Republican—to face up to that dilemma and come up with a workable solution, we would applaud him to the very echo. He would probably go down in history as the savior of the American democratic system.

There is reason to hope, however, that the disagreements can be ironed out, and the program made effective. It's worth earnest cooperation.

The commission has plans to participate in the search for a better way. The commission's report, soon to be completed with a third release, deserves thoughtful note by every American. Much of the commission's recommendation should gain broad public support.

The new initiative thus offers municipal governments and citizens of the entire metropolitan area the chance to make a contribution of lasting significance.

In any case, it is an issue which we must keep pressing.

The need is there.

So the cosmic question intrudes: Where will it all end?

The Masthead 14 (Summer 1972): 27–28
Reprinted by permission.

The world would still be wondering "with bated breath" if it had to depend upon such an ambiguous editorial for illumination or guidance about what's to be done in regard to some public issue or problem.

Summary and Conclusion

It can be argued that if the editorialist learns the facts about an issue, shouldn't common sense and reflection be enough to insure his drawing the right conclusions. And if common sense, as a type of natural logic, be sufficient, why then be concerned with all the fallacies and intricacies surrounding logical thinking which might better be left to the logician. Here is the answer of one logician:

> Though common sense is a necessary prerequisite to all effective thinking, it is not sufficient by itself to insure correct procedure, particularly when the matters under consideration are profound and

> complicated. Common sense is the guide of our workaday existence. It is unreasonable, however, to expect it to guide us equally well along the tortuous and thorny paths of science and wisdom. For so exalted a purpose common sense is too unreflective and uncritical . . .[20]

The editorialist must, therefore, check his common sense conclusions against what the logician calls "the science and art of right thinking"—formal logic. He needs, as far as possible, to avoid verbal and statistical fallacies in making his deductions. He needs to be aware of the type of question with which he deals. He needs to take care with causal relationships. He needs to beware of and generally avoid the devices of the propagandist. He needs to avoid stylistic errors and faults which tend to mar his efforts to communicate his straight thinking about an event or issue to his readers or listeners. He needs to do all these things if he is to be an effective persuader.

NOTES for Chapter 7

1 Nicholas Capaldi, *The Art of Deception,* 2d ed. (Buffalo, N.Y.: Prometheus Books, 1975), p. 171.

2 For a fuller discussion of fallacies arising from unwarranted assumptions, see Chilton R. Bush, *Editorial Thinking and Writing* (New York: Appleton, 1932), pp. 176–205.

3 For other examples of the use of "Red Herrings," see Capaldi, *The Art of Deception,* pp. 128–29.

4 Bush, *Editorial Thinking and Writing,* p. 184.

5 *Ibid.,* pp. 189–90.

6 For a discussion of the methods of attacking an argument, see Capaldi, *The Art of Deception,* pp. 71–114.

7 See, e.g., W. Ware Fearnside and William B. Holther, *Fallacy: The Counterfeit of Argument* (Englewood Cliffs, N.J.: Prentice-Hall, 1959): 152.

8 Raymond J. McCall, *Basic Logic,* 2d ed. (New York: Barnes & Noble, 1952), p. 29.

9 *Ibid.,* pp. 29–30.

10 Bush, *Editorial Thinking and Writing,* p. 195.

11 Philip Meyer, *Precision Journalism* (Blommington, Ind.: Indiana University Press, 1973), p. 16.

12 Darrell Huff, *How to Lie with Statistics* (New York: W. W. Norton, 1954), p. 101.

13 For another book on a related subject, see Darrell Huff, *How to Take a Chance* (New York: W. W. Norton, 1959).

14 See "What Needs to Be Known About a Poll," *Columbia Journalism Review,* 7 (Summer 1968): 22.

15 For a discussion of the fallacies of causal reasoning, see Capaldi, *The Art of Deception,* pp. 162–70.

16 For a discussion of the role of questions in expository writing, see Harold F. Graves and Bernard S. Oldsey, *From Fact to Judgment,* 2d ed. (New York: Macmillan, 1963).

17 James Howe, *The Making of Style* (New York: Chilton Book, 1972), p. 3.

18 For a discussion of "faults to avoid," see Curtis D. MacDougall, *Principles of Editorial Writing* (Wm. C. Brown, 1973), pp. 99–140.

19 Creel C. Black, "Maybe Too Little, Too Late," *The Masthead* 14 (Summer 1972): 27–28.

20 McCall, *Basic Logic,* p. xviii.

8

Editorial Credibility: *Perceptions Make a Difference*

A TALENTED YOUNG columnist for the *Chicago Tribune,* who had won a following among many of that newspaper's readers during a two-year period, resigned suddenly after what was termed "a breach of professional journalistic standards." The resignation came after the columnist was charged by an anonymous letter writer with substantial plagiarism from the work of another journalist which had been published in an anthology. While the charge and the resignation may not have been unusual, the response by the newspaper was. In a story under a four-column headline, Clayton Kirkpatrick, editor of the *Tribune,* explained to readers that while the columns in question were not about matters of great significance, the basic standards of good faith and veracity must still apply. "The standards that we look for in others, particularly public officials," Kirkpatrick wrote, "cannot, in fairness, be denied application to us. We condemn deception in others; we cannot accept it among our own without penalty."[1]

To what "penalty" was the *Tribune* editor referring? He was concerned, no doubt, with the future credibility of the *Tribune* and its editorial staff. Credibility is a valuable attribute, not only to a newspaper or other news media, but to the individual communicator as well. A serious credibility gap can remove a President of the United States from office, can alienate parents from their children, teachers from their students, or an editorialist or commentator from his audience.

The journalist's role, of course, has never been blessed with a surplus of prestige (a concept generally related to credibility) despite the romantic Hollywood treatment often given to journalists, particularly the newspaper reporter. The newspaper columnist, for example, was ranked 46th among 90 occupational roles surveyed during the 1960's—just below the farmer, undertaker, and welfare worker. The daily newspaper reporter and the radio announcer fared even worse than the columnist—coming up in 48th and 49th positions. The garbage collector, street sweeper and shoe shine boy brought up the bottom of the occupational listing. On the other hand, the three most prestigious occupations were supreme court justice, physician, and nuclear physicist.[2] The relative rankings among occupations, the report noted, had changed little in 1963 from a survey conducted in 1947, and there is little reason to think that the newsman's prestige improved greatly during the 1970's.

Journalists, however, were rated fourth of eleven professional categories in a 1976 Gallup poll which asked 1,524 adults, "How would you rate the honesty and ethical standards of the people in these different fields?" Journalists were rated "very high" or "high" by 33 percent of those surveyed, below doctors, engineers, and college teachers.[3] A Harris poll in 1977 reported that, for the first time in a number of years, confidence in the leadership in the nation's major institutions had begun to rise. Confidence in the news media, however, continued to wane. Both television news and the print media had been riding high during the Watergate era when 41 percent expressed confidence in television news and 30 percent in the press, according to a 1973 Harris poll. In 1977 television news leveled out at 28 percent and the press fell to 18 percent, an 8 percent decline since 1973 and a 2 percent drop since 1976. Ranking ahead of the press were doctors (43 percent), college presidents (37), the White House (31), the Supreme Court (29), organized religion (29), television news (28), the military (27), and business (20). Organized labor, the Congress, lawyers, and advertising agencies all ranked below the press.

Findings of an Associated Press Managing Editors national "image" study are tied even more closely to the credibility issue as it affects the media opinion writer. The study indicated, among other things, that 51 percent of the respondents did not believe newspapers confined their opinions to their editorials and 49 percent believed that their newspaper's stand on politics affected the news stories in the paper.[4] Media critics, of course, continue to harp on the perceived shortcomings of both the print and broadcast media. Despite national surveys which indicate that more and more people are relying on television for their news, however, there are a number of studies which indicate that, at least for some, newspapers are still more believable and trusted than are the broadcast media.[5]

Why all this concern for source credibility? Why should the media opinion writer or commentator be concerned with what members of his audience think of him? Why should editors be concerned with perceptions which audiences have about the news media?

Credibility and Persuasion

More than 2,000 years ago, Aristotle wrote: "Persuasion is achieved by the speaker's personal character when the speech is so spoken as to make us think him credible. We believe good men more fully and more readily than others."[6] Good character, good sense, and concern for the welfare of the audience, Aristotle wrote, are the three constituents of ethical appeal. "Men either form a false opinion through want of good sense," the philosopher observed, "or they form a true opinion, but because of their moral badness do not say what they really think; or finally, they are both sensible and upright, but not well disposed to their hearers, and may fail in consequence to recommend what they know to be the best course."[7] Aristotle's classic writing on *ethos* (the distinguishing character, tone, or guiding beliefs of man), evince an astuteness that may not be apparent upon first reading.

A more contemporary analysis of attitude formation and attitude change indicates that generally there will be more opinion change in the desired direction if the communicator (whether he be a teacher, a preacher, or an editorialist) has high credibility than if he has low credibility. Researchers in the Yale Communication Research Program, whose work dominated the attitude area during the 1950's and continues to be highly influential, found in a number of early studies that high credibility sources had a substantially greater immediate effect on the audience's opinions than low credibility sources. A classic Yale study found, for example, that a communication arguing the feasibility of atomic submarines was much more persuasive when attributed to J. Robert Oppenheimer (whom the audience had previously rated as high in credibility) than when attributed to *Pravda* (which the audience had previously rated as low in credibility).[8]

Variations in source credibility seem to influence primarily the audience's motivation to accept the conclusions advocated, researchers theorized, since information tests revealed equally good learning of what was said regardless of the credibility of the communicator.[9] In more recent research based upon the earlier Yale studies, message sources perceived to be credible (i.e., trustworthy and qualified) have been consistently found to be more influential in changing the attitudes of recipients than sources perceived to be low in credibility.[10]

In discussing how and why source credibility affects the persuasive impact of a message, another scholarly researcher identified three motivational bases for audience acceptance of an advocated persuasive position. They are (1) a desire to be correct on a given issue, (2) a desire to identify with or otherwise form an emotionally satisfying relationship with the source, and (3) the communicator's power, as perceived by the reader or listener, to reward or punish the recipient's compliance or lack of compliance.[11] The mass media opinion writer might benefit in the first area to the extent he is viewed as expert and objective, two components of source credibility. He might benefit in the second area to the degree his readers or listeners know him and view him as being similar to themselves or as being likable. As to the third area, it is doubtful that the opinion writer or commentator would often be in a position to bring about compliance—as might a political boss or public official playing a more authoritative role.

Recent scholarly research would indicate, however, that it is not always an easy task to determine who has credibility and who does not. Credibility, for one thing, is not a single characteristic of an individual, such as age or sex, nor a set of characteristics, such as socioeconomic position, although these might be among the components of credibility under a given situation. Credibility is a set of perceptions about a source held by receivers of a communication, and they become relevant only when they are perceived by the audience.[12] While contemporary researchers do not always agree on the labels given the dimensions of the concept, there is a general agreement that credibility is one of the most potent variables in the study of persuasive communications.[13]

Dimensions of Credibility

One of the problems in determining the parameters of source credibility is that the concept must be defined in terms of the perceptions of the receiver of the persuasive message, not in terms of objective characteristics of the source. The former task, of course, is far more difficult. A group of researchers during the 1960's, extending the work of Hovland and the Yale Communication Research Program, established three dimensions or factors which people use in judging the credibility of various sources. These factors were labeled *safety, qualification,* and *dynamism.* Using 128 pairs of adjectives, the factor analytical study attempted to measure the connotative meaning of the concept—source credibility.

Communicators rated high in the study on the *safety* dimension, for example, were described in choices between the adjective pairs as kind, congenial, friendly, warm, agreeable, pleasant, gentle, unselfish, just, forgiving, fair, hospitable, sociable, ethical, calm, and patient. Communicators rating high on the *qualification* dimension were described as trained, experienced, skillful, informed, authoritative, able, and intelligent. Those rating high in *dynamism* were described by receivers as aggressive, emphatic, frank, forceful, bold, active, energetic, and fast.[14] To achieve credibility, according to these researchers, a communicator would not have to rank high on each of the listed traits, but he would have to score well on the majority of them—as perceived by the recipient.

In a more recent study examining the relationships between the dimensions of source credibility, *safety* (or general trustworthiness) was found to be the predominant factor associated with task-oriented communications. The *dynamism* factor, labeled as general activity, was found to be more associated with increased social interaction rather than being task oriented. The *qualification* factor was labeled as expertise.[15] The qualification-expertise factor is sometimes labeled as *competence* or *authoritativeness* by researchers. *Dynamism* is often labeled as *charisma,* or listed as a separate fourth factor.[16]

Charisma is undoubtedly a more familiar concept to the layman, particularly in the political area, than is the term *dynamism.* To say that someone has charisma is to say that he seems to possess characteristics that cannot be easily defined or explained. President John F. Kennedy, Martin Luther King, Winston Churchill, and Mao Tse-Tung were all said to be charismatic leaders. The term originally was associated with powers of leadership thought to derive from some unusual sanction: divine, magical, or diabolic. Today the term is usually removed from the realm of magic. It is used rather to refer to unusual credibility or to unique personal influence of an individual.[17] While the term is more often used in regard to political leaders, editors such as Benjamin C. Bradlee of the *Washington Post* and Joseph Pulitzer III of the *St. Louis Post-Dispatch* would be perceived by many of their journalistic peers to have charisma. Many readers may likewise view various syndicated opinion columnists, for example Jack Anderson or James J. Kilpatrick, as charismatic. Editorialists, unfortunately, are seldom as well known by their audience.

The various dimensions of source credibility as a persuasive variable are linked by one researcher to two of the motivational areas discussed above. The desire to be correct on a given issue is related to both the perceived expertise and perceived objectivity of the communicator—of not only knowing the truth but being objective enough to tell it as he sees it. The desire to identify with or otherwise form an emotionally satisfying relationship with the source is tied to two elements of communicator attractiveness. One element is labeled *likableness,* an assumption that if one person likes another he will tend to agree or accept that person's likes or dislikes. The other is the doctrine of "common ground" or *source similarity,* an assumption that the recipient will be more persuaded by a source which he perceives as being similar to himself, ideological as well as demographic similarity.[18]

Other contemporary scholars have conducted scores of experimental studies, some utilizing factor analysis, resulting in surprising consistency. Although the words and the number of factors may vary, the findings are not only consistent with one another, they also tend to confirm Aristotle's ancient empirical judgments. Good sense, good moral character, and goodwill still go a long way toward establishing credibility as a communicator.[19]

Editorialists also often voice concern about the credibility of their work, though they may use different terms. Appearing on a National Conference of Editorial Writers panel discussing the question, "What's Wrong with the Editorial Page?" Reed Sarratt, Executive Vice President of the Southern Newspaper Publishers Association, had no trouble at all with his answer. The problem with editorial pages, he said, is "editorial writers." In accusing editorial writers of "not fulfilling a time-honored tradition," Sarratt, tongue-in-cheek, used this list of adjectives in describing the newspaper editorialist: tentative, uncertain, insecure, provincial, isolated, uninformed, unimaginative, insensitive, illiterate, shallow, lazy, arrogant, overbearing, doctrinaire, self-righteous, narrow-minded.[20] Such a perception of newspaper opinion writers by a majority of readers would indeed pose a credibility problem.

Source credibility, however, has a wider application than the reader's perception of the editorialist. In any case, the newspaper opinion writer, except for the syndicated writer or the local columnist, is too often anonymous.[21] However, source credibility, for better or for worse, is also applicable at the level of the news medium itself.

Credibility and Media Use

As with communicator credibility, media credibility and media use have received much attention from communications researchers for many years. The Roper Organization has reported credibility estimates of the various news media since 1959.[22] Even as early as the 1930's the Gallup and Fortune polls and surveys by the National Opinion Research Center reported on the public's perception of the accuracy, believability, truthfulness and reliability of radio and newspapers.[23] These surveys, plus a more recent study commissioned by the American Newspaper Publishers Association, give a good idea of the basis for the public's perceived credibility of the news media.

The ANPA study, for example, found five distinct components of media credibility:

(1) The media themselves; e.g., the permanently recorded convenience of newspapers or the highly visual aspects of television.
(2) The channel, or channels, of each medium that a person is acquainted with or uses most frequently.
(3) The news content: Is it judged to be complete, substantial, informative, true—or incomplete, superficial, uninformative, false?
(4) The treatment given the news: Is it presented in a boring or interesting manner, difficult or easy way, with emphasis on people or on events?
(5) The source or disseminator of the news: Is the individual communicator whose message is transmitted by the medium a credible source?[24]

A 1976 ANPA study considering these five domains simultaneously found no common characteristics of newspaper and television crediblity which ran across all five areas. Using fifty descriptive scales in testing the perceived credibility within each separate domain, as few as one and no more than four characteristics were found in common within a given domain. Only ten of the fifty descriptive scales provided significant differences between newspaper and television. Several of the differences were perhaps predictable. It was found, for example, (1) that people regarded television as a faster medium, (2) that the newspaper's content is more substantial and complete, (3) that television's news presentation is more interesting and dramatic, and (4) that broadcasters are more energetic. Not so predictable, however, was the finding that a newspaper's presentation is perceived to be more public spirited and more optimistic while television newsmen are perceived as being more expert and more informed.[25]

Audience characteristics found to differentiate newspaper from television users were summarized in one study as follows: (1) Young people find newspapers less credible; older readers find newspapers more useful; (2) women are more oriented toward television and men to newspapers in both credibility and usage; and (3) the more educated, the higher in socio-economic status, and the socially upward-mobile user of the news media place more reliance upon the print media and may also trust them more.[26]

The difficulty in measuring media credibility, however, is indicated in Roper surveys which show that since 1959 television has steadily moved ahead as "the people's choice" among media. Since 1961 television has led steadily as the most believable news medium, according to Roper. By 1974, television had widened its margin over newspapers to a two-and-a-half-to-one advantage. The 1976 Roper findings, announced in May of 1977, showed that 51 percent of the national sample (the same as in 1974) rated television to be "most believable." The believability of newspapers, however, rose from 20 percent in 1974 to 22 percent in 1976. By contrast, newspapers were found to be "most believable" in 1959, the first time Roper conducted the survey, with 32 percent of the national sample while television was found "most believable" by only 29 percent.[27]

Print media researchers have belatedly objected to the phrasing of Roper's questions because they allow for a multiple response. Using a modification of the Roper questions, a more recent study suggests that the Roper questionnaire may have distorted credibility responses.[28] Other studies conclude that newspapers are perceived as being more credible than the Roper studies suggest.[29] A number of critics point out that some of the underlying assumptions of media credibility research may be questionable. The public, one researcher notes, has a fundamentally different orientation toward television than toward newspapers. The public turns to television primarily to be entertained; it turns to the newspaper for information. It is also noted that in the national research samples the respondents may be evaluating network television news, which is national in scope, against the more localized news content of newspapers. Other problems face the researcher attempting to measure the use and believability of the news media.

The opinion writer and commentator need to be aware of this ongoing research because their effectiveness as persuaders depend in part upon the perceived credibility of the medium for which they work. This isn't to agree with Marshall McLuhan that the medium is the message. Media characteristics, however, and the perceptions which audiences hold of those characteristics make a difference. There is some evidence, for example, that high credibility may be more important for the broadcast communicator than for the newspaper editorialist. It has been found that when a broadcast audience distrusts the motives of the communicator the communication is seen as more of a threat. The researcher reasoned that this may be true because the more "live" the speech the more involved the audience feels.[30]

Believability and Credibility

There are strong indications that the editorialist's believability may be reflected by the extent to which his editorial message or commentary is perceived as being factually correct and in accord with empirical evidence. This in turn depends upon the ediorialist being perceived as both knowing what is correct and being motivated to communicate what he knows to his audience. Or, in more specific terms, source credibility (and believability) is ultimately based upon the source's perceived expertise and objectivity.[31] Expertise (competence or qualification) may be perceived as being general in nature, or it may be associated with and limited to a specific subject area.

An anti-alcohol message communicated by a former alcoholic, for example, may be more persuasive than the same message delivered by a non-convert, simply because of the special expertise the convert is perceived to have acquired on that subject. Alcoholics Anonymous routinely uses "reformed" addicts as persuasive agents for this reason.[32] It has also been found that jurors, on fairly subtle cues, often tend to assign a more general expertise to other members of the jury who appear to be better educated or whose occupations are on a higher socioeconomic level than their own.[33] The very nature of the editorialist's role often casts the editorial writer and commentator as an expert of sorts, better educated than many members of their audience, having acquired, perhaps, a higher social status than many of them. Too much expertise, however, might be detrimental. An editorial opinion leader, as other chiefs, must not get too far ahead of the Indians.

For maximum believability, the editorialist-commentator must also be perceived as not only knowing the truth as an expert, but he must be objective enough and sufficiently motivated to tell it as he sees it. This dimension, as noted above, has been labeled *safety* or *trustworthiness*. In keeping with this common sense assumption, several research studies have demonstrated that communicators may be more persuasive when they are perceived as being disinterested parties or when they are arguing against their own best interests. As a part of one study, for example, General William Westmoreland, a "hawk" on the Vietnam War, was found to be more persuasive in making a statement that the number of United States casualties in the war far exceeded that reported in the press than when that same statement was presented anonymously.[34]

Persuasiveness may even be enhanced by a communicator who unexpectedly attempts to dissuade an audience from engaging in some activity. A liberal author, for example, was found to be more persuasive than a conservative author in attempting to dissuade an audience of college students from engaging in the illicit use of drugs. Advocacy of an unexpected position, it was concluded, bolstered the sincerity and trustworthiness of the author in the eyes of the audience. The expectancy-violation position was found to encourage yielding by the audience to the persusive appeals of the message.[35]

An editorialist, likewise, will often be perceived as being more objective and more trustworthy if the position he is arguing editorially is unexpected or if it is viewed as not being one from which he or his medium is likely to profit. Related to this perception is the common sense notion that an editorial message will have more impact if its persuasive intent is masked or disguised. While this argument has support, one researcher has noted that there are circumstances under which precisely the opposite should occur, for example, when one is praising some action. In any case, comprehension of a persuasive message is usually enhanced, and the persuasive impact increased, by a straightforward, open editorial appeal.[36]

One long held research-based finding concerning source credibility, the so-called "sleeper effect," has been all but discarded by subsequent research. It held that the impact of a persuasive communication from a low credibility source tended to increase with the passage of time as the reader or listener dissociated the message from its source. It may indeed be that as a consequence of dissociation, over time, the message content is no longer connected to a source, but there is little evidence that this dissociation hypothesis requires that there be an increase in persuasion. The conclusion of more recent research is that if there is a sleeper effect, it cannot be a robust phenomenon.[37]

Attractiveness and Credibility

Another variable related to credibility which has been actively pursued by communications researchers is source attractiveness, usually defined in terms of likability and similarity. A communicator may be so liked or admired, for example, that the recipient of a message would receive gratification by identifying with him through shared beliefs, hopefully to include those being communicated. Or a communicator may be perceived as being so familiar or so similar that the recipient is willing to assume the position or adopt the views advocated by the communicator.[38] Relating this perception to the role of the media editorialist, an "attractive" editorialist may be said to be a more persuasive communicator to the extent he is liked or admired by his audience. On a common sense plane, the assumption is simply that people tend to agree with those whom they like.

Just why people become more favorably disposed toward a communicator, however, is a far more complex matter. In the 1968 presidential election, for example, neither Humphrey nor Nixon were popular candidates. Despite their unpopularity, researchers found the electorate more favorably disposed toward both the winner and loser after the election. It was speculated that sympathy toward the loser may have been translated into a generally more favorable attitude, or perhaps the repeated exposure of the candidates may have been sufficient to make both of them better liked.[39]

One researcher has noted that few propositions in the study of persuasion have obtained the degree of support enjoyed by the statement that "communicators who are perceived as similar to their audiences are more likely to effect persuasion than those sources who are seen as dissimilar." The impact of similar as compared to dissimilar sources has been examined in two principal contexts: (1) the relation between interpersonal similarity and attraction, and (2) the relation between interpersonal similarity and persuasion. At least thirteen studies are cited in support of the proposition that sources perceived as similar to their audiences are more persuasive than those perceived as dissimilar.[40]

Other studies, however, take a divergent view of the role of interpersonal similarity, at least as it relates to information processing. Attribution theory, for example, holds that the communicator who departs from the situational norm will have greater weight in determining response, though not necessarily greater agreement. Information theory, likewise, implies that greater dissimilarity of the source or higher newness of the message produces more arousal, more interest, and more response. Such theories dealing with information processing, however, do not deny that likability and similarity, as components of source attractiveness, tend to bolster the credibility of the mass media editorialist who is attempting to persuade and change attitudes rather than merely imparting information.[41]

Similarity vs. Dissimilarity

The concept of credibility (meaning source believability, expertise, competence, authoritativeness, trustworthiness) and the concept of source-audience similarity (the common ground concept, whether conceived of in demographic, attitudinal, or experiential terms, or based upon personality factors) pose a relational problem for communications researchers. The generalization asserting increased persuasiveness for more credible sources, for example, can be viewed as also being supportive of the proposition that dissimilarity, at least in regard to the various dimensions of credibility, also promotes persuasion. On a topic such as world politics, for example, undergraduate audiences were found to be influenced more by a Ph.D. in political science than by an undergraduate speaker. While the undergraduate was, without doubt, more similar in many respects to his audience, the Ph.D. was found to be more persuasive.[42]

On the other hand, recent trends in mass media persuasion seem to suggest that peer group representatives, for example, subjects from the same age group as the audience, more like their target audiences in physical features, in social behavior, or with similar demographic characteristics, are more effective persuaders. Children, it was noted, are used to sell breakfast cereals to other children via television, teenagers sell other teenagers tooth-whiteners, and middle-aged men tell their middle-aged audiences to watch their cholesterol level. In one experimental study involving evaluation of the intrauterine device as a part of a public health campaign it was found that peer appeal was more effective than a persuasive attempt by a source from a different age group. The study also suggested that first-hand experience with the subject of a persuasion campaign may increase a communicator's effectiveness.[43]

The contradictory results generated by research into source credibility and interpersonal similarity based upon the common ground doctrine has itself been a focus of various research studies. One study suggests, for example, that the effects of similarity could be better predicted if two distinctions are maintained: (1) between subjective similarity—comprised of shared attitudes, interest, or values—and objective similarity, including demographic factors such as sex, age, and economic background, and (2) between relevant similarities—those logically related to the proposition being advocated—and irrelevant similarities. For example, the fact that a speaker and his undergraduate audience are similar in height is probably irrelevant to acceptance of the speaker's stand on an economic issue, whereas his Ph.D. in economics is probably a relevant dissimilarity.[44]

Whether or not an expert source or a similar (peer) source is likely to be most effective in a given situation has been the concern of several researchers. One approach has been to test source appropriateness in terms of various message types. In reviewing the results obtained in these studies, one researcher formulated a "pedagogic model" which might have some application to the media persuader. The model adopts the two message types used in several of the studies: (1) the belief message, and (2) the value message. The definition of these message types by researchers become complex, but an example used in reference to the "pedagogic model" formulated by one researcher helps to make the distinction. In an attempt to persuade a high school audience not to use drugs, a doctor (expert source) might discuss the medical effect of drugs (a belief message), it is argued. A high school student (a similar peer), on the other hand, might better discuss the life style of the drug scene (a value message).[45] The pedagogic model would suggest that if the media communicator can establish himself as an expert, his persuasive appeal should be in a belief message. If, on the other hand, he views himself to be cooriented with his audience on a given topic or issue (that he shares similar views or can establish a peer relationship), then he should cast his persuasive appeal in a value message.

In any case, the "ideal" communicator may embody a combination of similarities and dissimilarities, all of which create appropriate ethos images if utilized wisely in terms of the circumstances of the communication engaged in.

Enhancing Source Credibility

If source credibility is of such importance in persuasion, how can a newspaper or broadcast station and its editorial staff improve its credibility rating? Actually a great many things may be done, most of them implied in the research findings set out above. Dozens of suggestions are made, for example, every time editorialists gather—although such proposals may not be tied explicitly to credibility. Based upon such experiences, here are a few specific suggestions which should be helpful in bolstering the credibility of the media editorialist:

1. Strive for expertise, as well as other pertinent characteristics enhancing credibility, when editorialists or commentators are recruited. Encourage participation by opinion writers in critique sessions and professional workshops to improve that expertise. Let readers and listeners know at every opportunity the excellent qualifications of editorial staffers.

2. Strive for diversity in the selection of the editorial staff. Editorialists, columnists, and commentators need not be gray and wrinkled to have credibility. They need not all be WASPish, certainly all your readers and listeners are not.[46] If the editorial staff is comprised of only one person, then strive for diversity of content in the selection of syndicated columnists and guest columnists.

3. Strive to establish an independent posture for the editorial staff, free from political, business, or other pressure group domination or the semblance of such influence. At the same time, however, be honest in making such claims. It has been found that the credibility of product claims is often enhanced by admitting inferiority on one or two attributes, preferably attributes which are of little consequence to the targeted market.[47]

4. Strive to be more objective. In terms of the NCEW's "Basic Statement of Principles," the editorialist should strive to "present facts honestly and fully," to "never knowingly mislead the reader, misrepresent a situation, or place any person in a false light," nor should "consequential errors" go uncorrected.[48]

5. Strive to be consistent. If the editorialist operates from a certain ideological position, a certain point of view, a certain perspective, that same yardstick should be applied to problems at *all* levels of government—national, state, and local—if readers or listeners are to view the editorialist as trustworthy and as a credible source.

6. Strive to be fair. This may mean giving both sides of an issue in a pro-con approach. Or, it may mean discussing various sides of more complex issues. It may mean safeguarding the reader or listener's desire to answer back. It may mean allowing staffers to take issue with the newspaper or broadcast station's position.

7. Strive to be honest. Don't let others use the editorial columns or broadcast commentaries for "canned" messages, using the good name of your medium to enhance *their* views. Don't engage in "freebies"; the economic savings aren't worth the cost to your own or your medium's credibility.[49] Remember, it's the public's interest, not private interests, upon which freedom of the press is based.

8. Strive to be more humanistic, remembering and acknowledging the interests, fears, problems, frustration of readers and listeners. In all your editorials and commentary, show the reader and listener what is in it for him. Do it, and your credibility will be greatly enhanced.

9. Strive to be more relevant. This may mean taking stands on local issues, investigating and analyzing all sides of controversial matters which make a difference to your readers or listeners. It may mean developing an Action Line column, getting involved in consumer interests, naming businesses and name brands, in your editorials, where pertinent.

10. Strive to operate the opinion function more openly, a condition the news media sometimes admire more in government than in themselves. Make the editorial columns a truly open forum. Take affirmative action to encourage access to the letters-to-the-editor column. Make provisions for feedback from listeners. Credibility is involved, and the news media's ability to persuade and lead is involved.

11. Strive to be more visible. If credibility is important, then anonymity for the mass media opinion writer is self-defeating. Why

shouldn't newspaper editorialists be as visible as broadcast editorialists and commentators? Why shouldn't editorials, for example, be signed?[50]

12. Strive to be more professional. Conflicts of interest, real or apparent, should be avoided. The NCEW's "Basic Statement of Principles," as revised in 1975, seeks to hold syndicates supplying editorial features to the same high standards as proposed for the opinion writers of newspapers.[51]

Such a list, of course, could run on endlessly. Others, for example, have suggested such attributes and goals as maturity of thought, avoidance of pretense, courage and forthrightness in responding to criticism, courtesy and appreciativeness, self-confidence without loss of modesty, the avoidance of triteness and banality, willingness to acknowledge mistakes, respect for the opinion of others, maintaining an even temper despite provocation, frankness and sincerity, dignity without pomposity, modesty without being apologetic, vitality and enthusiasm, a sense of humor.[52]

Indeed, behavioral research dealing with source credibility indicates that any action tending to enhance the prestige, general trustworthiness, expertise, or attractiveness of the communicator, or which works toward establishing a common ground of shared beliefs, values, or attitudes between the communicator and his audience should improve the overall credibility rating of the communicator. Such a goal seems worthy of the effort of the media opinion writer since a more credible and attractive editorialist is a more persuasive communicator.

NOTES for Chapter 8

[1] *Chicago Tribune*, December 7, 1975, p. 25.

[2] See Robert W. Hodge, Paul M. Siegel, and Peter R. Rossi, "Occupational Prestige in the United States, 1925–1963," *American Journal of Sociology* 70 (November 1964): 286–302.

[3] Report in *ANPA Public Affairs Newsletter*, October 1976.

[4] *ANPA News Research Bulletin* 21 (November 19, 1970): p. 74.

[5] For a critical interpretation of the Roper studies of public attitudes toward television and other mass media, see Vernon A. Stone, "Sources of Most News: Evidence and Inferences," *Journal of Broadcasting* 14 (Winter 1969–70): 1–4; and Alex Edelstein, "Media Credibility and the Believability of Watergate," *ANPA News Research Bulletin* 1 (January 10, 1974).

[6] Richard McKeon, ed., *The Basic Works of Aristotle* (New York: Random House, 1941), p. 1329.

[7] *Ibid.*, p. 1380.

[8] Carl I. Hovland and Walter Weiss, "The Influence of Source Credibility on Communication Effectiveness," *Public Opinion Quarterly* 15 (Winter 1951): 635–50. For a critical analysis of this and other research regarding communicator credibility in gen-

eral, see Philip G. Zimbardo, Ebbe B. Ebbesen, and Christina Maslach, *Influencing Attitudes and Changing Behavior,* 2d ed. (Reading, Mass.: Addison-Wesley, 1977), pp. 125–27. The authors note that in order to demonstrate a measurable effect upon attitudes, researchers often have had to create extreme differences in communicator credibility that, nevertheless, gave only a slight edge to the credible source in producing attitude change. They ask: "In real-life situations, where the naturally existing differences between communicators would be much less extreme, would there still be enhancement of the communication by virtue of its attribution to a slightly more credible source?" Some of the data suggest that there would not, the authors contend.

[9] C. I. Hovland, I. L. Janis, and H. H. Kelley, *Communication and Persuasion* (New Haven: Yale University Press, 1953), pp. 269–70.

[10] See, e.g., John R. Baseheart and Robert N. Bostrom, "Credibility of Source and Self in Attitude Change," *Journalism Quarterly* 49 (Winter 1972): 742–45.

[11] William J. McGuire, "Persuasion, Resistance, and Attitude Change," in *Handbook of Communication,* eds.: Ithiel de Sola Pool and Wilbur Schramm (Chicago: Rand McNally College Publishing Co., 1973), pp. 229–32.

[12] Erwin P. Bettinghaus, *Persuasive Communication,* 2d ed. (New York: Holt, Rinehart and Winston, Inc., 1973), pp. 103–4.

[13] For a recent study restating the importance of source credibility, see Douglas G. Bock and Thomas J. Saine, "The Impact of Source Credibility, Attitude Valence, and Task Sensitization on Trait Errors in Speech Evaluation," *Speech Monographs* 42 (August 1975): 229–36.

[14] David K. Berlo, James B. Lemert, and Robert J. Mertz, "Dimensions for Evaluating the Acceptability of Message Sources," *Public Opinion Quarterly* 33 (Winter 1969–70): 563–76.

[15] Charles A. O'Reilly and Karlene H. Roberts, "Relationships Among Components of Credibility and Communication Behaviors in Work Units," *Journal of Applied Psychology* 61 (February 1976): 99–102.

[16] Christopher J. Tuppen, "Dimensions of Communicator Credibility: An Oblique Solution," *Speech Monographs* 41 (August 1974): 253–60.

[17] Bettinghaus, *Persuasive Communication,* pp. 110–11.

[18] For a discussion of these concepts, see McGuire, "Persuasion, Resistance, and Attitude Change," pp. 231–32.

[19] For a comparison of the "Constituents of Ethos" as found by six modern-day researchers, see Wayne N. Thompson, *The Process of Persuasion: Principles and Readings* (New York: Harper & Row, 1975), pp. 60–61.

[20] Paul B. Hope, "We're the Problem," *The Masthead* 26 (Winter 1974–75): 6–8.

[21] Ernest C. Hynds, "Editorial Pages Remain Vital," *The Masthead* 27 (Fall 1975): 19–22.

[22] Roper Organization, *Trends in Public Attitudes Toward Television and Other Mass Media, 1959–1974* (New York: Television Information Office, 1975).

[23] For a summary of these surveys, see Hazel Erskine, "The Polls: Opinion of the News Media," *Public Opinion Quarterly* 24 (Winter 1970–71): 630–43.

[24] Bradley S. Greenberg and Michael E. Roloff, "Mass Media Credibility: Research Results and Critical Issues," *ANPA News Research Bulletin* 6 (November 4, 1975).

[25] Eugene F. Shaw, "The Popular Meaning of Media Credibility," *ANPA News Research Bulletin* 3 (October 22, 1976).

[26] Greenberg and Roloff, "Mass Media Credibility," p. 27.

[27] Roper Organization, *Changing Public Attitudes Toward Television and Other Mass Media, 1959–1976* (New York: Television Information Office, 1977), pp. 4–5.

[28] Eugene F. Shaw, "Media Credibility: Taking the Measure of a Measure," *Journalism Quarterly* 50 (Summer 1973): 306–11.

[29] See, e.g., sections on credibility and accuracy in the six volumes of *News Research for Better Newspapers,* published by the ANPA Foundation.

[30] Stephen Worchel, Virginia Andreoli, and Joe Eason, "Is the Medium the Message? A Study of the Effects of Media, Communicator, and Message Characteristics on Attitude Change," *Journal of Applied Social Psychology* 5 (April–June 1975): 157–72.

[31] McGuire, "Persuasion, Resistance, and Attitude Change," p. 230.

[32] John M. Levine and Ronald S. Valle, "The Convert as a Credible Communicator," *Social Behavior and Personality* 3 (1975): 81–90.

[33] James M. Gleason and Victor A. Harris, "Race, Socio-Economic Status, and Perceived Similarity as Determinants of Judgements by Simulated Jurors," *Social Behavior and Personality* 3 (1975): 175–80.

[34] Gary F Koeske and William D. Crano, "The Effect of Congruous and Incongruous Source-Statement Combinations upon the Judged Credibility of a Communication," *Journal of Experimental Social Psychology* 4 (October 1968): 384–399.

[35] Paul M. Kohn and Suzi Snook, "Expectancy-Violation, Similarity, and Unexpected Similarity as Sources of Credibility and Persuasiveness," *Journal of Psychology* 94 (November 1976): 185–93.

[36] William J. McGuire, "Suspiciousness of Experimenter's Intent as an Artifact in Social Research," in *Artifacts in Behavioral Research,* eds.: Robert Rosenthal and R. L. Rosnow (New York: Academic Press, 1969), pp. 13–57.

[37] Paulette M. Gillig and Anthony G. Greenwald, "Is It Time to Lay the Sleeper Effect to Rest?" *Journal of Personality and Social Psychology* 29 (January 1974): 132–39.

[38] William J. McGuire, "Persuasion, Resistance, and Attitude Change," p. 231.

[39] James M. Dabbs, Jr., "Attitudes Toward Winner and Loser After an Election," *Social Behavior and Personality* 3 (1975): 45–48.

[40] Stephen W. King and Kenneth K. Sereno, "Attitude Change as a Function of Degree and Type of Interpersonal Similarity and Message Type, *Western Speech* 37 (Fall 1973): 218–32.

[41] Clark Leavitt and Karen Kaigler-Evans, "Mere Similarity versus Information Processing: An Exploration of Source and Message Interaction," *Communication Research* 2 (July 1975): 300–6.

[42] King and Sereno, "Attitude Change," p. 220.

[43] Joanne R. Cantor, Herminila Alfonso, and Dolf Zillman, "The Persuasive Effectiveness of the Peer Appeal and a Communicator's First-hand Experience," *Communication Research* 3 (July 1976): 293–309.

[44] Herbert W. Simons, Nancy Berkowitz, and R. John Moyer, "Similarity, Credibility, and Attitude Change: A Review and a Theory," *Psychological Bulletin* 73 (January 1970): 1–16.

[45] Stephen W. King, "Source Appropriateness: A Pedagogic Model," *Speech Teacher* 21 (September 1972): 221–24.

[46] John Millhone, "How WASPish Are We?" *The Masthead* 25 (Winter 1973–74): 39–42.

[47] Kenneth J. Roering and Robert J. Paul, "The Effect of the Consistency of Product Claims on the Credibility of Persuasive Messages," *Journal of Advertising* 5 (Spring 1976): 32–36.

[48] NCEW's "Basic Statement of Principles," adopted in Philadelphia, October 10, 1975, *The Masthead* 27 (Winter 1975), back cover. Reprinted as frontispiece of this book.

[49] See, e.g., Symposium, "Junkets—One Way of Getting There," *The Masthead* 28 (Winter 1976): 3–9; and "More on Junkets," *The Masthead* 29 (Spring 1977): 32–33.

[50] Warren G. Bovee, "The Mythology of Editorial Anonymity," *The Masthead* 24 (Winter 1972–73): 54–65; and Ernest C. Hynds, "Editorial Pages Remain Vital, *The Masthead* 27 (Fall 1975): 19–22.

[51] See also James J. Kilpatrick, "Life and Times with Cranberg Rule," *The Masthead* 27 (Winter 1975): 9–12.

[52] See "Specific Suggestions for Enhancing Ethos," Thompson, *The Process of Persuasion,* pp. 82–83.

9

The Editorial Appeal: *How You Make It Is Important*

Two MAJOR STRATEGIES for bringing about a change in beliefs, attitudes, and, hopefully, behavior, have attracted the attention of behavioral science researchers: (1) the use of active participation and (2) the use of persuasive communication.[1] Since the first strategy focuses upon bringing about change through such stimuli as interaction with other people or the observation of the behavior of others, it is largely outside the scope of this chapter. It should be noted, however, that in contrast to active participation where a person gains information by observing people, things, or events in a more or less neutral environment, information in a persuasive communication usually is viewed as coming from an outside source and as generally designed to manipulate or to influence a reader or listener. The editorialist, for example, can hardly mask his manipulative persuasive intent as he evaluates the deplorable record of the city council or the town board. Since persuasive communication has always been viewed as the major strategy for influencing people, particularly via the mass media, it has held the interest of both scholars and practitioners for many years. In fact, much of the impetus for controlled research in this area came from the Yale Communication Research Program during the 1950s under the direction of psychologist and persuasion researcher Carl I. Hovland.[2]

The Yale Program Approach

Hovland and his associates at Yale University, who published several volumes of their research findings during the 1950s, including *Communication and Persuasion* outlining their conceptual approach, have had a profound influence in shaping contemporary research and theory on attitude change. Concepts such as source credibility and various message characteristics such as primacy-recency effects, the order of presentation of arguments, the one-sided vs. two-sided approach to argumentation, fear arousing appeals, conclusion drawing, as well as variables dealing with the persuasibility of audiences were all of concern. Hovland and his coworkers, however, explicitly stated that they were not presenting a systematic theory of persuasive communication, though their work has been criticized for a failure to do so. What they did was to present a broad program of empirical research organized around the theme: *Who* says *what* to *whom* with *what* effect?" Their focus upon the message (oral or written) as the stimuli for attitude or opinion change makes the Yale approach of particular interest and importance to the media persuader.[3]

The Yale approach placed the variables that influence the acceptance of persuasive arguments into four categories: (1) the source of the communication, (2) characteristics of the persuasive message, (3) the persuasibility of the audiences and individuals making up a given audience, and (4) audience reactions to the communication. The first category of variables was discussed in Chapter 8. The third and fourth categories will be the focus of Chapter 10. Message characteristics are the primary concern of this chapter.

The Yale approach also specified four steps or processes which determine the extent to which a person will be persuaded by a communication. The effect of a given persuasive message, it was hypothesized, depends upon the extent to which the communication is read, understood, accepted, and remembered. The implication is that the effect of a newspaper editorial or broadcast commentary is mediated by what the social science researchers call *attention, comprehension, acceptance* (or *yielding*), and *retention.* While common sense would dictate that a message must be heard or read—and understood—before it can be persuasive, the techniques for achieving the degree of attention and comprehension necessary to illuminate a complex public issue is quite another matter. Without such understanding, of course, there may be no acceptance or attitude change—the desired goal. The focus of this chapter will be upon the various processes which determine the extent to which a person will be persuaded by a written or oral communication and the various message content characteristics which behavioral researchers have experimented with through the years in an effort to determine a message's persuasive impact.

Attention and Comprehension

A frequently overlooked fact is that before any persuader can apply his techniques in an effort to break down the motivational defenses of readers or listeners he must first get their attention. There is considerable evidence that the newspaper editorialist may have more difficulty in gaining that needed attention than does the broadcast commentator. Many of the external factors tested in attention getting, for example, seem more adaptable by the broadcaster, particularly the television broadcaster, than the print media editorialist.

Intensity of sound, light, and color; the element of contrast and change; the attraction of movement through gestures and other nonverbal cues, all are attention compellers which the television commentator might best use. The newspaper editorialist may have to rely upon such external factors as the size of a headline, capitalization, the use of italics, type size, or the length of an editorial to apply the factors of intensity and contrast, while he is shut out entirely from using movement. Repetition, however, can be used as an attention compeller by both the print and broadcast commentator. The advantage of repetition is two-fold: (1) a stimulus (written or oral) that is repeated has a better chance of catching a reader or listener during a period when his attention may be waning, and (2) repetition increases the reader's or listener's sensitivity or alertness to the stimulus.[4]

There are numerous internal factors or determinants of attention which have been found to be fairly constant from individual to individual. Some topics and issues—for example, a direct threat with loss of security or safety—are so vital that they immediately attract attention. Some news events dealing with conflict, drama, or suspense which have an aspect of theater about them can be counted on to attract the attention of an audience. The unusualness of an event or issue may in itself arouse the curiosity of a reader or listener. A need for resolution, completion, or rebalancing may result in increased attention to an issue when such imbalance becomes psychologically intolerable. Humor also may be an effective attention getter if, for no other reason, audiences are drawn to such materials in an effort to escape from their fears, frustrations, and hostilities. Other editorials or commentaries may be attended to simply because to do so requires a minimal effort. The top-of-the-column editorial may be read by some people, for example, simply because it is there, and the television set often remains tuned to the same channel, and the commentary is heard because it takes less effort to listen to it than to turn off the television set.[5]

Even though the audience attends to the message, such attention may be useless if the intent of the communication is not fully understood. Poor organization, for example, may destroy the effectiveness of a message, rendering it incomprehensible. Textbooks stress the importance of message organization upon comprehension. Various empirical investigations also add support to prescriptions dealing with the concept of order.[6] The effect of the order of presentation of arguments within a given message on its persuasive impact is treated elsewhere in this chapter.

While it is important for a persuasive message to have something to say—to have content, the *matter* of the editorial or commentary—it is also vitally important how, and in what *manner,* the message is presented if it is to be understood. There are numerous formulas designed to measure the readability of all types of communications, a challenging undertaking because of the variability of the intended audience of mass communications.[7] Robert Gunning, for example, has formulated a "Fog Index" with scores correlated with the various grade reading levels. Rudolf Flesch, as a consultant to Associated Press, designed two readability formulas which have been widely used by the mass media—the "Reading Ease" score and the "Human Interest" score.[8]

Readability formulas, however, are not necessarily dictates of good style, indeed, may make poor formulas for writing. By design, a readability formula is a means of rating a piece of writing after it has been written. The first rule of thumb for the opinion writer should be to make sure that the manner of his persuasive communications—its style and tone—is appropriate to the subject matter being treated. The approach used tends to tip off the reader or listener of the editorialist's or commentator's attitude about the event or issue being evaluated. The style and tone of a persuasive message, as a display of the writer's attitude, also should be related to the writer's perception of what his readers or listeners already know about the subject or what attitude the audience already holds toward the issue, for example, a worsening community problem. For most topics a straightforward, serious approach may be more appropriate, but the editorial rapier of satire might be more effective in dealing with other problems or issues.[9]

There is some indication that audience comprehension of a message, particularly a message dealing with relatively complex materials, may pose more of a problem for the broadcast commentator than for the newspaper editorialist. Early "communication modality" research found that live or videotaped messages induced greater opinion change (more yielding) than written messages, perhaps because of nonverbal vocal and visual cues which tended to enhance the broadcast communicator's image. More recent research, however, indicates that any communication difficult enough to create comprehension problems through use of videotape or audiotape will be more persuasive if written because complex materials can be made more comprehensible to a reader.[10]

Acceptance and Retention

The acceptance of a persuasive message, or yielding to it, as some behavioral researchers identify the process, is the most extensively studied variable in the voluminous research on attitude formation and attitude change. Though acceptance cannot occur without reception of the message—attending to it and understanding it—the amount of acceptance is not necessarily positively related to the amount or degree of reception. Indeed, the most common research finding appears to be a lack of any clear relationship between reception and attitude change.[11]

One classic study, much relied upon by other researchers in the field, conceptualizes attitude change as including not one but three types of yielding: (1) *compliance,* which occurs when an individual accepts a persuasive appeal because he hopes to achieve a favorable reaction from the communicator or institution the communicator represents, (2) *identification,* which occurs when an individual accepts a persuasive appeal because he wants to establish or maintain what psychologists call "a satisfying self-defining relationship" with the communicator, and (3) *internalization,* which occurs when an individual accepts a persuasive appeal because the content of the message corresponds with his value system.[12] The media editorialist would seldom be in a position to bring about compliance through his persuasive appeals, a process defined by one source as public yielding to an influence attempt without private acceptance with the expectation of gaining rewards or avoiding punishment. The mass media editorialist normally isn't that powerful. If the editorialist is sufficiently attractive, however, as that term was defined in Chapter 8, he would be more likely to produce yielding through identification. If the editorialist is viewed as being a highly credible source (perceived as being both expert and objective), he should be more likely to produce yielding through the process of internalization.[13]

Numerous message characteristics have been studied by researchers as potential factors influencing the final acceptance or yielding of readers or listeners to a persuasive message. The most promising of these approaches provides the basis for the discussion in the remainder of this chapter. However, one general area of concern touching upon both comprehension and yielding, the effect of amplification and documentation of arguments in persuasive communication, needs to be discussed here. It should not be surprising that studies of the effects of evidence and documentation in persuasive communication have not always produced consistent findings.

Amplification, of course, may be achieved in a number of ways, all of which are attempts to provide greater clarity and effectiveness, at least in terms of the comprehension of the message. A topic sentence, for example, may be followed by an accumulation of specific items documenting the statement. Amplification may also be obtained through a series of restatements in which the communicator repeats the idea with changes in wording but without alterations in substance. The amplification, in this instance, comes essentially through the repetition of the idea. Or amplification may be gained by building upon an issue or concept through use of additional materials and examples, reinforcing the basic assertion of the message. The problem for the writer becomes, how much documentation and evidence is needed? How much repetition and expansion is enough?

One researcher argues that documentation is not only necessary, it needs to be specific and it needs to be verifiable else the reader or listener is being invited to supply the specificity needed to make the otherwise ambiguous message more meaningful and relevant to him. While nonspecific, even ambiguous discourse may generate what has been called "an empirically based motivation for a desired persuasive goal," it creates no new beliefs which the recipient did not already hold. Its effectiveness is the result of perceptions of reality already stored in the mind of the receiver. For a message to be persuasive, it is argued, the assertions being made need to be amplified through specific evidence which allows for the statements to be verified by the receiver. Such specificity, coupled with the necessary references to make the statements potentially verifiable, generates more attitude change because the message supplies new information and is more credible.[14]

Another study suggests that supplying evidence may be more important under some conditions than under others. If the audience is concerned about getting truthful, factually correct information relevant to a problem he wants to solve, for example, then evidence may assume the role ascribed to it by traditional theory. A highly credible source or an authoritative source, on the other hand, may be persuasive whether he uses evidence or not. A source with low credibility, however, may improve on the impact of his persuasive appeal, particularly on a long-term basis, through the careful documentation of his assertions.[15] Another study suggests that while documentary evidence may not have an immediate impact on attitude change, it does seem to have a predictable impact as an inhibitor against later efforts toward counterpersuasion.[16]

Retention, in contrast to yielding, has been one of the least-studied variables in attitude change research. It has been determined, however, that after a period of four to six weeks the amount of attitude change retained may range from only one-third to two-thirds of the original change, although a few studies have found attitude change lasting as long as six months. These empirical studies deal with attitude change brought about by a single persuasive message communicated only one time. The research findings also indicate that a delayed reexposure of a persuasive message or the repetition of an appeal will strengthen and prolong the prior opinion change.[17] The media editorialist through experience is well aware that the effectiveness of his persuasion is, at best, short lived and that the primary purpose of many of the editorials he writes is to reinforce attitudes already formed rather than to bring about a change in attitudes.

Primacy-Recency Effects

One of the first empirical generalizations to be studied by early researchers in regard to persuasive communication involved the question of order-effect: In constructing a persuasive message in which both sides of an issue are to be considered, which is most effective, the side presented first or the side presented last? The argument that when two sides of an issue are presented successively the side presented first is most effective constitutes what researchers have labeled a "primacy effect." The argument that the side presented last (most recent) is most effective constitutes a "recency effect." While it is difficult to generalize about the various experiments because of numerous contingent conditions linked to the findings, a review of primacy-recency research suggests the following order effects as they might apply to persuasive writing in the news media.

As far as learning is concerned, there tends to be a primacy effect in that the earlier part of a message tends to be better learned than the later part. There is some indication that in persuasive messages dealing with controversial topics or interesting subject matter there is a pronounced tendency for items presented first to dominate the impression received. There also tends to be a "set" effect: a crystallizing of opinion, with this "set" tending to interfere with the reception of a subsequent opposing argument. A primacy effect may also be triggered through public commitment. If after being exposed to one side of a controversial issue, for example, a public response is made in some way by the reader or listener which indicates agreement on the issue, such a commitment to an associate, either verbally or in writing, tends to reduce the effectiveness of any subsequent argument attempting to present the other side of the issue.

Recency effects, on the other hand, may result in persuasive messages dealing with less controversial topics, with less familiar issue, with less interesting subject matter, even though these topics may be of importance to members of the audience. In the absence of novel stimuli, it is argued, the sensory reaction needed to bring about strong first impressions is reduced, allowing the last (most recent) arguments to prevail.

The ordering of arguments within a given message is sometimes approached from the perspective of either the desirability of the positions being advocated, from the point of view of the communicator, or the extent to which those positions are perceived to be in agreement with members of the audience. Ordering on the basis of the desirability of the various solutions, positions, or alternatives being advocated has been shown to bring about greater total agreement over the whole range of issues presented in the message. Here a primacy effect tends to aid the communicator and perhaps the ordering also better attracts the attention of the audience. The ordering of a persuasive message on the basis of perceived audience agreement, however, may be counterproductive if such an ordering forces the communicator to place the least desirable solution, position, or alternative in a primacy position.[18]

More recent order-effect research tends to add even further to the complexity of earlier findings. It is argued, for example, that a strong persuasive argument will maintain its strength no matter what position the argument is assigned. While reasonably accurate predictions of audience response to messages may be made through a particular structuring of those messages, it is argued that serial order, by itself, is seldom suffieient.[19] The timing of pro- and con-arguments is another factor of continuing interest. Earlier research, which demonstrated generally that if two sides of an issue were presented successively, recency effects would prevail, has been challenged. The order-effect findings become even more conditional when a greater lapse of time occurs between the pro- and con-arguments.[20]

The order of presentation, in any case, is only one aspect of the primacy-recency consideration. The persuasive writer should, above all, be as timely as he can with his comments. Since he seldom knows with certainty if his audience already has been exposed to arguments he is advocating, often the best he can do is to define primacy as the first presentation of the argument by his own medium and follow up by doing his best to be as timely as possible in commenting upon public issues to take advantage of primacy effects. In addition, he might diminish the primacy effects of prior arguments which his audience has been exposed to in other media or through personal communications by casting his own arguments in different terms or by presenting a fresh point of view.

One-Sided vs. Two-Sided Appeals

Should the editorialist present both sides of an argument concerning a community problem or public issue he is attempting to illuminate or should he only present the side of the argument supporting the conclusion he plans to draw? Early research on the subject suggests that the media persuader would be well advised to refute rather than ignore opposing arguments (to take a two-sided approach) when (1) the audience has already been made aware of those arguments or (2) members of the audience can be expected to subsequently expose themselves or be exposed to arguments on the other side. Acknowledging and refuting all opposition arguments is particularly to be preferred when the audience is perceived as either being highly intelligent or generally hostile to the views being expressed.[21]

A two-sided persuasive message may also convey more credibility than a more biased, one-sided approach, an important consideration for the editorialist. A two-sided approach affords the opportunity for better documentation and examination of evidence. It has also been found that a two-sided communication, by distracting the listener or reader from his "silent rehearsal of the counterarguments," tends to focus more attention upon the supportive arguments in the persuasive message, making them more effective.[22] A two-sided, refutational message should also result in a more sustained attitude change in the face of counterpersuasion which often comes in what researchers call "small group communication" settings by inoculating message recipients against such subsequent arguments.[23] A two-sided argument should also tend to reduce audience resistance to yielding by masking the manipulatory intent of the communication—at least until the conclusion is reached—facilitating attitude change to the extent that the masking succeeds. A one-sided approach, it is argued, would immediately tip off the reader or listener as to the intent of the communicator.[24]

The recurring theme in on-going research into the effectiveness of one-sided vs. two-sided appeals, however, is audience familiarity with the pros and cons of the issue being discussed. While audiences unfamiliar with the issues may be more persuaded by a one-sided appeal, those familiar with the issues are usually more persuaded by a two-sided appeal.[25] In another recent study designed to test the relative efficacy of one-sided vs. two-sided appeals, it was concluded that while a two-sided communication may be superior in most circumstances, the "sidedness" of a persuasive message may be of only secondary importance. The most important factor (and this should not be surprising) was found to be the substance, the content, of the message itself.[26] In another study dealing with the effectiveness of television editorials, it was found that presenting relevant facts to back up the editorial stance being taken was rated more highly by viewers than presenting both sides of the issue, though both considerations were found to be important.[27]

The Effect of Repetition

The repetition of a persuasive appeal, within reasonable limits and with variation, tends to make words more positive, food more appetizing, and ideas more acceptable. There is some indication that the newness associated with uncertainty, which is likely to produce tension and negative feelings, is erased by repeated exposure.[28] Such repetition may be contained within a given message or may come from repeated exposure to the same message. Not only is repetition useful, it may be essential for full comprehension of many complex issues. Without repetition, it is also argued, readers and listeners would soon forget information they initially understood. Indeed, the most impressive finding of the research on repetition may not be that repetition enhances persuasion, or at least has some effect, but that it has so little lasting effect.

There is also some indication that with a captive audience comprehension of a message is quickly maximized by the first several repetitions. Not only is there nothing to be learned, or gained, by more repetition, but an audience may respond negatively to further repetition. Moderate exposure to a political message, for example, has been found to produce a more favorable rating and more desire for information about a candidate than high exposure. This determination suggests the possibility that repeated exposure to such political persuasion, which conventional wisdom has held will make them more familiar, may also generate dislike and decrease the chances that voters will try to find out more about them.[29] In many respects, however, the mass media audience isn't truly captive and repetition, at different times, may be more extensive since the audience of the persuasive message is constantly changing.[30]

Repetition can also be an important structural device to gain emphasis within a single persuasive message: repetition of a slogan or key phrase central to the theme of the message, repetition used as a transitional device linking important arguments being projected, repetition used in connection with parallel construction or in the enumeration of various items in the message. But such repetition needs enough variation to prevent it from becoming monotonous and distracting. Redundancy in a news story may be frowned upon, but the research findings clearly indicate that redundancy in persuasive writing can be an effective agent of attitude change.

The importance of repetition in editorial persuasion has been repeatedly demonstrated by Pulitzer Prize winning editorialists. The basis for judging the annual winner for "distinguished editorial writing" is "clearness of style, moral purpose, sound reasoning, and power to influence public opinion in what the writer conceives to be the right direction." While judging takes into account the whole volume of the editorial writer's work during the year, the focus is upon a packet of editorials submitted by the newspaper. Those packets often contain editorial campaigns with editorial after editorial in a sustained series hammering away repeatedly upon a single issue or problem.

The 1977 Pulitzer winner, the *Nevada State Journal* and *Reno Evening Gazette,* for example, published a series of twenty hardhitting editorials written by three different editorialists challenging the power of a local brothel keeper. Phil Kerby of the *Los Angeles Times* won the Pulitzer Prize in 1976 for a series of editorials making eloquent pleas in support of a free press, individual privacy, and open government. John D. Maurice of the *Charleston* (W. Va.) *Daily Mail* won the Pulitzer Prize in 1975 on the basis of editorials from a series of more than fifty written during the year concerning the textbook controversy in local schools. Repetition was clearly an important element in the effectiveness of each of these editorial campaigns.

Fear Arousing Appeals

A message characteristic which has been the subject of extensive research for twenty-five years or more is the effect of fear arousing appeals on attitude change. These fear arousal studies have dealt with such diverse topics as dental hygiene, cigarette smoking, tetanus inoculations, safe driving practices, fallout shelters, safety belts, population growth, mental health, cancer, roundworms, tuberculosis, syphilis, proper viewing of the sun during an eclipse, and the use of stairway handrails for safety. A 1969 survey of thirty-five studies, while noting conflicting findings and inconsistencies, listed a number of conclusions, including the following:

1. That the widely cited conclusion that high fear arousal creates a "defensive-avoidance reaction" (causing high fear to be less persuasive than low fear) is simply not true in most situations.

2. That the specificity and ease with which the recommendations to alleviate the fear can be implemented tends to increase the effectiveness of the fear appeals, regardless of the level of fear resorted to in the message.

3. That responses to fear arousal differ among individuals with self-esteem, feelings of vulnerability to danger, and the coping style of members of the audience suggested as important variables.

4. That high fear arousal appears to be consistently more effective than low fear arousal when the message source is perceived by recipients as highly credible.[31]

While there is little doubt that fear arousing appeals—particularly when such threats involve possible physical consequences—have persuasive impact, a number of studies suggest the desirability of the fear arousing message pointing out means of alleviating those fears. When fear is strongly aroused by a communication but is not fully relieved by reassurances contained in the message, the audience may become motivated to ignore or to minimize the importance of the threat. Indeed, a higher level of fear arousal may be optimal when highly specific and detailed recommendations are made concerning actions to be taken to reduce the fear.[32] Another study suggests, however, that fear arousal per se, and not fear reduction, is a sufficient condition for greater acceptance of a persuasive message.[33]

The magnitude of the noxiousness of a threatened event and the probability of its occurrence are two communication variables often used in testing the effect of fear arousal on attitude. A recent experimental study, for example, found that although increases in the perceived likelihood of an energy shortage (the subjective probability of its occurring) had no significant effect on attitude change, that increments in the perceived noxiousness or severity of such a crisis strengthened intentions to reduce energy consumption.[34]

One problem facing the mass media editorialist attempting to use fear arousal as a persuasive technique may be the question of how to determine when a message will actually induce the necessary degree of fear on an audience. Two researchers who recently failed in their attempt to test higher levels of fear arousal noted that "The relationship between aroused fear and the effectiveness of a persuasive communication has proven to be a complex one."[35] Another problem for the editorialist may be the determination of whether or not such events as the Equal Rights Amendment, or gay rights, or cigarette smoking have the "magnitude of noxiousness" to warrant even an attempt to use a fear arousing appeal.

The Effect of Humor

While textbooks on speech recommend humor as a persuasive device and politicians and advertisers employ it extensively, there seems to be a paucity of research on the subject. It may be as E. B. White has observed in an essay, "Some Remarks on Humor," that:

> Analysts have had their go at humor, and I have read some of this interpretative literature, but without being greatly instructed. Humor can be dissected, as a frog can, but the thing dies in the process and the innards are discouraging to any but the pure scientific mind.[36]

A handful of studies which have been done on the persuasive impact of humor and/or wit, either alone or inserted in otherwise straightforward messages, suggest that humor has little, if any, persuasive impact.[37]

A few studies have dealt with the use of satire as a persuasive device, and while most indicated no significant attitude change, humor can bolster a dull speech or message by enhancing interest in the communication.[38] It should be noted, however, that to entertain is no doubt a prime purpose of satire. Such an approach might be expected to enhance attention and boost readership, which it apparently does. But a satiric approach, by its ironic nature, is indirect. The intended discrepancy between inner thought and outward expression—that is, saying one thing while intending another—while humorous and entertaining, such a message may often be misread or misunderstood. The problem in using satire for the purpose of persuasion, therefore, is that whatever gain there may be in interest and readership may be lost through the indirectness of the approach to the extent the communication is misunderstood.[39]

A recent survey of the research literature dealing with humor's persuasive impact, while acknowledging that the general "no difference" findings could not be ignored, found methodological problems with some studies which might well have masked actual differences had they existed. The survey also noted, as reported above, that the inclusion of humor into a persuasive message may serve as a pleasant distraction, preventing readers from formulating counterarguments, resulting in greater impact of the message arguments. The survey also noted that even though prior research findings suggest that a humor-persuasion effect is, at best, never likely to be robust, that "even a small effect could be significant for messages delivered to the multitude."[40]

A few studies have dealt with the question of whether or not the use of humor added to or detracted from the credibility of the communicator. In some instances humor appeared to increase the ethos of the communicator.[41] In a few instances, however, the use of humor was found to lower ethos.[42] The credibility of the communicator is most likely to suffer where the use of humor is viewed as being excessive or in poor taste or where humor is viewed as being used to cover up for a lack of knowledge.

A moderate use of satire, however, has been found to be an effective method of immunizing an audience against counter-persuasion. The method of satire is to present and then point out the folly of the opponent's position. Even though the indirect, humorous method may hinder the audience in perceiving the message, these elements apparently enhance the inoculation effect of the satirical message.[43]

The tentative nature of the research findings in regard to the use of humor as a persuasive technique suggests that the media persuader should use caution before he attempts to emulate such opinion writers as Art Buchwald, Russell Baker, or Arthur Hoppe. Humor as a pleasant distraction or as an attention getter may enhance persuasion, but what is gained here may be lost in comprehension of the message or in the credibility of the communicator unless great care is used.

Conclusion Drawing

The research findings involving conclusion drawing indicate that there will probably be more opinion change in the direction intended if the communicator explicitly states his conclusion than if he leaves it to the audience to draw their own conclusions. In the opening of the persuasive message there may be good reason to approach an issue obliquely, but in closing the arguments the findings have been generally consistent that an explicit conclusion will elicit significantly more attitude change than will simply implying the conclusion.[44]

Arguments have been advanced, it should be noted, for allowing the reader or listener to participate in the conclusion drawing process. Such a non-directive approach, it is argued, will better convince readers or listeners of the rightness of the conclusion. Such participation will facilitate learning and will give more permanence to the materials presented. Leaving an obvious conclusion unstated may even augment yielding to the persuasive appeal.[45] But for the editorialist convinced of the validity of his arguments, who isn't fearful of the risk involved in calling for a certain course of action, who knows the consequences of and is willing to take responsibility for his or her arguments, there are many good reasons for drawing explicit conclusions.

In one study, for example, more than twice as many subjects changed their opinions in the direction advocated when an explicit conclusion was drawn than when the conclusion was left to the audience.[46] There is some indication that the editorial which doesn't draw an explicit conclusion may suffer the same fate as the often misunderstood editorial cartoon. One study demonstrated an overwhelming failure of a selection of nationally syndicated cartoons to get their message across. Interpretations ran a gamut of meanings which often differed markedly from the meaning intended by the cartoonist. Editorial cartoons have been found to be more effective, however, when accompanied by an editorial reinforcing the message contained in the cartoon, in effect, drawing the conclusion more explicitly.[47]

There is some evidence that even the degree of explicitness may be a factor in conclusion drawing. In one study, for example, it was found that greater change in opinion was produced by larger than by smaller amounts of advocated change, but the result obtained may best be generalized to situations where a highly credible communicator is involved.[48] In another study it was demonstrated that readers may often be confused by the use of too many "qualifiers" in verbal or oral assertions. If a reader or listener, for example, lacks knowledge on the topic under discussion, he must rely more heavily on the probability suggested by the qualifying words used in the assertion. This reliance leads to problems to the extent that such qualifiers (for example, distinguishing between likelihood of an event occurring and the possibility of its occurrence) are viewed as being similar. In short, qualifiers in conclusions, or elsewhere, may present barriers which fog assertions containing such words.[49]

The conclusion about conclusion drawing: persuasive messages which draw explicit conclusions are more likely to be effective than those which allow readers or listeners to draw their own conclusions.

Summary and Conclusion

The successful politician, according to Theodore Roosevelt, is "he who says what everybody is thinking most often and in the loudest voice." Such message-tailoring by politicians, particularly American presidents, is becoming more and more difficult in today's diverse society. But to some extent, one study suggests, the audience *is* the message in American politics.[50] The mass media editorialist, however, is not in the business of making consensus statements, but he is attempting to tailor his message as persuasively as he can, and he is attempting to speak in a loud voice. The research findings discussed above suggest many techniques and devices for tailoring a persuasive message to make it more effective. They may be summarized as follows:

1. The mass media persuader needs to cast his persuasive message in a provocative and interesting manner, taking care to write clearly and understandably. If a message isn't read or isn't comprehended, the arguments presented and the position advocated by the opinion writer cannot possibly be accepted—the ultimate goal of the persuasive communication.

2. The persuasive message should be as timely as possible, particularly when it deals with controversial topics or interesting subject matter where primacy effects have been most often noted. The media persuader, however, should be aware also of the recency effects of a persuasive communication—that the last (most recent) argument, under some circumstances, tends to have the greater impact.

3. The media persuader should likewise consider the advantages of the two-sided approach to argumentation, particularly when his audience can be expected to be hostile to the views being expressed or when the audience is highly intelligent. A two-sided appeal may also add credibility to the message as well as inoculate members of the audience against the future counterarguing by others.

4. The beneficial effects of repetition, particularly repetition with variation, should be utilized at every opportunity. This repetition may be employed in two ways: (a) within the persuasive message itself as a structural or transitional device placing emphasis on key positive assertions, or (b) through re-exposure of the audience to the same persuasive appeal over time, but with variation.

5. The media persuader should remember that while strong emotional appeals, such as threats or other fear arousing appeals, may sometimes be warranted and even be effective, such appeals should be used sparingly. And, if fear is evoked in a persuasive message, experimentation has indicated that a means of alleviating the fear needs to be extended in the same message for the maximum persuasive effect to be realized.

6. The use of satire or other forms of humor, while sometimes useful as attention compellers, or sometimes suitable as a change-of-pace approach, or as a pleasant distraction against counterarguing, such an approach may often be counterproductive as a persuasive technique. What is gained in readership through humor, for example, may be lost in the overall indirectness of a satiric approach.

7. The media persuader, to be most effective, should normally draw explicit conclusions, both to help clarify and summarize his per-

suasive arguments as well as to assist members of the audience in arriving at the proper conclusion, solution, or answer.

These general propositions may be conditioned, of course, by other variables related to source credibility and various factors influencing the persuasibility of mass media audiences. Despite the tentativeness of many of the experimental and survey findings of behavioral researchers discussed in this chapter, particularly as these findings have been applied to the media editorialist, this review of the techniques, strategies, and intricacies of the persuasive process should serve to reinforce and expand the convention wisdom gleaned from the shop talk of media professionals. The newspaper editorialist and broadcast commentator, after all, need all the help they can get.

NOTES for Chapter 9

[1] Martin Fishbein and Icek Ajzen, *Belief, Attitude, Intention, and Behavior: An Introduction to Theory and Research* (Reading, Mass.: Addison-Wesley, 1975), p. 451.

[2] See, e.g., Carl I. Hovland, et al., *The Order of Presentation in Persuasion,* Yale Studies in Attitude and Communication, vol. 1 (New Haven, Conn.: Yale University Press, 1957).

[3] For an evaluation of the Yale program approach, see Charles A. Kiesler, Barry E. Collins, and Norman Miller, *Attitude Change: A Critical Analysis of Theoretical Approaches* (New York: John Wiley & Sons, 1969), pp. 103–18.

[4] C. T. Morgan and R. A. King, "Characteristics of Attention and Attention-Getting," in *The Process of Persuasion: Principles and Readings,* ed.: Wayne N. Thompson (New York: Harper & Row, 1975), pp. 347–50.

[5] For a discussion of the factors influencing attention, see Herbert W. Simons, *Persuasion: Understanding, Practice, and Analysis* (Reading, Mass.: Addison-Wesley, 1976), pp. 170–81.

[6] See, e.g., Arlee Johnson, "A Preliminary Investigation of the Relationship Between Message Organization and Listener Comprehension," *Central States Speech Journal* 21 (Summer 1970): 104–7.

[7] George R. Klare, *The Measurement of Readability* (Ames, Iowa: Iowa State University Press, 1963), pp. 94–95.

[8] Rudolf Flesch, *The Art of Readable Writing,* rev. ed. (New York: Harper & Row, 1974).

[9] Dorothy Markiewicz, "Effects of Humor on Persuasion," *Sociometry* 37 (September 1974): 407–22.

[10] Shelly Chaiken and Alice H. Eagly, "Communication Modality as a Determinant of Message Persuasiveness and Message Comprehensibility," *Journal of Personality and Social Psychology* 34 (October 1976): 605–14.

[11] Martin Fishbein and Icek Ajzen, "Attitudes and Opinions," in *Annual Review of Psychology,* eds.: Paul H. Mussen and Mark R. Rosenzweig (Palo Alto, Calif.: Annual Reviews, Inc., 1972), p. 521.

[12] Herbert C. Kelman, "Compliance, Identification, and Internalization: Three Processes of Attitude Change," *Journal of Conflict Resolution* 2 (1958): 51–60.

[13] Judson Mills and John Harvey, "Opinion Change as a Function of When Information About the Communicator Is Received and Whether He Is Attractive or Expert," *Journal of Personality and Social Psychology* 21 (January 1972): 52–55.

[14] Paul I. Rosenthal, "Specificity, Verifiability, and Message Credibility," *Quarterly Journal of Speech* 57 (December 1971): 393–401.

[15] Thomas B. Harte, "The Effects of Evidence in Persuasive Communication," *Central States Speech Journal* 27 (Spring 1976): 42–46.

[16] James C. McCroskey, "The Effects of Evidence as an Exhibitor of Counter-Persuasion," *Speech Monographs* 37 (August 1970): 188–94.

[17] For an evaluation of research dealing with retention, see Stuart Oskamp, *Attitudes and Opinions* (Englewood Cliffs, N.J.: Prentice-Hall, 1977), pp. 150–51.

[18] For a discussion of order effects, see Samuel Himmelfarb and Alice H. Eagly, eds. *Readings in Attitude Change* (New York: John Wiley & Sons, 1974), pp. 262–92; Ithiel de Sola Pool and Wilbur Schramm, *Handbook of Communication* (Chicago: Rand McNally College Publishing Co., 1973), pp. 236–37; and Marvin Karlins and Herbert I. Abelson, *Persuasion: How Opinions and Attitudes Are Changed* (New York: Springer, 1970), pp. 27–29.

[19] Anthony J. Clark, "An Exploratory Study of Order Effect in Persuasive Communication," *Southern Speech Communication Journal* 39 (Summer 1974): 322–32.

[20] See, e.g., Abraham S. Luchins and Edith H. Luchins, "The Effects of Order of Presentation of Information and Explanatory Models," *Journal of Social Psychology* 80 (February 1970): 63–70.

[21] For representative studies of earlier research, see Carl I. Hovland, Arthur A. Lumsdaine, and Fred D. Sheffield, *Experiments on Mass Communication* (Princeton: Princeton University Press, 1949), pp. 213–15; Arthur A. Lumsdaine and Irving L. Janis, "Resistance to 'Counterpropaganda' Produced by One-Sided and Two-Sided 'Propaganda' Presentations," *Public Opinion Quarterly* 17 (Fall 1953): 311–18; and Elliott McGinnies, "Studies in Persuasion: III. Reactions of Japanese Students to One-Sided and Two-Sided Communications," *Journal of Social Psychology* 70 (October 1966): 87–93.

[22] Robert D. Dycus, "Relative Efficacy of One-Sided vs. Two-Sided Communication in a Simulated Government Evaluation of Proposals," *Psychological Reports* 38 (June 1976): 787–90. Counterarguing, which one researcher notes may amount to "a theoretical fiction," can also be resisted by forewarning and distraction. See, e.g., Norman Miller and R. S. Barron, "On Measuring Counterarguing," *Journal for the Theory of Social Behavior* 3 (April 1975): 101–18; George J. Szybillo and Richard Heslin, "Resistance to Persuasion: Inoculation Theory in a Marketing Context," *Journal of Marketing Research* 10 (November 1973): 396–403; Chester A. Insko, William Turnbull, and Ben Yandell, "Facilitative and Inhibiting Effects of Distraction on Attitude Change," *Sociometry* 37 (December 1974): 508–28; and Richard E. Petty and Timothy C. Brock, "Effects of Responding or Not Responding to Hecklers on Audience Agreement with a Speaker," *Journal of Applied Social Psychology* 6 (January–March 1976): 1–17.

[23] James C. McCroskey, Thomas J. Young, and Michael D. Scott, "The Effects of Message Sidedness and Evidence on Inoculation Against Counter-Persuasion in Small Group Communication," *Speech Monographs* 39 (August 1972): 205–12.

[24] Ralph L. Rosnow, "One-Sided Versus Two-Sided Communication Under Indirect Awareness of Persuasive Intent," *Public Opinion Quarterly* 32 (Spring 1968): 95–101.

[25] See, e.g., Robert L. Dipboye, "The Effectiveness of One-Sided and Two-Sided Appeals as a Function of Familiarization and Context," *Journal of Social Psychology* 102 (June 1977): 125–31.

[26] Dycus, "Relative Efficacy," p. 790.

[27] Hershel Shosteck, "The Structural Dimensions of Television Editorial Effectiveness," *Journalism Quarterly* 52 (Spring 1975): 37–43.

[28] Robert Zajonc, "Brainwash: Familiarity Breeds Comfort," *Psychology Today* 3 (February 1970): 22–25.

[29] Lee B. Becker and John C. Doolittle, "How Repetition Affects Evaluations of Information Seeking About Candidates," *Journalism Quarterly* 52 (Winter 1975): 611–17.

[30] William J. McGuire, "Persuasion, Resistance, and Attitude Change," in *Handbook of Communication,* eds.: Ithiel de Sola Pool and Wilbur Schramm (Chicago: Rand McNally College Publishing Co., 1973), p. 235.

[31] Kenneth L. Higbee, "Fifteen Years of Fear Arousal: Research on Threat Appeals, 1953–1968," *Psychological Bulletin* 72 (December 1969): 426–44.

[32] Brian Sternthal and C. Samuel Craig, "Fear Appeals: Revisited and Revised," *Journal of Consumer Research* 1 (December 1974): 22–34.

[33] Clyde Hendrick, Martin Giesen, and Richard Borden, "False Physiological Feedback and Persuasion: Effect of Fear Arousal vs. Fear Reduction on Attitude Change," *Journal of Personality* 43 (June 1975): 196–214.

[34] James W. Hass, Gerrold S. Bagley, and Ronald W. Rogers, "Coping with the Energy Crisis: Effects of Fear Appeals upon Attitudes Toward Energy Consumption," *Journal of Applied Psychology* 60 (December 1975): 754–56.

[35] Kenneth H. Beck and Clive M. Davis, "Effects of Fear-Arousing Communications and Topic Importance on Attitude Change," *Journal of Social Psychology* 104 (February 1978): 81–95.

[36] *Essays of E. B. White* (New York: Harper & Row, 1977), p. 243.

[37] Charles R. Gruner, "The Effect of Humor in Dull and Interesting Informative Speeches," *Central States Speech Journal* 21 (Fall 1970): 160–66.

[38] See, e.g., Charles R. Gruner and William E. Lampton, "Effect of Including Humorous Material in a Persuasive Sermon," *Southern Speech Communication Journal* 38 (Winter 1972): 188–96; and Charles R. Gruner, "Ad Hominem Satire as a Persuader: An Experiment," *Journalism Quarterly* 43 (Spring 1971): 128–31.

[39] Charles R. Gruner, "An Experimental Study of Satire as Persuasion," *Speech Monographs* 32 (June 1965): 149–53.

[40] Markiewicz, "Effects of Humor," p. 420.

[41] See, e.g., Gruner, "The Effect of Humor in Informative Speeches."

[42] Pat M. Taylor, "An Experimental Study of Humor and Ethos," *Southern Speech Communication Journal* 39 (Summer 1974): 359–66.

[43] See, e.g., Larry Powell, "Satirical Persuasion and Topic Salience," *Southern Speech Communication Journal* 42 (Winter 1977): 151–62; and "The Effects of Ego Involvement on Responses to Editorial Satire," *Central States Speech Journal* 26 (Spring 1975): 34–38.

[44] Stewart L. Tubbs, "Explicit Versus Implicit Conclusions and Audience Commitment," *Speech Monographs* 35 (March 1968): 14–19.

[45] McGuire, "Persuasion, Resistance, and Attitude Change," pp. 234–35.

[46] Carl I. Hovland and Wallace Mandell, "An Experimental Comparison of Conclusion Drawing by the Communicator and by the Audience," *Journal of Abnormal and Social Psychology* 47 (July 1952): 581–88.

[47] LeRoy M. Car, "Editorial Cartoons Fail to Reach Many Readers," *Journalism Quarterly* 45 (Autumn 1968: 533–35; and Del Brinkman, "Do Editorial Cartoons and Editorials Change Opinions?" *Journalism Quarterly* 45 (Winter 1968): 724–26.

[48] Carl I. Hovland and Henry A. Pritzker, "Extent of Opinion Change as a Function of Amount of Change Advocated," *Journal of Abnormal and Social Psychology* 54 (March 1957): 257–61.

[49] Jerry D. Feezel, "A Qualified Certainty: Verbal Probability in Arguments," *Speech Monographs* 41 (November 1974): 348–56.

[50] Lawrence W. Miller and Lee Sigelman, "Is the Audience the Message? A Note on LBJ's Vietnam Statements," *Public Opinion Quarterly* 42 (Spring 1978): 71–80.

10

The Editorial Audience: *Selective, Skeptical, Obstinate*

BOTH THE PRACTITIONERS of persuasion as well as scholars involved in research concerning attitude change and behavior are often appalled by the success and lack of success of their efforts in influencing and/or predicting human behavior. The editors of a book-length review of various experiments in persuasion, for example, have noted:

> Some people are extremely gullible. They tend to accept unreservedly almost anything authoritative they read, see, or hear. They adopt one opinion, then its very antithesis. Like the branches of a willow in the wind, they seem to sway first one way, then the other. Others though more reserved in their reaction to persuasion, tend to be highly susceptible to special appeals.[1]

Emotional appeals, it was pointed out, affect some people more than others. Some are more susceptible to the subtle coercion of a fear appeal than others. Still others seem to be impervious to all intentional efforts, going out of their way not to react to any persuasive message. If they do grudgingly respond, it may be in just the opposite direction recommended.

Editors of another study focusing upon the effects of mass media communication observe that

> the process and effect of mass communication must be seen today against the background concept of an intensely active audience, seeking what it wants, rejecting far more content than it accepts, interacting both with the members of the groups it belongs to and with the media content it receives, and often testing the mass media message by talking it over with other persons or comparing it with other media content.[2]

The reaction of the audience to a persuasive message, of course, is the prime focusing point, indeed, the ultimate concern of effective communication. The media persuader has long been aware that not everyone exposed to an editorial or commentary pays any attention to it, that some readers and listeners who do expose themselves to the message understand it differently than others, that they remember it differently, that they may react to it differently. Researchers and theorists in communications, psychology, sociology, as well as related disciplines, have also given considerable attention to the often selective, sometimes skeptical, even obstinate role played by audiences in the communications process. Today a considerable body of literature deals with concepts such as the likes and dislikes of the audience, the audience as mediator, the audience as information processor, the audience as defender of its ego, the audience as pleaser of others, the audience as problem solver, the audience as members of a group, the audience as a system, etc.[3]

The primary purpose of this chapter is to examine selected theories and approaches taken by social science and communications researchers of primary interest to the mass media persuader. The process will involve an examination of pertinent concepts related to the mechanisms of attitude and behavioral change as well as theoretical considerations involving the persuasibility of individuals making up mass media audiences. A plausible beginning point appears to be a consideration of the nature of the concept labeled "attitude."

The Nature of Attitudes

Wilbur Schramm, a pioneer communications researcher, defined attitudes as "inferred states of readiness to react in an evaluative way, in support for or against a given situation."[4] The word "inferred" is used, Schramm explained, because there is no way to observe an attitude directly. Attitudes are assumed as a class of intervening variables in order to explain how the human nervous system converts a given stimulus (an editorial appeal, for example) into a given response (hopefully the action called for in the editorial). The term "states of readiness" is used, Schramm said, because attitudes are envisaged as operating as predispositions to action. If an editorialist knows the nature of an individual's (or audience's) attitude toward a given object or situation, he can predict that the individual (or audience), stimulated by the object or situation, and being free to act, will act in the direction of the attitude. The term "react in an evaluative way" is used, Schramm noted, because attitudes are envisaged as being concerned with the relative values of life situations. And finally, Schramm concluded, since these states of readiness to react in an evaluative way to a given stimulus are learned, that under appropriate conditions they may presumably be reinforced, generalized, or even forgotten.

Countless other definitions of attitude might be cited,[5] and while the emphases may vary, most define attitude as a mental set or disposition, as a readiness to respond, as being evaluative in nature, as being learned, and as relatively enduring.

Attitudes are likewise conceptualized by most theoreticians as having three components: (1) a *cognitive* component consisting of a person's factual knowledge of and beliefs about an object or person; (2) an *affective* component consisting of a person's evaluation of, liking for, or emotional response to that object or person; and (3) a *behavioral* component involving a person's overt behavior directed toward that object or person.[6] The reader of an editorial evaluating the voting record of a local congressman, for example, may already have formulated an attitude toward the politician to include (1) information about his voting record and what legislation he now supports (the cognitive component), (2) a critical evaluation or feeling about the congressman's performance (the affective component), and (3) involvement to the extent of writing a letter critical of the congressman's voting record and threatening to withhold his vote at the next election (the behavioral component).

Attitudes are often related—sometimes in ambiguous ways—to three other concepts: opinions, beliefs, and values. An opinion is usually considered to be the verbalization of an attitude or a more specific manifestation of a broader attitude. A belief is usually distinguished from an attitude on the basis of the various components of attitude discussed above. An attitude, for example, always includes an evaluation of an object (the affective component), whereas a belief does not. For example, a person is expressing a belief about the Equal Rights Amendment when she says, "Both President and Mrs. Carter are working for ratification of the Equal Rights Amendment." The belief becomes an attitude when she adds, "I like the position they have taken."

A value, on the other hand, usually refers to one's orientation toward a series or class of related objects. Values are generally viewed as more permanent and enduring than attitudes—for example, one's religious values. A common view is that a value is an important life-goal or standard of behavior toward which a person has a strong positive attitude. It may be helpful to think of these concepts as representing successive points along a single continuum from the narrower and least enduring to the broader and most permanent, respectively: opinions, beliefs, attitudes, and values.

Although the definitions of attitude may vary considerably among disciplines and researchers, there has been general agreement that a person's attitude toward some object constitutes a predisposition on his part to respond to the object in a more or less consistently favorable or unfavorable manner. A few recent studies, however, have questioned the assumption that there is a strong relationship between attitude and behavior. One problem with establishing an empirical attitude-behavior relationship, it is noted, has been that a given attitude may elicit any of a number of responses consistent with the attitude. To measure a person's attitude in terms of a single behavior, as many research studies have attempted, is to misjudge the attitude-behavior relationship.

In studies, however, where multiple-act criteria have been used, more evidence of a significant relation between attitude and behavior has been reported. Multiple-act behaviors are usually measured by asking persons involved in the research their intention to perform various acts. Indeed, it is argued by some that a better predictor of behavior than attitude might be to learn one's intentions.[7] The term behavioral intention, however, has not been defined consistently in the research literature. Some view intention, for example, as a variable flowing from an attitude with each specific intention related to a specific behavior.[8] Others view intentions as being within the behavioral component of attitude, as discussed above.

Despite this questioning of the assumed relationship between the attitudes one holds and one's overt behavior, the mechanisms of attitude and behavioral change continue to play a central role in behavioral research. Attitudes are generally seen as more or less enduring predispositions affecting behavior, but since they are essentially learned rather than innate, they are susceptible to change. Attempting to explain how the overall process works has been the focus of scores of attitude change theories.

The Role of Theories

Theory formulation in scientific inquiry helps the researcher to better focus his study and to more clearly understand his findings by providing a meaningful context. Ultimately, the worth of a theory, however, rests upon its ability to predict what will happen under various conditions. Theories are said to be supported (they are never proved) if research data confirm their predictive value. Theories, of course, vary according to their scope or range of applicability. Some theories are broad, such as learning and consistency theory approaches in attitude change. Some are relatively narrow, for example, the theory of inoculation against persuasion, as involved in the two-sided argumentative approach. Other theories might better be classified as middle-range theories.

Approaches taken by some researchers, such as in the Yale program discussed in Chapter 9, or the group dynamics approach to be discussed later, are more empirically oriented than theoretically based.

There is, however, no overall classification of attitude change theories generally agreed upon by researchers or in textbooks.[9] One author discusses twelve different theoretical approaches, for example, while another has listed thirty-four specific theoretical contributions involving emphasis on different psychological processes.[10]

Theoretical approaches in attitude change are often classified as either functional, learning, perceptual, or cognitive. Functional theories focus on the personality or motivational needs which attitudes serve, among them, for example, a knowledge function based upon a person's need to acquire information and to organize it in a way that gives meaning to a potentially absurd and confusing environment. Learning theories, which unlike functional theories have been the subject of much research, assume that the learning of new information in a persuasive communication will change beliefs. Or, in the terms of the definition of attitude discussed above, the affective component of attitudes is held to be influenced or changed by altering the cognitive (or knowledge) component. Generally, this was the approach of the Yale program of research discussed in Chapter 9. Learning approaches are important to the media persuader because of the theoretical emphasis upon stimulus-response connections and the attention given to the content of the persuasive message.[11]

Perceptual approaches to attitude change focus upon how people perceive and interpret other people, objects, and situations. Social judgment theory, for example, focuses upon the discrepancy of a message from the recipient's position and the degree of ego-involvement of the recipient. Attribution theory attempts to explain the way in which people try to account for human actions—one's own as well as the actions of others. While attribution theory has enjoyed a wave of popularity during the 1970s, perceptual approaches generally are not of primary interest to the mass media persuader. On the other hand, cognitive theories—labeled consistency theories by some and dissonance theories by others—are of more interest. These theories, in general, are concerned with inconsistencies that arise between, or among, related beliefs (bits of knowledge) about an object or an issue. One cognitive theory in particular, the theory of cognitive dissonance, which has stimulated a prolific outpouring of research on attitude change, may help to explain the limitations which the media persuader often faces in attempting to influence his audience.

Cognitive Dissonance Theory

Dissonance theory, based upon theoretical contributions of Leon Festinger, deals with the relationship between so-called "cognitive elements"—items of knowledge, information, or belief that a person holds about himself or about his surroundings. Such cognitive elements can be either consonant (compatible or consistent) with each other, or they can be dissonant. Dissonance may be the result of logical inconsistency, of personal experience, or of cultural norms and values. Two basic situations giving rise to cognitive dissonance of interest to the media persuader are (1) the voluntary or involuntary exposure of individuals to dissonant information and (2) the process of decision making. The basic principle of the theory is that dissonance, being "psychologically uncomfortable," will motivate the individual to try to reduce the dissonance and achieve consonance and to avoid situations and information which would likely increase the magnitude of the dissonance. If the dissonant message cannot be avoided, a reader or listener may attempt to evade the issue psychologically by simply choosing not to understand the dissonant appeal.[12] There are many ways, unfortunately, for editorial readers or listeners to accommodate the discomforting arguments put forth by the media persuader short of changing their views to conform with the discrepant editorial appeal.

A person who continues to smoke, for example, while being bombarded with editorial persuasion based upon reports from the Surgeon General that smoking is injurious to one's health, may decide he enjoys smoking so much that it is worth the risk, that the chances of his health suffering are not as serious as some would make out, that he can't always avoid every possible dangerous contingency and still live, or that if he stopped smoking he would put on weight which might be equally injurious to his health.

Dissonance theory generally holds that individuals will attempt to avoid information which tends to be discrepant with their knowledge and understanding of a person or issue. Communication theorists have long held that readers and listeners tend to expose themselves more to persuasive appeals with which they are already in substantial agreement, avoiding exposure to information which is at variance with their predispositions.[13] While there may be this so-called "selective-avoidance tendency," other researchers have pointed out that there seems to be an equal or greater opposite tendency to seek out surprising or discrepant information.

Selective exposure, in any case, may include enough latitude for a range of opinions on any one issue falling within a given zone or band, with only opinions falling outside such borderlines being systematically rejected. If the persuasive argument falls within the latitude of acceptance, these researchers say, the reader or listener will often perceive the argument as being closer to his own position than it actually is. The recipient may also tend to assimilate the difference between the opinion being expressed and his own by shifting his own position closer to the new point of view. If the persuasive message falls outside the acceptance zone, however, the reader or listener—in rejecting—may perceive the view being expressed as lying farther from his own position than it actually does.[14]

There is some indication that the perceived vulnerability of a non-supportive message may also be a factor in a reader's or listener's willingness to expose himself to a discrepant message. An easy to refute message, even though non-supportive of the individual's views, for example, might be received while a non-supportive, difficult to refute message would be avoided.[15] However, even where exposure to a message is high, as in television political advertising, the overall effect of such a communication may be more a reinforcing of beliefs than a conversion of views. A "non-believer," because of the principle of selective retention, may be exposed to a message but selectively recalls or forgets discrepant portions of the information. It has been found, for example, that viewers of political advertising can more readily recall information in agreement with their voting preference and predispositions than information which is incongruent.[16]

Indeed, selective exposure is a much more complex measure than originally conceived, recent studies suggest. For example, such factors as novelty or usefulness of the information, the degree of choice open to the individual and the attractiveness of decision alternatives—as well as the discomfort arising from cognitive dissonance—have been found to influence the willingness or lack of willingness of individuals to expose themselves to dissonant information.[17]

The media persuader should be aware that he may be confronted with the selective exposure process every time he attempts to communicate his message to an audience. While the potential audience of media editorials is enormous, only about one in every three newspaper readers regularly reads editorials. Television and radio editorials do not penetrate much better, although some variation has been reported according to the time of day and placement in relation to surrounding programs.[18] Aware that an audience can ignore his message, can reject its conclusions, or can even derogate the communicator himself, the media editorialist needs to take care not to fall victim to what one group of behavioral researchers calls the "MUM Effect"—that is, the communicator tends to keep "Mum about Unpleasant Messages."[19] The MUM effect may lead the communicator to slant his message so as to make the position argued seem minimally discrepant from the audiences, or he may omit discrepant statements.

But there are other more effective communication strategies for masking discrepancy; for example, the message can be made less specific, taking a less extreme position, or using less explicit language. The editorialist can spend more time on issues and problems (rather than solutions), de-emphasizing the audience's awareness of the communicator's opposing position. One study suggests that while there is strong evidence that message strategies often are planned with possible audience rejection in mind, a difficult audience may also challenge a communicator, under some conditions, to try even harder to convert obstinate recipients. The ideal technique, the study concluded, might be to use the strongest possible arguments within the audience's "range of acceptance" or to maximize the communicator's credibility.[20]

Counter-Attitudinal Advocacy

The strategy of persuasion is normally based upon a sequence calling for a source to communicate a message to an audience with the intent of changing attitudes which in turn will modify behavior. If the process fails, the communicator tries again. Recent research spawned by the "forced compliance" aspects of Festinger's cognitive dissonance theory, however, has taken a different approach, focusing more upon the inducement of an individual to do or say something contrary to his opinion or belief. Though the effect being studied is often called "forced compliance," this is a misnomer since it is important in the purposive creation of dissonance that a person not feel "forced" to comply. A more appropriate term, it has been suggested, is counter-attitudinal behavior or counter-attitudinal advocacy. Although contentions about the conditions under which people may be induced to engage in such self-persuasion remain a matter of lively debate, this mini-theory is of interest to the media persuader to the degree he may be able to create attitude-behavior discrepancies and therefore coax or pressure readers or listeners into various counter-attitudinal activities.

Festinger hypothesized that two things must happen before attitudes will be modified by counter-attitudinal activities: (1) the person must be under enough pressure to comply with the request, but not "forced" so much that he will feel he had no choice, and (2) the person must be prevented from reducing the dissonance he experiences from the counter-attitudinal activity in ways other than changing his attitude, for example, through receipt of a substantial payment or reward. In general, according to Festinger, the less justification provided to a person for complying with a counter-attitudinal request, the greater the likelihood that dissonance will lead him to modify his attitude. In a classic study, for example, it was found that paying a person one dollar to say something contrary to his beliefs produced more dissonance than paying him twenty dollars. It was reasoned that the one-dollar payment produced more dissonance since the advocate had less justification for engaging in the counter-attitudinal behavior than did a person paid twenty dollars.[21]

While the research findings in counter-attitudinal behavior are complex and sometimes confusing, they suggest that dissonance effects generally are more likely to occur when counter-attitudinal behavior is performed under the following conditions: (1) providing for low incentive, (2) allowing a high perceived choice, (3) with unpleasant consequences of the behavior, and (4) with an awareness by the advocate that he is personally responsible for the consequences of his behavior.[22]

Counter-attitudinal advocacy appears to hold important implications for the mass media persuader. On the one hand, it suggests that when direct persuasion by the editorialist fails, he may be able to modify the attitudes of his readers or listeners by encouraging—even pressuring—them to become engaged in some aspect of the problem or issue being discussed—by speech making, essay or letter writing, or other public activity which calls for role playing or posturing in a manner incongruent with their opinions or beliefs. At least, under the conditions described above, an editorialist may bring about attitude modification by creating attitude-behavior discrepancies.

Counter-attitudinal advocacy research also suggests that in addition to the problem arising from the selective exposure limitations of dissonance theory, making it difficult to reach those who disagree with the views the editorialist wishes to advocate, that a person engaged in counter-attitudinal advocacy or behavior may be even more difficult to convince of the rightness of the editorial advocacy. Cognitive dissonance arising under such circumstances is more likely to be reduced by the behavior engaged in by the message recipient (his self-persuasion resulting from his counter-attitudinal activity) rather than from the editorial advocacy of the media persuader.

The Role of Interpersonal Influence

In contrast to the more formalized "who said what to whom with what effect" approach taken in the Yale program studies which viewed the individual as processor of information whose attitudes flow from being exposed to logical arguments, other theories emphasize the important role of interpersonal influence in attitude formation and attitude change. Face-to-face interaction in small groups, for example, particularly the intimate association and cooperation which sociologists call primary groups, has been the subject of scores of research studies during the past twenty years.[23] This group dynamics approach contends that a major factor that causes people to change their beliefs and attitudes is the discrepancy that exists between an individual's attitude or behavior and a group's norms.[24]

While a general discussion of interpersonal communication and group dynamics is beyond the scope of this chapter, the media editorialist needs to recognize that most persuasion involves change, and that most change advocated by the media involves social change. To the extent that the change advocated is supported by informal or formal groups or by organizations, that information should be used in support of the persuasive message. One study concluded, for example, that the media alone are seldom able to effect substantial changes in strongly held attitudes or overt behavior without at least the assistance of interpersonal communication.[25] The media have long been viewed by some researchers as one of several "mediating influences" working together to bring about opinion change.[26] One of the most important of these mediating influences may be person-to-person communication.

An individual reads or listens to an editorial appeal, for example, and talks about it with other people. These more active members of the mass media audience are referred to as "opinion leaders" or "influentials" who, for whatever reason, tend to expose themselves to the news media more frequently than do others and in turn pass on to others, often in an informal or primary group context, the information and opinions stemming from such exposure.[27] The importance of person-to-person communication, therefore, may be that it enhances the function of the editorialist to the extent that the opinion leaders are among the one-in-three or one-in-four who expose themselves to editorial comment in the mass media. This relay function, often referred to by researchers as the "two-step flow of information," is effective for a number of reasons, research studies indicate.

The opinion leader informing others through face-to-face contact, for example, can usually choose the occasion for passing along the information better than can the editorialist. He can better adapt the information he has gained from the editorialist to his listeners, he can even offer counter-arguments to dislodge resistance, and he can do all this in a more personal way than can the more remote mass media communicator. The opinion leader also can often mask the purposiveness of this approach better than can the editorialist. At the same time, he may bring about compliance with his arguments without necessarily changing the listener's views.[28] In other words, the opinion leader, through face-to-face communications, while using the editorialist's basic arguments, can often get the desired results where the editorial message alone may fail.

Commenting on the important role of these influentials in the persuasive process, a team of journalism researchers had two suggestions for maximizing this two-step flow influence: (1) on important and complex issues, persuasive arguments should be directed consciously to the influentials expected to be in the audience, and (2) on matters of content, the message should be long enough to accommodate all the pertinent arguments and their supporting facts. Such arguments should include refutations of anticipated counter-arguments to inoculate the audience against future exposure to such arguments.[29]

A more recent review of interpersonal influence in election campaigns, however, indicates that the classic two-step flow hypothesis as originally formulated may not be entirely accurate. The study revealed, for example, that while one segment of the electorate may operate solely through interpersonal channels in which the mass media's role is somewhat unclear, a second segment relies more directly upon the mass media, particularly newspapers, for their political information. The general conclusion seems to be that a generation after the formulation of the two-step flow hypothesis, Americans rely much more directly on mass media for political campaign news than originally thought.[30]

Personality and Persuasion

Every editorialist soon becomes aware that even his most persuasive appeals are sometimes received and acted upon differently by different members of his audience. Scores of research studies have been conducted during the past fifteen years dealing with the complex and fascinating relationship between personality and persuasibility. While the editorialist is seldom in a position to know who is reading a given editorial, or listening to a broadcast commentary, or how such individuals might rate on various personality scales, a general awareness of the research findings in this area may still prove helpful.

One research study notes, for example, that one of the most persuasive aspects of personality is the manner in which an individual views himself—the degree of self-esteem he displays. A person displaying confidence, optimism, and competence is said to have high self-esteem. One who displays feelings of inadequacy, social inhibition, or anxiety is said to have low self-esteem. Most research tends to support the hypothesis that individuals with low self-esteem are more willing to agree with the opinions of others, since they have little confidence in their own opinions.[31] The term self-uniqueness, generally defined as the willingness to be different, is related to self-esteem by a few researchers. The more "non-unique" a person is the more readily susceptible to the appeals of persuasive communications he will be.[32] While self-esteem is an important variable, especially in interpersonal communication where the recipient of a communication can be observed, its effect in mass media persuasion may be limited to the extent that low self-esteem depresses attention and comprehension to the message.

A second personality trait, the so-called *authoritarian* personality, has been the subject of a number of experiments in persuasion. An individual possessed with such a trait tends to have an unquestioned respect for people in authority and therefore are more easily swayed by an appeal from such an authority. An individual possessing an authoritarian personality not only relies on the moral authorities in his own reference groups, he also tends to adhere rigidly to middle-class values, is preoccupied with the relative power and status of people around him as well as with his own power and status. He may also tend toward absolute judgments regarding the values he holds and is not easily swayed by messages that contradict the authorities he trusts.[33] Persons who are not themselves authoritarian in nature, on the other hand, may be more influenced by an information-type appeal. The media persuader, therefore, might be well advised to appeal to authority, when such sources are appropriate, while carefully mustering his editorial facts to satisfy the non-authoritarian members of his audience.

A third trait, the more extroverted-type of personality, particularly when combined with high intelligence, has been found to be more persuasive and less persuasible than the more introverted personality. An extroverted individual, the research findings indicate, is more apt to argue his point of view with a would-be persuader, changing his opinion less frequently than the person with a more introverted personality.[34]

A fourth personality trait, the way a person thinks, may affect his susceptibility to persuasion, or at least affect the way in which he seeks and utilizes information. Members of a mass media audience, for example, who are more flexible, more original, more creative in their thinking are said to be high in *integrative complexity*. Those who are rigid and close-minded, on the other hand, are labeled *concrete* thinkers. In contrast to the abstract (creative) thinker, the concrete thinker is less able to utilize information in new and meaningful ways. The research findings indicate that the concrete thinker, being low in integrative complexity, is more vulnerable to persuasive appeals.[35]

Some researchers have gone further, testing the possibility that susceptibility to persuasion may itself be a personality trait, that certain persons may be highly susceptible to persuasive appeals in a variety of contexts. Thus far, however, no general trait of susceptibility to persuasion has been established.

Motivations and Attitudes

A Harris or Gallup public opinion poll may give the editorialist specific information about the nuances of opinion members of his audience hold about a given issue or problem, but a determination of the reasons underlying such opinions may be a far more complex matter. The research findings suggest, for example, that there are a number of different motivational bases underlying otherwise identical attitudes or opinions. Some attitudes, obviously, are more enduring than others because of the reasons underlying their formation. Among the implications flowing from the more important motivational bases identified by researchers are these:

1. To the extent that attitudes and opinions are held as the best explanation of a given factual situation, the opinions may be susceptible to change by exposing the person to new facts so that he can see things

in a different light. Editorials written to illuminate the facts of an issue, for example, may be persuasive in such instances merely on the basis of communicating the needed facts.

2. Some attitudes and opinions may be held because they make the individual more acceptable to various social groups or civic organizations with whom he associates, or with whom he desires to associate. The editorialist, therefore, may bring about a change in such socially-derived attitudes if he can show that the proposed change is also acceptable to members of the groups or organization in question.

3. Some attitudes and opinions are apparently held to provide a rationalization for individual disappointments or shortcomings, making it possible for that individual to face the world and/or himself. Researchers label this kind of attitude as *ego-defensive* in function. Ego-defensive persons, in general, have been found to respond better to material which attempts to help them understand themselves than to material which is purely informational. One researcher suggests, however, that the extreme ego-defensive attitudes might better be left to a persuasive psychiatrist.[36]

Motivational research theorists have also tested the hypothesis that subliminal stimulation can affect behavior, particularly buying behavior. A New Jersey movie theater, for example, claimed to have increased popcorn and soft drink sales after commands of "EAT" and "DRINK" were flashed on the screen at 1/3000 of a second, too rapidly for the eye to see but supposedly communicated below the level of consciousness or apprehension. One critic charges that through subliminal techniques "tens of millions of humans are daily massaged and manipulated without their conscious awareness."[37] A recent empirical study, however, experimenting with the phrase "HERSHEY'S CHOCOLATE" flashed on the screen in letters six inches high at 1/50 of a second, found no basis for the claim of a subliminal stimulation toward buying.[38] The media persuader, the study suggests, must deal with the motivation of the individual members of his audience more openly. In any case, subliminal approaches, even if ethical, may be more apparent than real.

Other Persuasibility Factors

A number of demographic and socio-economic factors also have been pursued by researchers in an attempt to isolate variables which enhance the susceptibility of the individual to personal influence or media persuasion. Characteristics such as race, socioeconomic class, and religion, for example, have been studied but with little success. Age, sex, and education (or intelligence) have yielded better, though limited, results. The limited nature of some research findings is indicated in reference to age and persuasibility. It has been found, for example, that there is a rising rate in persuasibility during the early, pre-adolescent years which is attributed to stronger motivation and an increased ability for attention and comprehension. There appears to be a slight decline during adolescence, a leveling off during the adult years, with a recurring decline in more advanced years when attention and comprehension diminishes.[39]

In regard to sex, where a difference has been found between the sexes, women tend to be more persuasible than men.[40] While older persons, regardless of sex, appear to be less persuasible than younger persons, female adolescents have been found to be more persuasible than male adolescents.[41] One researcher was quick to point out that he found no evidence that female persuasibility was a function of physiological factors. It is more likely that such increased readiness to conform to a persuasive message is the result of cultural expectations which, in America, reinforce women to act submissively.[42] It has also been pointed out that a woman, though swayed in a psychological experiment, is not necessarily as easily swayed in the "real world" where more relevant issues may be involved. The recent assertiveness of the feminist movement may be closing the apparent persuasibility gap between the sexes. Recent research, in fact, questions the popular stereotype depicting females as passive and more susceptible to influence. Not only has the female been found to be as resistant to yielding as her male counterpart, one study reports she may be an even more effective persuader in a small group context than is the male.[43]

Any importance which may be attached to the fact that women have been, or are, more persuasible than men is further diminished, at least from the newspaper editorialist's point of view, by survey findings in a national study sponsored by the ANPA News Research Center. The findings indicate that male readers of editorials outnumber female by almost three to two. The average readership of editorials in relation to total newspaper readers was reported as 30 percent for males and 21 percent for females.[44]

Various indices of intelligence—chronological age, mental age, years of school—also have been investigated in relation to persuasibility. The general hypothesis has been that the more intelligence, the more ability, or the more education a person has, the more resistant to persuasion he will be. The research findings, however, have been mixed. One researcher suggests that people of moderate intelligence may be more persuasible than persons of either extremely high or low intelligence. The level of intelligence at which maximum persuasibility occurs, however, is viewed as sliding upward as the complexity of the issue or situation involved in the communication increases.[45]

One of the reasons advanced for the mixed results in research findings is that while intelligence may make a reader more susceptible to persuasion because of increased attention, and perhaps greater comprehension of the persuasive message, the better educated and presumably more intelligent reader is, at the same time, often more resistant and less yielding to the persuasive message. Highly intelligent readers, however, because of their ability to draw valid inferences, have been shown to be more influenced than readers with low intellectual ability when exposed to messages which rely primarily on logical arguments.[46] Unsupported generalizations, or false, illogical, irrelevant argumentation, on the other hand, are unlikely to impress the intelligent reader or listener because of his higher critical ability.[47] Faced with an intelligent, more educated audience, the media persuader, therefore, is well advised to present a more balanced two-sided, logical argument if he hopes to be effective.

Summary and Conclusion

If theoretical concepts and empirical studies concerning the recipient of persuasive messages do nothing else, they should focus attention on the audience of communications as an active, selective, skeptical, often obstinate group of individuals. It is obvious, for example, that not everyone exposed to editorial comment in the mass media pays any attention to it. Of those who do stop to read or listen, some perceive the message differently from others, remember it differently, react to it differently. And it can be assumed that members of the mass media audience, as people generally, react to a persuasive message not just as isolated individuals, but as members of the various social groups located in the community.

The successful media editorialist, whether he wants to or not, becomes engaged in a type of psychological warfare, interacting with members of his audience, being changed by them as he attempts to bring about change. The more he understands his audience, the more he knows about their individual needs and interests, the more he knows about the groups with whom they associate, the more successful he is likely to be in his primary role as an influential persuader. The various theories of attitude change and empirical research probing the relationship between attitudes and behavior should provide the editorialist with additional insights into this complex process of persuasion.

NOTES for Chapter 10

[1] Ralph L. Rosnow and Edward J. Robinson, eds., *Experiment in Persuasion* (New York: Academic Press, 1967), p. 195.

[2] See introduction to "The Nature of an Audience" in *The Process and Effects of Mass Communication,* rev. ed., eds.: Wilbur Schramm and Donald F. Roberts (Urbana: University of Illinois Press, 1971), pp. 191–387.

[3] For a summary of research on these topics, see Raymond A. Bauer, "The Audience," in *Handbook of Communication,* eds.: Ithiel de Sola Pool and Wilbur Schramm (Chicago: Rand McNally College Publishing Co., 1973), pp. 141–52.

[4] Wilbur Schramm, ed., *The Process and Effects of Mass Communication* (Urbana, Ill.: University of Illinois Press, 1954), p. 209.

[5] See, e.g., Samuel Himmelfarb and Alice Hendrickson Eagly, eds., *Readings in Attitude Change* (New York: John Wiley & Sons, 1974), pp. 2–8; Charles A. Kiesler, Barry E. Collins, and Norman Miller, *Attitude Change: A Critical Analysis of Theoretical Approaches* (New York: John Wiley & Sons, 1969), pp. 1–8; Stuart Oskamp, *Attitudes and Opinions* (Englewood Cliffs, N.J.: Prentice-Hall, 1977), pp. 7–9; and William J. McGuire, "Persuasion, Resistance, and Attitude Change," in *Handbook of Communication,* eds.: Ithiel de Sola Pool and Wilbur Schramm (Chicago: Rand McNally College Publishing Co., 1973), pp. 219–20.

[6] Philip G. Zimbardo, Ebbe B. Ebbesen, and Christina Maslach, *Influencing Attitudes and Changing Behavior,* 2d ed. (Reading, Mass.: Addison-Wesley, 1977), pp. 20–21; and Richard V. Wagner and John J. Sherwood, eds., *The Study of Attitude Change* (Belmont, Calif.: Brooks-Cole, 1969), pp. 2–3.

[7] For a discussion of recent research on the attitude-behavior relationship, see Martin Fishbein and Icek Ajzen, "Attitudes Towards Objects as Predictors of Single and Multiple Behavioral Criteria," *Psychological Review* 81 (January 1974): 59–74.

[8] Charles A. Kiesler and Paul A. Munson, "Attitudes and Opinions," in *Annual Review of Psychology,* eds.: Mark R. Rosenzweig and Lyman W. Porter (Palo Alto, Calif.: Annual Review, 1975), pp. 418–19.

[9] For a discussion of approaches to attitude change theory, e.g., see Oskamp, *Attitudes and Opinions,* pp. 165–90.

[10] See Chester A. Insko, *Theories of Attitude Change* (New York: Appleton-Century-Crofts, 1967); and T. M. Ostrom, "The Emergence of Attitude Theory: 1930–1950," in *Psychological Foundations of Attitudes,* eds.: A. G. Greenwald, T. C. Brock, and T. M. Ostrom (New York: Academic Press, 1968), pp. 1–32.

[11] See, e.g., Zimbardo, Ebbesen, Maslach, *Influencing Attitudes,* pp. 56–57.

[12] For a more complete discussion, see Leon Festinger, *A Theory of Cognitive Dissonance* (Stanford, Calif.: Stanford University Press, 1957).

[13] Joseph T. Klapper, *The Effects of Mass Communication* (New York: The Free Press, 1960), pp. 19–21, 64–65. See also, Lewis Donohew and Philip Plamgreen, "A Reappraisal of Selective Exposure Hypothesis," *Journalism Quarterly* 48 (Autumn 1971): 412–20.

[14] Carolyn W. Sherif, Muzafer Sherif, and R. E. Nebergall, *Attitude and Attitude Change* (Philadelphia: Saunders 1965).

[15] For a discussion of the refutation concept, see Randall R. Kleinhesselink and Richard E. Edwards, "Seeking and Avoiding Belief-Discrepant Information as a Function of Its Perceived Refutability," *Journal of Personality and Social Psychology* 31 (May 1975): 787–90.

[16] Stuart H. Surlin and Thomas F. Gordon, "Selective Exposure and Retention of Political Advertising," *Journal of Advertising* 5 (Winter 1976): 32–37.

[17] See, e.g., Dieter Frey and Robert A. Wicklund, "A Clarification of Selective Exposure: The Impact of Choice," *Journal of Experimental Social Psychology* 14 (January 1978): 132–39; and Timothy C. Brock, Stuart M. Albert, and Lee A. Becker, "Familiarity, Utility, and Supportiveness as Determinants of Information Receptivity," *Journal of Personality and Social Psychology* 14 (April 1970): 292–301.

[18] See *Straus Editor's Report,* "Ingredients of the Good Editorial," *The Masthead* 23 (Spring 1971): 40–41. Another survey places readership of editorials by adults at only one in four. See *ANPA News Research Bulletin* 8 (July 12, 1973).

[19] Abraham Tesser and Sidney Rosen, "Similarity of Objective Fate as a Determinant of the Reluctance to Transmit Unpleasant Information: The MUM Effect," *Journal of Personality and Social Psychology* 23 (July 1972): 46–53.

[20] Michael D. Hazen and Sara B. Kiesler, "Communication Strategies Affected by Audience Opposition, Feedback and Persuasibility," *Speech Monographs* 42 (March 1975): 56–68.

[21] For a discussion of various experiments in counter-attitudinal advocacy, see Himmelfarb and Eagly, *Readings in Attitude Change,* pp. 18–19, 472–592.

[22] See, e.g., Barry E. Collins and Michael F. Hoyt, "Personal Responsibility-for-Consequences: An Integration and Extension of the 'Forced Compliance' Literature," *Journal of Experimental Social Psychology* 8 (November 1972): 558–93; and Kiesler and Munson, "Attitudes and Opinions," pp. 421–25.

[23] For a survey of research, see Fred L. Strodtbeck, "Communication in Small Groups," in *Handbook of Communication,* eds.: Ithiel de Sola Pool and Wilbur Schramm (Chicago: Rand McNally Publishing Co., 1973), pp. 646–65.

[24] For a discussion of the group dynamics approach, see Zimbardo, Ebbesen, and Maslach, *Influencing Attitudes,* pp. 62–66.

[25] Everett M. Rogers, "Mass Media and Interpersonal Communication," in *Handbook of Communication,* eds.: Ithiel de Sola Pool and Wilbur Schramm (Chicago: Rand McNally College Publishing Co., 1973), pp. 290–310.

[26] See, e.g., Klapper, *The Effects of Mass Communication,* pp. 7–9.

[27] Elihu Katz and Paul F. Lazarsfeld, *Personal Influence* (Glencoe, Ill.: The Free Press, 1955), pp. 32–34.

[28] Paul F. Lazarsfeld, Bernard Berelson, and Hazel Gaudet, *The People's Choice,* 2d ed. (New York: Columbia University Press, 1948), pp. 150–58.

[29] D. F. Douglas, B. H. Westley, and S. H. Chaffee, "An Information Campaign That Changed Attitudes," *Journalism Quarterly* 47 (Autumn 1970): 479–87.

[30] John P. Robinson, "Interpersonal Influence in Election Campaigns: Two-Step Flow Hypothesis," *Public Opinion Quarterly* 40 (Fall 1976): 304–19.

[31] See, e.g., Howard S. Friedman, "Effects of Self-Esteem and Expected Duration of Interaction on Liking for a Highly Rewarding Partner," *Journal of Personality and Social Psychology* 33 (June 1976): 686–90; Carl I. Hovland and Irving L. Janis, eds., *Personality and Persuasibility* (New Haven: Yale University Press, 1959), pp. 229–32; and Erwin P. Bettinghaus, *Persuasive Communication,* 2d ed. (New York: Holt, Rinehart and Winston, 1973), pp. 65–66.

[32] Fredric A. Powell, "The Perception of Self-Uniqueness as a Determinant of Message Choice and Valuation," *Speech Monographs* 41 (June 1974): 163–68.

[33] Bettinghaus, *Persuasive Communication,* pp. 69–71.

[34] D. W. Carment, C. G. Miles, and V. B. Cervin, "Persuasiveness and Persuasibility as Related to Intelligence and Extraversion," *British Journal of Social and Clinical Psychology* 4 (February 1965): 1–7.

[35] See, e.g., Marvin Karlins and Herbert I. Abelson, eds., *Persuasion: How Opinions and Attitudes Are Changed,* 2d ed. (New York, Springer, 1970), pp. 101–5.

[36] *Ibid.,* pp. 92–96.

[37] Wilson Bryan Key, *Subliminal Seduction* (Englewood Cliffs, N.J.: Prentice-Hall (Signet Book) 1972), p. 1.

[38] Stephen G. George and Luther B. Jennings, "Effect of Subliminal Stimuli on Consumer Behavior: Negative Evidence," *Perceptual and Motor Skills* 41 (December 1975): 847–54.

[39] McGuire, "Persuasion, Resistance, and Attitude Change," p. 238.

[40] For a summary of early research on sex differences, see Hovland and Janis, *Personality and Persuasibility*, pp. 238–40.

[41] James O. Whittaker and Robert D. Meade, "Sex and Age as Variables in Persuasibility," *Journal of Social Psychology* 73 (October 1967): 47–52.

[42] Karlins and Abelson, *Persuasion*, pp. 90–91.

[43] Roberta Steinbacher and Faith D. Gilroy, "Persuasibility and Persuasiveness as a Function of Sex," *Journal of Social Psychology* 100 (December 1976): 299–306.

[44] *ANPA News Research Bulletin* 8 (July 12, 1973), p. 57.

[45] For a concise summary of ability factors in persuasion, see McGuire, "Persuasion, Resistance, and Attitude Change," p. 238.

[46] Barry Fish and Henry Orloff, "Who Is Cognitively Consistent?" *Personality and Social Psychology Bulletin* 1 (1974): 130–31.

[47] Karlins and Abelson, *Persuasion*, pp. 98–99.

11

The Syndicated Opinion Columnist: *A Necessary Ingredient*

EVER SINCE THE *New York Herald Tribune* introduced the first political columnist, Walter Lippmann, in 1931, the role of the political opinion columnist has grown and expanded. The process of syndication made such growth possible; economic considerations provided the incentive for the wholesaling process. It is interesting that early syndication to newspapers was of a more literary nature, for example, S. S. McClure, founder of *McClure's* magazine, formed his own syndicate during the 1880s to market the writing of authors such as Rudyard Kipling and Robert Louis Stevenson. Syndication has changed in many ways today, but the rationale remains much the same as stated by McClure almost a century ago:

> A dozen, or twenty, or fifty newspapers—selected so as to avoid conflict in circulation—can thus secure a story for a sum which will be very small for each paper but which will in the aggregate be sufficiently large to secure the best work by the best authors.[1]

Today a columnist may write for as many as 1,000 newspapers, for example, Jack Anderson, author of the muckraking "Washington Merry-Go-Round," whose column is distributed by United Features Syndicate. Not only has the number of newspapers using syndicated opinion columns grown, the number of columnists has increased despite the general decline in the number of daily newspapers through the years.

The eighty-page "Directory of Syndicated Services" published by *Editor & Publisher* in 1977, which includes three categories of columns ("Columns," "Editorial (Text)," and "History-Politics"), lists a total of more than 1,200 columns in the three categories. An undetermined number, however, are duplicated in two or more categories. In contrast, Bagdikian reported only 715 columns in these three categories in 1965, only 412 in 1949, and 320 in 1940. Fewer than 100 of these syndicated columnists, however, deal consistently with current public affairs. The majority of these political opinion columnists live and work in Washington. Their columns are usually distributed through the mail, or—if the newspaper will pay—by wire service. A few of the columnists living outside of Washington reproduce and distribute their own columns, for example, Paul Greenberg, editor of the editorial page of the *Pine Bluff* (Ark.) *Commercial*.

Syndication not only makes available to newspapers an increasing number of public affairs columns, such wholesale marketing also reduces the cost of these columns to newspapers. Smaller daily newspapers can often buy a three-times-a-week column, for example, for as little as five dollars. Most newspapers can purchase any column for less than it would cost to put a good columnist on their own payroll. In fact, syndication discourages the development of local columning talent. A related economic factor encouraging the use of syndicated columns is that most editorial pages are, to begin with, woefully understaffed. A survey conducted in 1971 by the National Conference of Editorial Writers showed that more than 53 percent of the responding newspapers in the 100,000-and-under circulation category had staffs of no more than a single full-time editorial writer. Only 20 percent of the over-100,000-circulation category had editorial staffs of five or more. The unavoidable conclusion is that many editorial pages are wretchedly understaffed.[2] With such a small staff, it can be argued, the syndicated opinion columnist is truly a necessary ingredient, particularly on slow days, just to produce the materials needed to fill the page. There are, of course, other advantages, as well as disadvantages, arising from the use of syndicated columnists, to be discussed below.

The Need for Columnists

A special critique group at the Charlotte, N.C., NCEW conference engaged in a day-long pursuit of this intriguing question: "The syndicated columnists—Who needs 'em?" The critique group first noted the shortcomings and faults of such syndicated writers: they were criticized for writing repeatedly on the same subject; too many of them, it was noted, were Washington based; their point of view was found to be too predictable; because of the mail distribution, they were often found to be untimely with their comments; columnists were not viewed as infallible oracles; they tended to all write columns of the same length, and most were found to be too long. But the conclusion of the group was that the syndicated columnist, despite all these shortcomings, was here to stay. Part of the reason for this conclusion, as noted above, was that syndicated material is generally more economical and that it helps to fill up the editorial page on a slow day. But there were other perceived advantages.

Highly regarded writers such as James Reston and Joseph Kraft, for example, are viewed by some editors as adding prestige to an editorial page while, at the same time, providing new sources and points of view not produced by the regular staff of most community daily newspaper editorial pages. Many syndicated columnists such as James J. Kilpatrick and Russell Baker are also viewed as excellent writers who have the time to research their subjects well and who have developed an interesting stylistic approach not found in most journalistic writing. Popular syndicated columnists such as Jack Anderson, Rowland Evans and Robert Novak provide a comfort factor, some editors say, which helps a new reader, who perhaps has just moved from another city or state, to feel comfortable reading a columnist he has grown accustomed to elsewhere through the years.

Donald W. Carson, journalism professor at the University of Arizona, surveyed NCEW members attending the Boston convention in 1971 in an attempt to find out what the typical editorial writer thought about columnists. Most respondents, Carson reported, thought that syndicated public affairs columnists made a significant contribution to the thought process they hoped that their pages provoked among readers. Sig Gissler, editorial writer for the *Milwaukee Journal,* for example, said of the columnist:

> He can raise issues with a bluntness and boldness that we sometimes find difficult to muster. Then, too, I think readers like the personalized journalism of the columnist. He's a person, not a remote institution.

Robert M. Heck, editor of the editorial pages for the *Rockford* (Ill.) *Morning Star,* thought the columnist adds breadth in filling the editorial page. He noted, however, that if he had enough letters to fill the rest of the page every day the columnists would be quickly discarded. A few editorialists, however, indirectly questioned the value of columnists. One said: "Their main value is to draw customers for our own editorials. Their value is secondary to in-depth, analytical pieces of a local, regional and state character." Another said: "Some days I think (they are used) only to fill the remaining space on pages after editorials and letters are dummied in. But on most days I realize that the columnists have followers who want insights into what's going on in the world." Still another said, tongue-in-cheek: "They are worth about what we pay for them." [3]

Selection of Columnists

Ben H. Bagdikian, press critic, formerly national news editor of the *Washington Post,* and now a journalism educator, has noted that

"For newspaper editors, choosing a columnist is like choosing a wife—maybe not so permanent and not so monogamous, but just as much by hunch and hope." Norman Cherniss, editor of the editorial page, *Riverside* (Calif.) *Press Enterprise,* is quoted as saying of "the mystical process" of selecting columnists:

> I try to buy people I have some reason to believe are good, as determined by a set of nebulous and difficult-to-define standards, and someone who will be read. We have about fourteen or fifteen public affairs columnists right now and I do bear in mind the need to present a broad spectrum of opinion without giving space to the nuts. What I am saying, I guess, is that it is in great measure a matter of by-guess-and-by-golly and we are all very fortunate that I am as wise as I am.[4]

One basis of selection for many editors is an attempt to balance political philosophies rather than to present only one point of view on the editorial pages. In the 1971 *Masthead* survey, for example, most respondents indicated that syndicated columnists were selected primarily on the basis of balancing political philosophies although readability, prestige, price, and other factors were also considered. One of the reasons given for balancing by most editorialists was a concern for the monopoly position of their newspapers. Typical was the response of R. W. Smith, editor of the *Minneapolis Star,* who said:

> We try to balance in the sense of presenting representation of all major strains of political ideology. We do not try to "balance" in the sense of so-many-conservatives vs. so-many-liberals. We think we have an obligation, especially since we are a single-ownership city, to give our readers the opportunity to examine as many ideological views as possible in addition to their own.

A few of the respondents to the *Masthead* survey failed to answer the balancing question. A check of the columnists they said their newspapers carried, however, usually indicated a one-point-of-view philosophy. One respondent who reported that his newspaper did seek to balance listed Paul Harvey as its liberal voice, indicating that balancing, at best, may be a highly subjective process.[5]

Bagdikian, in his earlier 1964 survey of data representing 85 percent of the country's total newspaper circulation concluded that most dailies pick syndicated columnists to support their own editorial views despite claims to the contrary. Among Republican papers he found four times as many with predominantly conservative columns as there were with predominantly liberal columns. Among Democrat newspapers there were almost twice as many with a majority of liberal columns as there were with conservative columns. Indeed, Bagdikian found only one newspaper in six that balanced columnists against the newspaper's own opinion.[6] Two years later, however, Bagdikian reported a growth of the idea that a paper should give a voice to "the other side," particularly among large metropolitan newspapers where the shift was toward the liberal point of view.[7]

In a few cities where there are competing newspapers with different ownership, the concern for balancing may be less relevant. In St. Louis, for example, the liberally-oriented *Post-Dispatch* is dominated with liberal columnists such as James Reston, Tom Wicker, Joseph Kraft, Anthony Lewis, and Marquis Childs, while the more conservative *Globe-Democrat* carries such conservative columnists as James J. Kilpatrick, William F. Buckley, Jr., M . Stanton Evans, Louis Kohlmeier, and Patrick Buchanan. Theoretically there is less need for a philosphic balancing of editorial page content where the reader has two local papers to choose from, particularly with editorial pages as different in orientation as those in St. Louis.

Smaller newspapers, however, often realy heavily upon syndicated columnists and obviously do attempt to bring a variety of views to their pages. Whether or not the columnists balance the editorial views expressed by the newspapers, of course, would take further investigation. The *Great Falls* (Mont.) *Tribune,* a morning newspaper with a circulation of 41,000 daily, two-thirds of that circulation out of the city, for example, publishes twelve or more political columnists. Bill James, executive editor of the *Tribune,* reported to NCEW critique group members in 1971 that the columnists included William F. Buckley, Jr., James Kilpatrick, Richard Wilson, Clark Mollenhoff, Evans and Novak, Max Lerner, Art Buchwald, James Reston, Tom Wicker, Anthony Lewis, Max Frankel, plus a couple of local columnists. In fact, critique group members found that the syndicated columnists on most days tended to dominate the *Tribune*'s editorial page.

The *Eugene* (Ore.) *Register-Guard,* an evening newspaper with a circulation of 54,000, also publishes a list of more than a dozen columnists, but obviously they are chosen on the basis of different criteria. Robert B. Frazier, editorial page editor of the *Register-Guard,* reported to NCEW critique group members in 1972 that the columnists included Tom Wicker, Max Lerner, James Reston, William Safire, C. L. Sulzberger, Anthony Lewis, Russell Baker, Joseph Kraft, Mary McGrory, Rowland Evans and Robert Novak, Carl Rowan, plus local columnists. This group is obviously more liberally oriented than the *Tribune* columnists discussed above.

It should not be surprising that editors view syndicated columnists differently, classify them differently, evaluate them differently. These subjective evaluations go into the mix when selections are made. Balancing of political ideologies, however, may be a goal which is more discussed than practiced.

Classification of Columnists

Factors which go into the selection of syndicated opinion columnists, as noted above, may vary from editor to editor and from newspaper to newspaper. There are a number of basic considerations, however, which often enter into the selection process leading to the classification of columnists into various groups from which the selection process takes place. The actual selection, of course, may or may not produce a balance within the various classifications. These basic classifications are based upon the following considerations: (1) the fairness and credibility of the columnist—for example, is he fair or unfair; (2) the philosophical approach—is the columnist a detached, analytical observer or is he a reporter, staying close to the news; (3) the writing style—does the columnist write in a formal, straightforward manner or is his style more informal, more personal, more entertaining; and (4) the political ideology of the writer—is the columnist liberal, conservative, or is he a moderate, a centrist. There are, of course, other factors which may go into the selection process. The prestige, reputation, or notoriety of the columnist, for example, or the perception and intelligence of the columnist, his skill at analysis and synthesis, his interests and experience. The list could go on and on.

The editors of *Seminar* magazine, then a quarterly publication of Copley Newspapers, surveyed subscribers in 1970 about their attitudes concerning the fairness of several facets of the mass media, including newspaper columnists and television commentators. The findings, while based upon the responses of 180 subscribers, are not scientific, but they are of interest. The five syndicated columnists rated as most fair from among the fifty listed in the survey were James Reston, S. I. Hayakawa, James J. Kilpatrick, William S. White, Rowland Evans and Robert Novak. The five viewed as least fair were Paul Harvey, Max Rafferty, Jack Anderson, William F. Buckley, Jr., and Barry Goldwater. Among the television commentators, the five viewed as most fair were Walter Cronkite, Harry Reasoner, Eric Sevareid, Howard K. Smith, and Frank McGee. Those viewed least fair were David Brinkley, Mike Wallace, Sander Vanocur, Chet Huntley, and Nancy Dickerson.[8] Fairness as a classification for choosing syndicated columnists, of course, is at least one valid yardstick since fairness is a dimension of source credibility and credibility is a factor in persuasion.

On the philosophical scale, columnists may range all the way from the ivory-tower, analytical approach of the pioneering columnist, Walter Lippmann, who liked to observe from a detached point of view separated from the hubbub of the marketplace, to such reporter types as Jack Anderson, who thrives on exposés derived from investigative reporting and from information from inside tipsters, to Evans and Novak, who specialize in less provocative information gleaned from inside tidbits provided by more establishment-oriented sources. Editors, based upon their wide usage, obviously like both types of columnists.

Lippmann, whose "Today and Tomorrow" column appeared for more than forty years, first in the *New York World* and later in the *New*

York Herald Tribune, epitomized the columnist as philosopher. Lippmann's two interests, one of philosophy which provided the context of his day-to-day observation on world events and one of journalism which provided the laboratory in which to test that philosophy and keep it from becoming too abstract, provided the impetus for what one commentator called his flawless interpretation of American public policy. A Britisher said of him:

> Lippmann's cast of mind . . . is that of a genuine inquirer with no axe to grind, a pioneer researcher who uses great knowledge of the past as a handy but treacherous guide to the present. . . . There is more of the forest ranger about him than the plant collector, and more of the skeptical, wise judge than either.[9]

An obvious successor to Lippmann is Joseph Kraft who worked for the *Washington Post, New York Times,* and *Harper's* magazine before launching his syndicated column in 1963 at the age of 39. Kraft, labeled "the most famous journalist in America" by one writer, is viewed as a proponent of the "heavy-weight 'analytical' style, of which Lippmann was an early representative." Such analysts are viewed as filling a genuine need by providing a detachment and perspective one seldom finds elsewhere in the press. Kraft, for example, was one of the first syndicated columnists to declare that the war in Vietnam was a mistake, that the Great Society programs during the 1960s were of limited value, and, in his first column after the Watergate break-in, to note that it defied logic to believe that President Richard Nixon was not deeply involved. Kraft's analyses, however, were often faulty and fraught with inconsistencies as were those of Lippmann.[10] There are, of course, other columnists who rely heavily upon analyses, for example, James Reston, George Will, Tom Wicker, and Anthony Lewis, but they are less philosophical and less detached than is Kraft.

The more non-analytical investigative column, pioneered by Drew Pearson and Robert Allen and carried forward by Jack Anderson, has reinstated muckracking as an honorable profession, one writer has noted. Anderson in three short months early in 1972, for example, published in his "Washington Merry-Go-Round" column:

> 1) Secret papers showing a strong anti-India bias in the administration's handling of the India-Pakistan war; 2) the story of a U.S. ambassador getting drunk on a commercial airliner; 3) a report that the Justice Department had settled an antitrust suit against ITT (International Telephone & Telegraph), on terms relatively favorable to the firm, at about the same time that ITT had promised a contribution to the Republican convention fund.[11]

On the fourth month Anderson rested and was awarded the Pulitzer Prize for his work on the India-Pakistan war papers. Muckraking, however, is the target of strong criticism, both from media critics as well as from those under attack. The "Washington Merry-Go-Round" column through the years, for example, has been the target of 107 libel actions, most of them against Pearson. Up until the time of Pearson's death in 1969, however, he had lost only one libel action; two others were settled after his death in an effort to close his estate. Anderson, by contrast, has been the target of only three libel actions since he took over the column in 1969.[12]

Representative of another type of opinion columnist is the generally non-analytical approach taken by Rowland Evans and Robert Novak in their "Inside Report" column published since 1963. While "Inside Report" is usually classified as opinion writing, Evans and Novak often take an informational rather than an interpretative approach. Novak explains "Inside Report" this way:

> We take a strong point of view on a situation, but we're not strongly doctrinaire. Neither Rowly nor I am terribly profound. I don't think we're in business to point up the good; we're trying to show the foibles of people. The conservatives claim that we're a liberal column and the liberals claim that we're a conservative column, which I think shows that we're doing a good job of stepping on a lot of toes.[13]

There are other reporter-types among the syndicated columnists, of course, among them Clark Mollenhoff and Louis Kohlmeier.

The analytical, non-analytical continuum, marked at the one end by the Lippmanns and the Krafts and at the other by the Andersons and Evans and Novak, is just one more method of classifying the syndicated columnist.

Syndicated columnists may also be classified by their writing style as it reflects their attitude and approach to a subject. Most columnists, whether liberal or conservative, analytical or non-analytical, engage in a more or less straightforward appeal to the reader's intellect. Expository or argumentative techniques are usually used; the tone is usually serious. There are a few columnists, however, who consistently employ a more change-of-pace approach. Some are merely attempting to be more provocative, for example, the sometimes irreverent and unpredictable comments on politics and government of Nicholas von Hoffman of the *Washington Post* who, one observer noted, "writes with the white heat of a *Rolling Stone* crusader."[14] The bold and brassy utterances of Jimmy Breslin, a former columnist for the *New York Post,* also appear to fall into this category. Breslin is often more interested in the emotional impact of an issue than with the issue itself.

A columnist may, on the other hand, take the more leisurely approach of the literary essayist. The "Strictly Personal" column of Sydney J. Harris, which originates on the editorial page of the *Chicago Daily News,* for example, has, through the years, presented a thoughtful, perceptive commentary on every aspect of contemporary life from the emotional complexities of marriage and child-rearing to the global issues of war and peace. At least seven collections of Harris' essays have been published in book form.[15] Though his columns usually appear on editorial and op-ed pages, they also appear from time to time in Sunday supplements, in anthologies, even on the Christmas card of a U.S. Congressman.

An even more marked departure from the straightforward appeal used in most syndicated opinion columns is the change-of-pace approach of such political satirists as Russell Baker of the *New York Times*, Arthur Hoppe of the *San Francisco Chronicle*, and Art Buchwald, whose humor column is distributed by the *Los Angeles Times* syndicate. For three such deft writers as Baker, Hoppe, and Buchwald to have been produced by one generation is, in itself, unusual. Baker is probably the most gifted writer of the three, but it has been noted that he sometimes has difficulty finding themes that will carry his wry commentary. Hoppe is viewed as having more and richer ideas than either of his rivals, perhaps because he is more of a political animal. His satire often carries an acid quality. Buchwald, the celebrity of the three, has been called the "greatest satirist in English since Pope and Swift." His columns and other writings have been published in more than a dozen books; he is a genuinely humorous person and is much in demand as a speaker. The three columnists, however, employ much the same techniques. Each carefully observes the foibles of men, especially the behavior of politicians and public figures, focus on one of their more dubious enterprises, and then imagine in print what would occur if it were carried to its absurd conclusion.[16] Mike Royko of the *Chicago Daily News*, a 1972 winner of the Pulitzer Prize for commentary, also frequently writes satirically, but his subjects are more often related to the Chicago scene.

While the fairness and credibility of columnists, their analytical and reporting techniques, and their style and approach to writing are all methods of evaluating columnists, the classification most frequently used by editors in seeking to balance the views being expressed on a given editorial page is the liberal-conservative continuum. Representative columnists falling to such liberal, conservative, or centrist positions are discussed briefly below.

Columnists: Liberal Voices

The liberal voices among syndicated opinion columnists are perhaps more prominent and more numerous than are their conservative counterparts. This may be due partially to attempts by editors to balance their generally more conservative editorial pages; it may be due to the fact that the columns of four of these liberal voices originate on the editorial pages of the *New York Times*. These four liberal columnists, all of whom are widely syndicated, are James Reston, Tom Wicker, Anthony Lewis, and C. L. Sulzberger. A fifth *Times* columnist, Russell Baker, may also fit the liberal mold, but he is more satirist than liberal. A sixth *Times* opinion columnist, William Safire, President Richard Nixon's former speech writer, is definitely not a liberal voice. The *Times* columnists are an interesting as well as a prominent and prestigious group.

James "Scotty" Reston, a vice president of the New York Times Co. and former Washington Bureau chief, is probably the most respected and influential correspondent in Washington. He not only sets the agenda and points the way for other Washington-based columnists, he often influences the actions of political leaders as well.[17]

Tom Wicker, an associate editor of the *Times* and Reston's successor as Washington Bureau chief, is perhaps the most liberal of the four *Times* columnists, especially in the area of civil rights. He was one of those summoned, at the demand of inmates, to act as an observer and mediator during the Attica Prison uprising in upstate New York in 1971. His book four years later about that experience, entitled *A Time to Die,* is considered by many to be a significant social document as well as an excellent example of the so-called "new journalism." Wicker is also the author of a number of novels, including a best-seller dealing with a journalist entitled *Facing the Lions.*

Anthony Lewis of the *New York Times,* winner of two Pulitzer Prizes for national reporting, the latest in 1963 for his coverage of the Supreme Court of the United States, has been a syndicated columnist since 1969. Lewis was head of the *Times'* London bureau from 1965 until 1972; during those years his column frequently was written from the perspective of an American abroad. As a former Nieman fellow at Harvard, Lewis concentrated on the study of law and frequently writes on legal subjects. His book, *Gideon's Trumpet,* is a classic study of a landmark Supreme Court case in which it was determined that an indigent has a right to a lawyer.

C. L. Sulzberger, a nephew of Arthur Hays Sulzberger, publisher of the *New York Times,* has covered international events for the *Times* for more than thirty years. As a globe-trotting columnist, Sulzberger usually writes on subjects somewhat off the news, attempting to place events in a more understandable frame of reference and to prepare the readers of his "Foreign Affairs" column for possible future flareups around the world. He was one of the few liberals who defended the war in Vietnam. Sulzberger's long memoirs and diary, *A Long Row of Candles,* published in 1969, provides many personal glimpses into the life of a columnist as well as a personalized history of the European scene from 1934 to 1954.

One of the oldest of the non-*Times* liberals among the syndicated opinion columnists is Max Lerner, a former professor of American civilization and world politics at Brandeis University and the author of more than a dozen books. Though an old-fashioned liberal of the New Deal stripe, Lerner does not hesitate to criticize a liberal position which he feels is wrong. Because of his academic background he can write in-depth commentaries on such varied issues as education, crime, disenchantment of the young, politics, skyjacking and terror tactics, each as it breaks in the news. Despite his age, or perhaps because of it, editors note that he can successfully bridge the generation gap.

Another scholarly columnist whose liberal orientation goes back to the New Deal years of Franklin Roosevelt is Marquis Childs who retired from the *St. Louis Post-Dispatch* in 1974 after a 47-year career. Childs was awarded the first Pulitzer Prize for commentary in 1970. He continues to write his syndicated column twice a week, an effort distinguished by careful research and documentation. Childs is also the author of several political novels as well as other books, including *Eisenhower: Captive Hero* in 1958.

The best known black columnist in the nation is Carl Rowan, a prize-winning reporter for his coverage of the civil rights movement for the *Minneapolis Tribune* before President John F. Kennedy named him deputy assistant secretary of state for public affairs and later ambassador to Finland. He later served as director of the U.S. Information Agency, a cabinet level position, in the Johnson administration. Few newsmen have better international connections, yet most of Rowan's columns deal with problems closer to home. One editor notes that Rowan is by no means a black columnist; he is a columnist who happens to be a black. Only about one out of six columns deals with racial topics.

Mary McGrory of the *Washington Star* is one of the few successful female opinion columnists and the only woman to win a Pulitzer Prize for commentary. Her column, "Point of View," often deals with the human factor behind behavior. Her impressions are combined with classical literary allusions in a style which has been described as the "poet's gift of analogy." Or, as another editor noted, her writing reflects the feelings that most people have but cannot express.

Space prevents the discussion of all the syndicated columnists whom many editors would place on the liberal list. Joseph Kraft and Jack Anderson, discussed above in other categories, would certainly be included as liberals by most editors. Others often listed as liberals include Tom Braden, former editor of the *Blade Tribune,* Oceanside, Calif., who began his syndicated column with Frank Mankiewicz in 1968; Norman Cousins, erudite editor of the *Saturday Review* magazine; Clayton Fritchey, former editor of the *New Orleans Item* and deputy chairman of the National Democratic Committee; John P. Roche, a professor of civilization and foreign affairs at Fletcher School of Law and Diplomacy at Medford, Mass.; Garry Wills, who spent five years in a Jesuit seminary, earned a doctorate at Yale, and is the author of the book, *Nixon Agonistes*.

Columnists: Conservative Voices

While the conservative syndicated columnists, as a group, may not be as prominent and as prestigious as their liberal counterparts, there are among them a number of articulate voices who command large audiences and who wield great influence on the nation's editorial pages. A few of them are well known for their broadcast commentary as well.

William F. Buckley, Jr., is probably the most prominent of the conservative voices, if for no other reason than his multimedia approach to persuasion. He has been the editor of the conservative *National Review* magazine since 1955. He has written his "On the Right" syndicated column since 1962. He has been the host of the weekly broadcast commentary "On the Firing Line" since 1966. In addition, he has written a score of books, some of them controversial as was his very first book about his alma mater, entitled *God and Man at Yale,* in 1951. Buckley has been called a "philosophical conservative" who at times comes through as more of a libertarian, often making little pretense of practicality in his ardent fight against liberalism and liberals.

One of the most articulate conservative voices is James F. Kilpatrick, former editorial writer and editor of the *Richmond* (Va.) *News Leader.* Once the standard bearer of the Old South's defense of racial segregation as an editorialist in Virginia, Kilpatrick's tone has changed through the years, but his innate conservatism continues to undergird his commentary. One of his special interests is the functioning of the courts; he often devotes an entire column, for example, in evaluating an important decision handed down by the Supreme Court. Kilpatrick, like Buckley, is also active as a broadcast commentator. In 1968 ABC named him one of that network's recurring critics of public events. He is a regular also on the point-counterpoint portion of CBS's "Sixty Minutes" program. He is also the author of several books, including *The Southern Case for School Segregation* in 1962.

One of the rising stars among conservative syndicated columnists is George F. Will, whose twice-weekly column has been syndicated since 1974 by the Washington Post Writers Group. Within three years his "Will Power" column was being distributed to 235 newspapers; in 1977 he received the Pulitzer Prize for commentary. Will received a doctorate in political science at Princeton in 1964 and taught at Michigan State University and the University of Toronto before becoming a columnist. As a contributing editor of *Newsweek* since 1976, he writes a biweekly column for that magazine. He frequently appears on "Agronsky & Company," "Meet the Press," and other television shows. He previously served as the Washington Editor of the conservative journal,

The National Review, and was special assistant to the chairman of the Republican Policy Committee.

Another even more recent conservative columnist is Patrick J. Buchanan, former editorial writer for the *St. Louis Globe-Democrat* and speech writer and consultant to Presidents Nixon and Ford. In his column, "The Dividing Line," distributed by the *New York Times* syndicate, Buchanan observes the current political, social, and economic scene. He is the author of two books, including *Conservative Votes, Liberal Victories* in 1975.

Another conservative columnist who takes a multi-media approach is M. Stanton Evans, former editor of the *Indianapolis* (Ind.) *News.* Evans, a graduate of Yale, has served on the editorial staff of Buckley's *National Review* and as editor of *Human Events* magazine. He has been a participant in CBS's "Spectrum" series as well as being involved with CBS Radio since 1971. He has written a number of books, including *The Future of Conservatism* in 1968.

A conservative columnist who has been around for a long time, but who is perhaps better known to some for his many books written since 1935, is Holmes Alexander who views the Washington Scene from the conservative side. Not all the conservative columnists, however, write from Washington. Paul Greenberg, editorial page editor for the *Pine Bluff* (Ark.) *Commercial,* a former editorial writer for the *Chicago Daily News,* and a Pulitzer Prize winner for editorial writing in 1969, began distributing his syndicated column from Pine Bluff in 1970.

Many editors would place other columnists strongly on the conservative side, for example, Jeffrey Hart, professor of English at Dartmouth, who writes from a campus viewpoint, often reflecting what youth thinks; William A. Rusher, publisher of *National Review,* whose "Conservative Advocate" column has been distributed by Universal Press syndicate since 1973; and a number of columnists distributed by the *Los Angeles Times* syndicate, including Paul Harvey, Jenkin Lloyd Jones, Roscoe Drummond, Max Rafferty, Ernest B. Furgurson, and Lt. Gen. Ira C. Eaker. These, as well as others, are available to editors desiring to bolster the conservative stance of their editorial pages.

Columnists: the Centrists

One of the criticisms of syndicated columnists which editors frequently voice is that they are too predictable, that they write from a liberal or conservative point of view so consistently that readers can predict what stance the columnist will take on any given issue even before the column is read. It can be argued, of course, that the columnist is often chosen to appear on the editorial page for the precise reason that he does write from a liberal or conservative bias. It may be unfair, therefore, to be critical when the columnist lives up to his reputation. Nicholas von Hoffman, writing in *The Masthead,* holds that, indeed, there is not enough bias among columnists. He noted, for example, that:

> [O]ne function of a columnist is to resonate, preferably with some elegance, the opinions he shares with others. This is the famous knee-jerk syndrome which displeases editors who'd rather have their columnists "unpredictable." Apparently most readers don't. At least it seems the most successful and widely read columnists can be anticipated with almost as much accuracy as the movements of the stars.[18]

Since politicians must mumble and fudge, Hoffman argues, columnists are left as the only strong expositors of points of view about issues of public concern. Editors may compensate for such biases, Hoffman noted, by balancing the points of view being expressed on their pages.

At least one syndicated columnist, however, responding to an invitation to comment on what columnists liked or disliked about today's editorial pages, expressed concern about the liberal-conservative approach for the selection of columnists. J. F. terHorst, former Washington newsman and short-time press secretary to President Ford, argued that editors should leave room for what he called the "centrists"—columnists who cannot properly be catalogued ideologically as either liberal or conservative. He related the centrists to the growing group of independent voters, which Gallup estimates at 37 percent, who are being wooed by both political parties. Among this middle group of independent voters are a high percentage of the best-educated, the wealthiest, the most influential, and the most newspaper-oriented segment of the general public, terHorst argued:

> Yet, as I see it, America's political centrists are very much underrepresented on most of the opinion pages of our daily newspapers. The conservatives in any city are comfortable with them. And liberal readers are quite likely to have the same pleasure. But why such a dearth of opinion columnists who can speak to—and for—the very large group of readers who occupy the high middle ground of political thought in America?[19]

One reason the centrists may be underrepresented, terHorst noted, is that editors are uncomfortable with them:

> We don't slot very neatly. We mess up the formula. In the competition for space on the page, an identifiable liberal or conservative writer will beat out a centrist nearly every time. So the temptation for the centrist is to slide left or right, to adjust to the economic realities of columnizing, because that's where the money is.

Who are these "centrist" columnists? Obviously terHorst, as a moderate, considers himself one of them, though some readers might consider him a conservative. He suggested that such reportorial columnists as Jack Anderson and Rowland Evans and Robert Novak might fit the centrist image. Editors responding to a *Masthead* survey in 1971 also place Jim Bishop, Tom Braden, David Broder, Marquis Childs, Roscoe Drummond, Joseph Kraft, Mary McGrory, Clark Mollenhoff, Victor Riesel, C. L. Sulzberger, Tom Thiede, and Nick Thimmesch in the reporter category. Obviously the editors were giving more weight to the analytical versus reporter continuum than to the liberal versus conservative classification. Even in terms of analytical writing, however, it is difficult to view such writers as Marquis Childs, Joseph Kraft or Mary McGrory as centrists.

There are other syndicated opinion columnists who have not been mentioned in any of the above categories. A few, for example, Louis Kohlmeier, obviously fit the reporter-centrist category. A newcomer such as William Safire, President Nixon's former speech writer, may fit the moderate-centrist category, but many editors would label him a conservative. There are others for which no classification has been suggested: Jack Cloherty and Bob Owens, Jim Fitzgerald, Anne Geyer, Sandra Haggerty, Smith Hempstone, Ron Hendren, Jesse Jackson, Victor Lasky, George Mair, Kevin P. Phillips, William Raspberry, and Joe Kingsbury Smith.

The Role of Syndicated Columnists

Once the editor chooses the group of syndicated columnists who are to grace his editorial page, or his op-ed page, how is he going to treat them, how is he going to edit them, how is he to determine what role they should play? The answer to these questions may depend upon the reasons why the columnists were chosen in the first place. The overall editorial policy of the newspaper may also provide guidance. If an array of six or eight syndicated columnists, for example, has been selected to balance the viewpoints being expressed in locally written editorials or columns, then obviously they should be edited toward that end. If they have been acquired simply to help fill up the pages on slow days, then the editing process may be of far less importance. If the columnists have been acquired to prevent competing media from using them, then there may be no strong motivation even to use them.

Generally speaking, however, syndicated columnists should be used to balance the page and to assist the staff in fulfilling its function in commenting upon state, national, and international events and issues of relevance to the page's readers. This is the reason most often given by editors for their use. In such a role the syndicated columnists should serve as visiting professors, helping to highlight the important issues, not as the star attractions on the page. The page's emphasis should be on the locally written editorials and columns, and the makeup and display of items on the page should highlight these efforts.

In editing, the syndicated columnists should be held to the same standards as the other writers on the page. Indeed, a few editors make the syndicated columnists compete against one another, choosing the best column on a given subject from among those available to them. A few editors edit syndicated columns heavily, cutting back their length as much as fifty percent. In doing so, editors say they are going after the quality of the columnist's reporting and judgments, forgetting whether he wears a liberal, a conservative, a moderate, an independent, a populist, or whatever label.

Editors are becoming increasingly aware also of the need to safeguard the credibility of the newspaper as a voice in the community, and that concern applies to the syndicated columnist as well as to regular editorial page staffers. The National Conference of Editorial Writers, in amending its "Basic Statement of Principles" in 1975, took special note that editors should seek to hold syndicates to the same standards as those proposed for editorial writers.[20] The proposed standard that a syndicated columnist has an obligation to provide an opportunity for reply to persons or institutions aggrieved by his mistakes or attacks, often referred to as the Cranberg Rule, has apparently been of some benefit.[21] Indeed, the person most responsible for the NCEW amendment concerning conflict of interest, Gilbert Cranberg, editor of the editorial pages of the *Des Moines* (Ia.) *Register & Tribune,* canceled Buckley's column in 1977 based upon Cranberg's concern about possible conflicts of interests caused by Buckley's non-journalistic activities.[22]

The editor's effort to balance, however, is sometimes hampered by a different sort of problem, the matter of exclusivity and denial of territorial rights to purchase a needed columnist in the first place. Several editors responding to the 1971 *Masthead* survey noted that the territorial rights of other papers had prevented them from buying such conservatives as Kilpatrick or Buckley, for example, while others complained of having been "frozen out" by being required to purchase a whole service in order to get one or two key features they sought. Richard B. Childs, editor of the editorial page for the *Flint* (Mich.) *Journal,* however, concluded that being frozen out wasn't all that bad since it forced him to turn to other sources, preventing his newspaper from becoming too loaded with regulars.[23]

Despite all the shortcomings of syndicated columnists, despite disagreements about the proper role for such outsiders on the editorial pages of community or regionally-oriented newspapers, despite ambiguity in the classification and the criticism about their selection, despite all these problems the use of syndicated columns continues to grow,[24] apparently because they are needed. They are needed, some say, to bolster the output of woefully undermanned editorial page staffs, especially on smaller newspapers. They are needed to balance the views being expressed by the editorial page staffs, especially in communities where there is no competing newspaper, a situation that exists in 96 percent of all communities having daily newspapers. They are needed to improve the quality of and to provide the variety needed if the editorial page is to be a smorgasbord of views that will better attract modern-day readers. The breadth of views and the variety of the offerings available to the editor provide a challenge to select those columnists who will best strengthen and balance the effectiveness and persuasibility of the page. Such a selection process, however, is no easy task.

NOTES for Chapter 11

[1] As quoted by Ben H. Bagdikian in "Journalism's Wholesalers," *Columbia Journalism Review* 4 (Fall 1965), p. 27.

[2] Laurence J. Paul, "Many Pages Wretchedly Understaffed," *The Masthead* 24 (Spring 1972): 1–4.

[3] See Donald W. Carson, "What Editorial Writers Think of the Columnists," *The Masthead* 23 (Spring 1971): 1–5.

[4] As quoted by Ben H. Bagdikian in "How Editors Pick Columnists," *Columbia Journalism Review* 5 (Spring 1966): 40.

[5] Carson, "What Editorial Writers Think of Columnists," p. 3.

[6] Ben H. Bagdikian, "How Newspapers Use Columnists," *Columbia Journalism Review* 3 (Fall 1964): 20–24.

[7] Bagdikian, "How Editors Pick Columnists," p. 42.

[8] "Is There a 'Fairest One' of All?" *Seminar* 17 (September 1970): 14–24.

[9] Alistair Cooke, "Mr. Lippmann's First Quarter-Century," *Nieman Reports* 10 (July 1956): 43–44.

[10] For an evaluation of Kraft and other syndicated columnists, see James Fallows, "The Most Famous Journalist in America," *Washington Monthly* 7 (March 1975): 5–22.

[11] Peter J. Anderson, *Research Guide in Journalism* (Morristown, N.J.: General Leraning Press, 1974), p. 7. For a less flattering view of Anderson and a number of other Washington-based columnists discussed in this chapter, see Barry Collier, *Hope and Fear in Washington (The Early Seventies): The Story of the Washington Press Corps* (New York: Dial Press, 1975).

[12] Douglas Anderson, "A 'Washington Merry-Go-Round' of Libel Actions" (Ph.D. dissertation, Southern Illinois University, 1977), p. 514.

[13] As quoted in Anderson's *Research Guide in Journalism,* p. 14.

[14] *Ibid.,* p. 25.

[15] For Harris' latest published columns, see *The Best of Sydney J. Harris* (Boston: Houghton Mifflin, 1975).

[16] William L. Rivers, Theodore Peterson, and Jay W. Jenson, *The Mass Media and Modern Society,* 2d ed. (San Francisco: Rinehart Press, 1971), p. 215.

[17] For a discussion of the influential role played by Reston, see William L. Rivers, *The Opinionmakers* (Boston: Beacon Press, 1965), pp. 69–91.

[18] Nicholas von Hoffman, "Not Enough Biases Among Columnists," *The Masthead* 27 (Winter 1975): 7–8.

[19] J. F. terHorst, "Leave Some Room for Centrists," *The Masthead* 27 (Winter 1975): 5–6.

[20] See page 15, "The NCEW's Basic Statement of Principles."

[21] James J. Kilpatrick, "Life and Times with Cranberg Rule," *The Masthead* 27 (Winter 1975): 9–12.

[22] For a discussion of this topic, see Gilbert Cranberg, "Why I'm Bouncing Buckley's Column," and William F. Buckley, Jr., "Columnist Buckley Begs to Differ," *The Masthead* 29 (Summer 1977): 14–19.

[23] Carson, "What Editorial Writers Think of Columnists," pp. 3–4.

[24] It is difficult to determine the number of subscribers for each column or to determine the cost of the columns since the syndicates generally refuse to divulge such information. One writer argues that the promotional materials often distort the actual distribution. See, e.g., Richard Weimer, *Syndicated Columnists* (New York: Richard Weimer, 1975), pp. 11–28.

12

Feedback: *The Need for an Open Forum*

IF EDITORIAL PAGES are to be storm centers of thought, as one writer has suggested they should be, if they are to provide a public forum where differing views may be presented, if they are to properly function as an adjunct to the marketplace of ideas where various solutions to problems and answers to questions of public policy may be tested against alternative solutions and counter proposals, then readers must have a right of access to newspapers, particularly in the letters to the editor columns of newspapers.

The need for access in the 1970s has been heightened, critics claim, because the number of media voices in the marketplace are being diminished through increasing monopolization, through cross media ownership of broadcast and print facilities, and through the expansion of chain ownership of newspaper properties. The growing trend toward consolidation in all these areas tends to lessen competition which historically existed among the media, discouraging competition in the reporting and analyzing of the events of the day as well as discouraging competition on the business side.[1]

In the face of this diminishing number of mass media voices, critics of the media clamor for a more socially responsible press, to be brought about through affirmative action by its own initiative or through governmental regulation designed to provide the most extensive dissemination of opposing viewpoints in the media which remain.

Theoretical Basis for Access

A basic assumption underlying the free speech and free press doctrine is that one of the important purposes of society and government is the discovery and spread of truth on subjects of general concern. John Milton argued in 1644 in his *Areopagitica* that freedom of expression is essential to the emergence of truth and the advancement of knowledge. Justice Oliver Wendell Holmes, in one of his noteworthy Supreme Court dissents, gave the marketplace concept of Milton a twentieth century interpretation. Justice Holmes said.

> [T]he ultimate good desired is better reached by free trade in ideas—that the best test of truth is the power of the thought to get itself accepted in the competition of the market, and that truth is the only ground upon which [such thoughts] safely can be carried out. That at any rate is the theory of our Constitution.[2]

Justice Holmes' theory is basically a *laissez-faire* idea. The clash of political ideas is, in this view, a self-righting and self-sustaining process. There have always been those, however, who have doubted the practicality of such a free expression doctrine. Judge Learned Hand, another noted American jurist, on one occasion wrote that the First Amendment

> . . . presupposes that right conclusions are more likely to be gathered out of a multitude of tongues, than through any kind of authoritative selection. To many this is, and always will be, folly; but we have staked upon it our all.[3]

Increasing press criticism during the twentieth century, however, has emphasized the need for, and hastened the adoption (or at least the espousal) of, the so-called "social responsibility theory" of the press. Critics say that the Hutchins Commission report in 1947 helped to awaken the press to the need for a more socially responsible performance. The theory, described as largely a grafting of new ideas on to traditional theory, has the major premise that:

> Freedom carries concomitant obligations; and the press, which enjoys a privileged position under our government, is obliged to be responsible to society for carrying out certain essential functions of mass communication in contemporary society. To the extent that the press recognizes its responsibilities and makes them the basis of operational policies, the libertarian system will satisfy the needs of society. To the extent that the press does not assume its responsibilities, some other agency must see that the essential functions of mass communication are carried out.[4]

The question of access to the editorial pages of newspapers is just one aspect of that social responsibility role perceived for the press. The question has both legal as well as practical implications.

Legal Implications of Access

One prominent critic who formulates his attack on the press from a legal basis is Jerome Barron, professor of law at the National Law

Center, George Washington University. In a law review article in 1967, Barron argued that to make viable the time-honored marketplace theory, a statutory right to access was needed. He concluded that:

> With the development of private restraints on free expression, the idea of a free marketplace where ideas can compete on their merits has become just as unrealistic in the Twentieth Century as the economic theory of perfect competition. The world in which an essentially rationalist philosophy of the First Amendment was born has vanished and what was rationalism is now romance.[5]

The equilibrium of the marketplace has been destroyed, Barron argued, by changes in technology, by the growing monopolization which denies the expression of minority views, and by the romantic interpretation of the First Amendment by the courts which denies a needed public forum.

Issues arising out of the publication of an editorial in the *Miami Herald* in September of 1972 provided Professor Barron with an opportunity to argue his access theories before both the Florida Supreme Court, where he won, and the Supreme Court of the United States in 1974, where he lost. The offending *Miami Herald* editorial read as follows:

LOOK WHO'S UPHOLDING THE LAW!

Pat Tornillo, boss of the Classroom Teachers Association and candidate for the State Legislature in the Oct. 3 runoff election, has denounced his opponent as lacking "the knowledge to be a legislator, as evidenced by his failure to file a list of contributions to and expenditures of his campaign as required by law.

Czar Tornillo calls "violation of this law inexcusable."

This is the same Pat Tornillo who led the CTA strike from February 19 to March 11, 1968, against the school children and taxpayers of Dade County. Call it whatever you will, it was an illegal act against the public interest and clearly prohibited by the statutes.

We cannot say it would be illegal but certainly it would be inexcusable of the voters if they sent Pat Tornillo to Tallahassee to occupy the seat for District 103 in the House of Representatives.

Tornillo, as a candiate for public office, asked to reply to the editorial under Florida's right to reply law passed in 1913. The *Herald,* considering the statute unconstitutional, refused to publish the reply and published a second editorial critical of Tornillo's candidacy. Tornillo went to court to compel the *Herald* to print his replies under the state statute. After the Circuit Court ruled that the statute was unconstitutional,

Tornillo appealed to the Florida Supreme Court, which reversed the lower court.

In June of 1974 the U.S. Supreme Court held the Florida right of reply statute unconstitutional because the law infringed upon the editorial control and judgment afforded the press under the First Amendment. The Court noted that:

> It has yet to be demonstrated how governmental regulation of this crucial process [editorial discretion] can be exercised consistent with First Amendment guarantees of a free press as they have evolved to this time.[6]

The Court pointed out that while a "responsible press is an undoubtedly desirable goal," that press responsibility is not mandated by the Constitution "and like many other virtues it cannot be legislated." In other words, privately owned newspapers are not legally obligated to provide access to candidates for public office, to letter writers, to public officials or public figures wishing to answer editorial attacks made upon them, or to anyone else for whatever reason.

Even though denial of access may be discriminatory and may constitute censorship in the guise of editorial discretion, private censorship is not forbidden by the First Amendment. If state action were involved, however, as in the case of a newspaper operated by a state university, then the person seeking access might be in a better position to argue a legal right of access, but editorial discretion has been recognized by the courts on even state operated media.[7]

Broadcast Fairness Doctrine

In contrast to the private newspaper press, the broadcast media do have a legal responsibility to provide access under a number of provisions of the broadcast regulations. The Federal Communications Commission in its 1974 report on the handling of public issues under the Fairness Doctrine stressed that two basic duties are involved: (1) the broadcaster must devote a reasonable percentage of time to the coverage of public issues and (2) his coverage of these issues must be fair in the sense that it provides an opportunity for the presentation of contrasting points of view.[8]

It is the broadcast licensee, however, who is called upon to make "reasonable judgments in good faith on the facts of each situation" as to whether a controversial issue of public importance is involved.[9] The 1974 report of the FCC goes on to discuss what constitutes a "controversial issue of public importance and what is meant by a "reasonable opportunity" for contrasting viewpoints. The broadcast commentator must be aware of these legal distinctions.

In at least two other areas the broadcaster is subject to even more specific right of reply obligations. One is the "personal attack" provision of the Fairness Doctrine which has been crystallized into a rule which states that:

> When, during the presentation of views on a controversial issue of public importance, an attack is made upon the honesty, character, integrity or like personal qualities of an identified person or group, the licensee shall, within a reasonable time and in no event later than 1 week after the attack, transmit to the person or group attacked (1) notification of the date, time and identification of the broadcast; (2) a script or tape (or an accurate summary if a script or tape is not available) of the attack; and (3) an offer of a reasonable opportunity to respond over the licensee's facilities.[10]

The episode involving the personal attack, however, must occur "during the presentation of views on a controversial issue of public importance." Personal attacks, therefore, which are unrelated to such a controversial issue do not invoke the rule, though they might lead to a defamation action.

Broadcast editorializing, first sanctioned by the FCC in 1949 in which the station's position is given on an issue, provides an even stronger case for the requirement that responsible persons be given a reasonable opportunity to reply.[11] It is when such interpretation, comments, or opinion are included in newscasts as commentary that the argument often arises about whether the commentary involved "a controversial issue of public importance." If an editorial endorses or opposes a political candidate, there is no question but that a reply must be afforded to the candidate being opposed or to other candidates for the same office in the case of an editorial endorsement. The FCC rules provide that:

> Where a licensee, in an editorial (i) endorses or (ii) opposes a legally qualified candidate or candidates, the licensee shall, within 24 hours after the editorial, transmit to respectively (i) the other qualified candidate or candidates for the same office or (ii) the candidate opposed in the editorial (1) notification of the date and the time of the editorial; (2) a script or tape of the editorial; and (3) an offer of a reasonable opportunity for a licensee's facilities.[12]

The regulations also provide that the broadcaster of such a political editorial presented within 72 hours prior to the day of election must comply with the provisions of the above paragraph sufficiently far in advance of the broadcast to enable him to have a reasonable opportunity to prepare a response and to present it in a timely fashion.

Section 315 of the Communication Act also provides a statutory access to all legally qualified candidates for any public office should the broadcast licensee permit any candidate for that office to use the broadcast facility. Such an equal time broadcast is beyond the power of the licensee to censor or edit in any way; neither is the licensee legally responsible for any defamation which may result from the broadcast.[13]

While the complexity of the Fairness Doctrine can only be fully understood in terms of the scores of cases litigated in the courts during the past twenty-five years, clearly the broadcast commentator and editorialist are faced with a far different access doctrine than that facing the print editorialist. In the case of the newspaper editorialist, it is a matter of providing access because it is socially responsible to do so. Though the sanctions of the Fairness Doctrine do not apply to the print media, critics continue to point out that the denial of access to opposing points of view makes a mockery of the role of a free press in the marketplace of ideas.[14] In response to such criticism the press, at least segments of the press, have taken a renewed interest in stimulating access to their editorial pages. The primary public forum provided by newspapers is the letters-to-the-editor column.

Letters to the Editor

Letters to the editor are found on the majority of the nation's editorial pages. Such columns may be simply headed "Letters to the Editor" or "Letters," or they may be labeled with such phrases as "Our Readers Speak," "In the Editor's Mailbag," "Over the Fence," "Readers' Viewpoints," "Voice of the People," "Everybody's Column," "Public Forum," "Your Opinion," "Feedback," or one of the seemingly endless variations on these and related themes. Other than the fact that they are usually present on most editorial pages, it is difficult to generalize about letters columns. In most columns, for example, the letters bear the name of the writer, but some do not. In most columns the letters show evidence of being carefully edited, but in some there has been an obvious effort to maintain the colloquial speech of the writer. In most newspapers the letters appear as a gray column of type below a standing, never-changing heading, but some letters are displayed with individual headlines, others with thumbnail illustrations to boost them graphically.

Despite such varied treatment of letters, most readers find them the most inviting feature on the editorial pages, if the findings of readership surveys can be so generalized. The question, however, remains: How effective are such columns as an open forum through which readers may express dissenting views? The answer, as indicated below, may depend upon the individual newspaper under consideration, upon the size of the newspaper, on the nature and personality of its readers, and upon the scope of its letters policy.

It is evident that the letters to the editor column provides a better opportunity for access to readers of small newspapers than of metropolitan newspapers. The *New York Times*, for example, receives about

40,000 letters each year but publishes only about six percent of them. Clifton Daniels of the *Times* has noted that if his newspaper published all the letters it receives the columns of the *Times* would be filled from January through April with no room for news.[15] The *Washington Post* receives from 75 to 100 letters a day and publishes only seven or eight of them.[16] A little better percentage, perhaps, but not much better. The *Manchester* (N.H.) *Union Leader,* by contrast, boasts that it publishes more letters from readers than any newspaper in the United States. In 1970 the *Union Leader* reported it published more than 6,000 letters, mostly just as they were written.[17]

A 1976 survey of the eighteen daily newspapers published in Nebraska showed that all but one printed 90 percent of the letters received. Only the state's largest daily, the *Omaha World-Herald,* fell below the 90 percent range. The *World-Herald* published 4,506 of the 6,940 letters received, about 65 percent of the total.[18] It becomes obvious that the small daily is in a position to provide the reader better access than the metropolitan daily where the volume of letters makes access more difficult. This is not to say that the community editor always provides such access.

Even newspapers with smaller circulations can thwart the efforts of readers to gain access through the adoption of a too restrictive letters policy. A letters policy, generally speaking, should be no more restrictive than the limitation of resources or the demands for access require. A typical letters policy statement is this from the *Alton* (Ill.) *Telegraph,* inviting readers to participate in its "What YOU think" column:

> The Telegraph welcomes prose expressions of its readers' own opinions to What YOU think. Writers should sign their letters. Writers' names and addresses must be published with their letters. The writer's telephone number will add to our convenience in rechecking. Contributions should be concise, preferably not exceeding 150 words, and are subject to condensation.

This policy apparently isn't too restrictive; at least it doesn't unduly discourage Alton letter writers. In fact, the "What YOU think" column provides a lively exchange of views. It is obvious that the *Telegraph*'s length limitation, however, is subject to inflation, as such limitations are on many editorial pages. One limit often placed on letter writers, which is not apparent in the above policy, is frequency of publication, for example, once a month or four times a year.

A poll of the members of the National Conference of Editorial Writers in 1970 revealed that 94 of the 130 respondents "almost invariably" publish the writer's name and home address. Some would publish the name with the city or the name alone. Only six of the respondents said they would use anonymous letters.

Fifty-six of the 130 respondents said they verified all letters; 74 replied that they verified only controversial or suspicious letters. Some editors said they generally processed "without hesitation" letters on personalized stationery or with business letterheads.

As for the editing of letters, 66 said they edited "sparingly," remaining very conscious of the writer's pride and lack of professionalism. Thirty-four said they edited "liberally," smoothing out sentences and tightening up paragraphs. Another 19 said they sometimes rewrote letters, or portions of them, in the interest of brevity, clarity, and readability.

Only 59 of the 130 respondents reported length limits. Most editors indicated that letters were judged individually. If they were interesting, length was not a major concern. If they were judged to be too long, the letter was edited down. Of those newspapers with length limitations, the most frequently reported limit was 300 words; 26 newspapers imposed that limit. Only 51 of the 59 newspapers had length limitations in excess of 300 words.[19]

Letters policies often take affirmative steps to encourage the flow of letters, according to the NCEW poll. The *Nashville* (Tenn.) *Tennessean,* for example, provided the best letter published each day with three stars and the writer with a cash prize. At the end of the year the three-star winners were invited to a "Forum Banquet." The *Cincinnati* (Ohio) *Enquirer* on at least two occasions has sponsored public meetings with an invited speaker for its letter writers. The speakers were syndicated columnists William F. Buckley, Jr., and John P. Roche. The *Arkansas Democrat* at Little Rock has encouraged readers to share their opinions with a $5 prize to the writer of the most original and thought-provoking letter each week.

A letters to the editor symposium compiled in 1976 by Herb Robinson, associate editor of *The Masthead,* emphasizes that editors are far from agreement about how letters to the editor should be handled. Paul Greenberg, editorial page editor of the *Pine Bluff* (Ark.) *Commercial* found that the arguments against editing of letters still outweighed the arguments for editing. He concluded, "It's more fun to run them that way, and one hopes it's more fun to read them that way." Jimmie Cox, editorial page editor of the *Fort Worth* (Texas) *Star-Telegram,* lamented that "Texans prefer talking to writing" and sometimes don't write letters to the editor at all. But, he noted, "During hot election periods, the multitudes do sometimes wax prolific. Then we're inundated." It's difficult to formulate a policy to satisfy both conditions.

James Clemon, editorial page editor of the *Omaha* (Neb.) *World-Herald,* defended his paper's policy in using initials and pseudonyms. "In my memory," he wrote, "no reader has ever questioned our liberal policy on sigs—probably because the reader's more interested in what's said than in who said it." He noted, however, that other editorialists have questioned the policy. Joanna Wragg of the *Miami* (Fla.) *News* reported that a recently installed tape-recorded answering machine for readers to phone in letters had produced "some fascinating results."

Both the phoned and written letters are transcribed by a typist into the VDT for editing, she reported. The phoned and written letters are published together in the column without distinction. Other symposium editorialists expressed various concerns about the publication of letters. One editor wrote, for example, of the need for making the readers feel more welcome while another posed the question, "Should madmen and illiterates be heard?"[20] The practice of editorial notes appended to letters is another controversial issue. It is generally held that editorial notes tend to discourage letters and should, except in unusual circumstances, be avoided.

Tom Horner, associate editor of the *Akron* (Ohio) *Beacon Journal,* reflecting upon the torrent of letters received by his newspaper after the Kent State shootings in 1970, noted that letters to the editor is a form of protest which never deprives anyone else of his right to protest. In fact, letters often invite response; so do editorials on controversial issues. The *Beacon Journal,* for example, devoted three special pages to letters in three issues of the newspaper during the week following Kent State. Reader response indicated that the letters were the best read feature in the newspaper. Part of the reason, Editor Horner believes, is that, "People do like to peek into other people's mail. Readers are curious about other readers' opinions. And readers like to read the prose of kindred amateurs."[21]

Non-media critics of letters, however, often question whether or not such columns actually provide access on a regular basis to those wishing to express views not reported or inadequately covered by the media. They ask, "When a person is not satisfied with press performance—when he has his own view of the way things are or ought to be—what recourse does he have?" One answer might be that the estimated eight million letters to the editor published each year surely represent a variety of points of view. The problem, of course, is that only one letter out of every ten mailed is printed, according to one estimate, with the percentage declining generally as the prestige of the publication increases.[22]

Indeed, the views expressed in published letters may be only "hazy reflections of public opinion," one research study concludes. Letter writers, at least the writers of letters which are published (usually the only letters available for study), are older, richer, better educated, more rooted in their community and more conservative than the general population. Since the editor chooses the letters to be published and since most of the 30 years' research on letters to the editor has been based on only those published, it may be that the profile which has emerged reflects less on the writers than the selection of editors.[23]

For newspapers which publish the majority of letters which they receive, however, and many of the small and medium size newspapers—perhaps the majority—do publish all the letters which meet their policy requirements, criticism of the editor as gatekeeper-censor seems unwarranted. The editor should strive to improve the quality and the usefulness of the letters column, however, and he may do so in many ways. The quality of letters increases as quality letters are printed. The quality of the letters also reflects the tone and quality of the editorials, the editing of the page, the integrity of the newspaper, the willingness of the editor to deal with controversial subjects, and the courage of the editor to print letters critical of the newspaper's stance on public issues. If the editor is too cautious about controversy, if he is a censor of criticism, the letters column as an open forum will soon lose its integrity and its appeal to readers.

The Pro-Con Approach

An outcropping of the concern which developed during the early 1970's about providing readers with a more balanced approach in analyzing public issues and for bolstering the credibility of newspapers, particularly monopoly newspapers, was the so-called "pro-con" editorial approach. Pioneering this movement was the *St. Petersburg* (Fla.) *Times,* whose predominantly conservative readers were being turned off by that paper's consistently liberal editorials. Robert Pittman, editor of the *Times* editorials, reported in *The Masthead* in 1974 that the *Times* pro-con package contained these elements:

> 1. A direct, objectively phrased question posing the issue.
> 2. An introductory statement of the issue and an explanation of how we are dealing with it.
> 3. The "yes" and "no" arguments, tightly organized and as direct in their rebuttal of each other as possible. (These are expansions of the familiar editorial technique of recognizing opposing arguments.)
> 4. Our editorial, briefer and stronger now that the opposing arguments already are on the page.
> 5. A coupon giving readers a chance to contribute their response, with a space for comment. These are tabulated and published. The comments appear as brief letters to the editor.
> 6. Background information when needed. This can take the form of an article, a listing of data or a chart.
> 7. An attractive illustration to draw readers to the package.[24]

As to reader response to questions posed by the *Times,* some ranged as high as 4,500, others as low as 1,000. The highest, a question about President Nixon's possible removal from office either by resignation or impeachment, brought 4,572 responses.

Pittman noted that three questions are often asked by editors about the *Times'* pro-con approach. First, isn't it wishy-washy? No, says Pittman, because it opens the reader's mind to persuasion and allows the newspaper to write more forceful and more effective editorials. Secondly, doesn't such an approach over-simplify some issues? Yes, says Pittman, unless a reasonably complete discussion can be framed in answer to a direct and objectively phrased question. Thirdly, who writes the various sides of the argument? Sometimes one editorial writer at the *Times* researches and writes the complete package, including the editorial. Sometimes editorialists volunteer for the sections of the package they prefer, Pittman reports.

Other newspapers have also experimented with the pro-con approach. The *Cedar Rapids* (Iowa) *Gazette,* for example, from time to time runs a "mini-ballot" soliciting readers' judgments and comments about an issue or question. The pro-con columns are formulated in a future issue on the basis of letters with the *Gazette*'s editorial opinion printed in between the pro-con columns. Other newspapers have adopted the question approach, for example, the *Milwaukee Journal* and the *Philadelphia Bulletin.* The letters in the *Bulletin* usually appear on the "Saturday Forum," a weekly feature with an editorial on the same subject. The question for the next week is also posed for readers to consider. The *Journal* has used a similar format except that letter writers are given two weeks to respond. The *National Observer* also experimented in 1975 with posing a question to readers, even publishing their responses on the front page.[25] Other newspapers pair columnists against each other, use excerpts from speeches and articles, recruit outsiders to write views which oppose the editorial stance taken by the newspapers; still others use the pro-con packages prepared by Congressional Quarterly.[26]

The Op-Ed Page

The op-ed page, the page opposite the editorial page, has been used by some newspapers for many years for letters to the editor, for syndicated columnists, for other editorial page features which get crowded off of the regular editorial page. The origin of the modern, still-evolving op-ed page has been traced to the *New York World*'s inclusion of political columns with such cultural offerings as movie, theatre, and book reviews on the page opposite the editorial page during the 1920's. An innovation during the 1970's, particularly among metropolitan newspapers, has been to open up the page to new voices, people other than professional journalists, making the op-ed page more of a public forum for outsiders.

The *New York Times,* for example, after several years of study, opened up the page opposite the editorial page to articles written by non-journalists in 1970. One source notes that five newspapers had ceased publication in New York City between 1949 and 1970, and the *Times* editors felt an increasing responsibility to provide their readers with a more diverse spectrum of opinion than that provided by their own generally liberal editorialists. The *Times*' own columnists first were moved from the editorial to the op-ed page, making more room for letters to the editor. The columnists were then complemented by two or three outside contributions from the 300 unsolicited manuscripts received by the op-ed page staff each week. The *Times* op-ed page article ranged from those written by congressmen, Pulitzer Prize-winning poets, foreign diplomats, and university professors to housewives, businessmen, construction workers, and people on welfare.[27]

The *Los Angeles Times, Washington Post, Boston Globe,* and *Chicago Tribune* are among metropolitan newspapers to open their daily op-ed pages to outside contributors during the 1970's. The *Los Angeles Times,* in contrast to the *New York Times,* prohibits advertising on its op-ed page, allows its own staff to contribute to the page, but strives for more personal experience pieces. However, the *New York Times* op-ed page, it has been pointed out, remains the "most cerebral" of the nation's op-ed pages. The *Washington Post,* which began its op-ed page at about the same time as its east coast competitor, the *Times,* continues to publish more political commentary by syndicated writers as well as by *Post* writers on its op-ed page than most newspapers, leaving less space for other articles. The *Boston Globe* publishes three or four outside pieces each week on its op-ed page, many of them dealing with local issues. The *Chicago Tribune*'s op-ed page carries four or five outside contributions each week, publishes a weekly "Speak Out" column by one of its readers, and carries a twice-weekly column written by a local construction worker. Such op-ed pages, by design, expand the public forum function of the traditional editorial page.

Many papers, however, still use the op-ed page merely to expand the space available for regular editorial features. The *Des Moines Sunday Register* has redesigned its op-ed page, for example, to carry a combination of letters and columns. The McClatchy newspapers—the *Sacramento, Modesto,* and *Fresno Bee*—use their daily op-ed pages for letters, three syndicated columnists, the "Another Viewpoint" column, and occasional excerpts from a speech or report of interest.[28]

Other Affirmative Approaches

Newspaper critics often argue that it isn't enough to provide space for letters and for the opinions of others, as on the page opposite the editorial page; newspapers should engage in affirmative actions to encourage the expression of minority views and should seek to foster a more wide-open, robust, uninhibited debate on important public issues. The pro-con editorial approach, linked with reader coupons seeking response on a question of the week or month, as discussed above, falls under such an affirmative action classification. Prizes for the best letter of the week or month might fall into the same category, as would any recognition of letter writers which encouraged future participation in the discussion of issues on the editorial pages.

Providing readers with the opportunity to telephone their responses for publication in the letter's column is another type of affirmative action designed to encourage access to the letter's column. The *St. Petersburg* (Fla.) *Times,* for example, provides a phone service it calls "Instant Access." When readers dial 893-8169 they get this message:

> Thank you for calling Instant Access. This service allows you to dictate your letter to the editor, or message to Hotline. Letters to the editor should be no more than 200 words long. Be sure to include your name and address, spelling it out clearly. Begin dictating after the tone. Thank you again for calling.[29]

Although such a service may not be suitable for many types of communication, the *Times* editorial page editor notes that such a technique is used by many newspapers for letters. It demonstrates to readers that the newspaper is receptive to their opinions and is willing to go to such an expense to get their response.

The employment of guest editorialists and guest columnists—outsiders invited to contribute their views for publication on the editorial page—is a type of affirmative action taken by a number of newspapers which do not have op-ed pages regularly devoted to the publication of the views of non-journalists. The invited guests often have some expertise on a subject or issue which is in the news and are asked to write on that subject. A few newspapers, however, allow the guests to choose their own topics.

The *St. Petersburg* (Fla.) *Independent* publishes a daily "My View" column written by one of a staff of about twenty-four guest columnists recruited to provide a variety of views. These nonjournalistic columnists include spokesmen for major segments of the community, leaders in public and private life, writers of letters to the editor who have demonstrated that they can articulate a point of view with some effectiveness, indeed, anyone with a capacity to express himself clearly on subjects of interest. Each columnist writes one column a month on a topic of his own choosing.

Guest opinions may take other forms. The *Winston-Salem* (N.C.) *Sunday Journal-Sentinel,* for example, did away with editorials in its Sunday edition in 1974 and turned the page over to readers who were urged to express their views in an article or essay—not a letter—on an assigned issue on the newly designated "Readers Write" opinion page. In his announcement of the first such feature, Jerry Adams, Sunday editor, explained that:

> Preference will be given to those contributions that persuasively argue their respective points and are most thoroughly documented. Personal experience is usually the best documentation, but we will help by making whatever research we have done available to you. Ask us for help. The idea is to break down the barriers that have prevented readers'

> views from being expressed, that have perpetuated the presumption that editorial writers have something to say simply because they control the forum.[30]

One of the troublesome aspects of the "Readers Write" page, Editor Adams reported, was that very few readers responded with essays on their own. It generally took affirmative action on the part of the newspaper to seek out and elicit the cooperation of knowledgeable persons related to the specific issue of the week.

Another form of recruiting guest editorials, if not guest editorialists, is the reprinting of editorials from other publications, an approach once considered a lazy method of acquiring fillers. The process, however, may also be viewed as the effort of an enlightened editor who desires to share the views of other editorialists with his readers—an editorial page editor who doesn't think he has all the good solutions or worthwhile ideas. Sometimes the process of selection becomes one of balancing the page. The *Louisville Courier-Journal,* for example, searches out editorials which disagree with its own views and publishes them under the heading, "Another Viewpoint." Other newspapers publish reprint columns of editorial comment regularly from regional or national publications, thereby providing their readers access to a better marketplace of ideas.

Ombudsman, Reader Advocate Columns

"We who live by the press have done a poor job of explaining what we do and why," according to Eugene C. Dorsey, publisher of Gannett Rochester Newspapers.[31] There has been a movement during the 1970's by newspapers to do just that through the establishment of ombudsmen, reader advocates, public editors, media critics—a few of the titles given to staffers assigned to such roles. *The Masthead* solicited the views of a group of pioneers in this field in a 1976 symposium in an attempt to determine the effectiveness of such an approach, questioning, for example, whether or not the ombudsman-media critic was a permanent fixture or just a passing fancy.

Ben H. Bagdikian, former ombudsman of the *Washington Post,* said that he believed most newspapers now considering an ombudsman, or which had done so in the past, would abandon such efforts when and if public criticism of the media subsided. But the idea will not disappear, Bagdikian argued, because such a function is needed. He noted that:

> There is no question in my mind that public appraisal of performance of individual papers by an experienced journalist will ultimately increase credibility of the press. It will help end the powerlessness that most readers feel, and it will diminish the feeling that papers are remote, corporate enterprises beyond the reach of ordinary social reaction.[32]

Bill Bransted, reader's advocate of the *St. Louis Post-Dispatch,* saw the ombudsman's role as promoting a higher level of reader acceptance. Indeed, a highly visible ombudsman makes clear to the reader that the paper is willing to invest money and energy in an effort to improve its situation. The ombudsman operation is indeed expensive, Bransted noted, but it is needed on the metropolitan newspaper where the reader has difficulty identifying with newspaper staffers. On community newspapers the disgruntled reader has an easier time of accosting the editor, Bransted concluded.[33]

Most ombudsmen, reader advocates, or media critics write a column from time to time explaining their newspaper's role to readers, usually focusing their comments on areas of operation bringing the most complaints and criticism from readers. More often, however, they handle public complaints on an individual basis. Sometimes they act as the middle man between the reader who feels he has been wronged and the news or editorial staff member responsible for the publication. Sometimes he serves more as an independent critic of his newspaper. Bob Schulman, news critic of the *Louisville* (Ky.) *Times,* for example, performs as a more or less independent critic. Schulman has a guaranteed access to the editorial page with responsibility only to the publisher for the content of his column. Ordinarily the publisher, Barry Bingham, Jr., sees the column only after it is published.[34]

For the ombudsman to be effective he needs to be recognized as a representative of the readers of the newspaper, handling their complaints on matters of fairness, accuracy, balance, professional performance, as well as serving as the paper's internal critic—the house conscience and gadfly. Charles B. Seib, ombudsman for the *Washington Post,* believes that the ombudsman should not be recruited from the newspaper staff. As an outsider (Seib was recruited from outside the *Post* staff), the ombudsman has more credibility with newspaper readers and his criticism of the newspaper is more acceptable to staffers who feel he has no axe to grind. Such credibility is important, Seib argues, if the ombudsman, media critic is to function effectively. The First Amendment serves to protect the press as the watchdog of government, a watchdog with certifiably sharp teeth. But who is to watch the watchdog? Lacking a better solution, Seib concludes, the media, through its ombudsman, reader advocate, media critic—whatever he is called—must watch itself:

> And that is what I am trying to do—in a small and faltering way on an important, bellwether paper. I am trying to give the press a little of the same kind of critical examination and exposure that the press gives the other institutions of our society. If it's healthy for them, it's healthy for us.[35]

Summary and Conclusion

If the newspaper is to be an effective voice of leadership and an instrument of persuasion in the community it serves, it must accept the responsibility of providing an open forum through which readers can express their views concerning issues of public interest and importance. Such an open forum will serve an important role in the marketplace of ideas from which truth hopefully emerges. As an open forum, the letters to the editor column should be open to the expression of all types of dissenting views from diverse groups within the community. The newspaper's policy toward letters should be consistent with this goal of encouraging letters to the editor. The newspaper should provide the space and should meet the cost of maintaining a viable letters column consistent with space and budget limitations of the newspaper and the demands for access to the newspaper.

Often the newspaper needs to take other steps to affirmatively encourage access to the editorial pages. Providing additional space through the page opposite the editorial page, for example, has been a movement toward providing more access during the 1970's. Adoption of a pro-con editorial approach, especially in communities where there is no competing newspaper, also fosters the marketplace concept by maintaining a diversity of views. Many newspapers are encouraging access through the use of questions and reader coupons seeking the reaction of readers to a specific question or public issue. Guest editorialists and guest columnists are often recruited to help balance the views expressed in the paper's editorials. And finally, a few newspapers have established ombudsmen, reader advocates, media critics to help explain to readers what newspapers do and why, and why they often fail in their efforts. All these approaches are, without doubt, beneficial. The limited extent that such measures have been adopted by the press, however, is still the subject of media criticism.

NOTES for Chapter 12

[1] For a discussion of the growing trend toward consolidation, see Bryce W. Rucker, *The First Freedom* (Carbondale, Ill.: Southern Illinois University Press, 1968).

[2] *Abrams v. United States,* 250 U.S. 616 (1919).

[3] *United States v. Associated Press,* 52 F. Supp. 362 (S.D.N.Y. 1943).

[4] Fred S. Siebert, Theodore Peterson, and Wilbur Schramm, *Four Theories of the Press* (Urbana: University of Illinois Press, 1956), p. 74.

[5] Jerome Barron, "Access to the Press—A New First Amendment Right," *Harvard Law Review* 80 (1967): 1641.

[6] *Miami Herald Publishing Co. v. Tornillo,* 418 U.S. 241 (1974).

[7] See, e.g., *Avins v. Rutgers, State University of New Jersey,* 385 F.2d 151 (3d Cir. 1967).

[8] "In the Matter of the Handling of Public Issues Under the Fairness Doctrine and the Public Interest Standards of the Communications Act," 48 F.C.C.2d 1 (1974).

[9] "Applicability of the Fairness Doctrine in the Handling of Controversial Issues of Public Importance," 29 Fed. Reg. 10415 (1964).

[10] 47 C.F.R., Sec. 73.123.

[11] "In the Matter of Editorializing by Broadcast Licensees," 13 F.C.C. 1246 (June 1, 1949).

[12] 47 C.F.R., Sec. 73.123(c).

[13] *Farmers Educational and Cooperative Union of America v. WDAY, Inc.*, 360 U.S. 525 (1959).

[14] For a summary of the arguments for legal access to the press, see Jerome A. Barron, *Freedom of the Press for Whom?* (Bloomington: Indiana University Press, 1973).

[15] William L. Rivers, Theodore Peterson, and Jay W. Jensen, *The Mass Media and Modern Society,* 2d ed. (San Francisco: Rinehart Press, 1971), pp. 5–6.

[16] F. B. Henry, "Letters to the Editor," in *The Editorial Page,* ed. Laura Longley Babb (Boston: Houghton Mifflin, 1977), p. 161.

[17] Daniel St. Albin Greene, "Dear Mr. Editor, You Fink: Masses of Letters Deluge Nation's Newspapers as Readers Speak Out." *The Quill,* 58 (July 1970): 16–19.

[18] Douglas Anderson, "Letters to the Editor," *The Nebraska Newspaper,* (July 1976): 4–5.

[19] Barney Waters, "Handling the Daily Mail," *The Masthead* 22 (Fall 1970): 44–48.

[20] For the responses of twelve editorialists, see "Letters to the Editor—When the Readers Write Back," *The Masthead* 28 (Fall 1976): 3–17.

[21] "A Matter of Conscience: A Report on Editorials in Knight Newspapers," August, 1970, p. 8. For a study of Kent State letters in the *Kent Record-Courier,* see Byron G. Lander, "Functions of Letters to the Editor: a Re-Examination," *Journalism Quarterly* 49 (Spring 1972): 142–43.

[22] For a survey of research on letters to the editor, see "Letter Columns: Access for Whom?" *Freedom of Information Center Report* 237, School of Journalism, University of Missouri, February 1970.

[23] David L. Grey and Trevor R. Brown, "Letters to the Editor: Hazy Reflections of Public Opinion," *Journalism Quarterly* 47 (Autumn 1970): 450–56.

[24] Robert T. Pittman, "10 Best Bets for Edit Pages," *The Masthead* 26 (Summer 1974): 30–38.

[25] *The National Observer,* March 1, 1975, p. 1.

[26] " 'Pro-Con' Technique Adds Sparkle to Editorial Pages," *Editor & Publisher,* December 8, 1973, p. 10.

[27] For a discussion of the development of the op-ed page, see David Shaw, "Newspapers Offer Forum to Outsiders," *Los Angeles Times,* October 13, 1975, p. 1 ff.; "The Op-Ed Page Gains in Popularity—A Report on New Trends," *The Masthead* 23 (Spring 1971): 29–34.

[28] Pittman, "10 Best Bets for Edit Pages," p. 31.

[29] Robert T. Pittman, "The Name of the Game Is Access," *The Masthead* 28 (Winter 1976): 23–25.

[30] Philly Murtha, "N.C. Daily Lets Readers Write Sunday Editorials," *Editor & Publisher,* June 8, 1974, pp. 13, 66.

[31] "Letters to the Readers," a brochure published by the *Democrat & Chronicle* and *Times Union,* Rochester, N.Y., 1976.

[32] Ben H. Bagdikian, "Press Profits from Self-Criticism," *The Masthead* 28 (Spring 1976): 3–5.

[33] Bill Bransted, "Creating a Climate of Fairness," *The Masthead* 28 (Spring 1976): 5–6.

[34] Bob Schulman, "Louisville Slugger Hits Home Runs," *The Masthead* 28 (Spring 1976): 12–13.

[35] Charles B. Seib, "Who Will Watch the Watchdog?" *The Masthead* 28 (Spring 1976): 13–15.

13

Editorial Policy: *A Basic Statement of Principles*

THE EDITORIAL POLICY of a newspaper or broadcast station, though vitally important in terms of how the medium operates, is often elusive and baffling to readers and listeners as well as to media researchers. The policy may be elusive because it is often unstated and can be determined only in terms of the editorial stances the medium takes on controversial issues, the political candidates or programs the medium endorses, or the types of issues in which the medium is willing to become involved. The policy may be baffling also because of the multitude of persuasive roles and positions of leadership editors and editorialists can, and often do, engage in. If these various stances and roles appear inconsistent, editorial policy may be even more difficult to determine. American journalists through the years have demonstrated the wide variety of persuasive roles open to the editorialist.

James Franklin, against the advice of friends but with their promise of support and with the help of his young apprentice, brother Benjamin, launched the nation's third newspaper, the *New England Courant,* in 1721. When the first issue of the *Courant* was distributed, Boston was near a panic over the worst smallpox epidemic in its history. The young publisher immediately became engaged on the anti-inoculation side of the controversy in opposition to the powerful clergy. In doing so, Franklin became the first American editor to question the authority of the church in matters of everyday life and effectively raised the question of the right of a newspaper to criticize unsparingly those in authority.[1]

During the past 250 years, however, it is clear that not all newspaper editors are willing to engage in such a crusading role against powerful institutions within their communities. A newspaper's persuasive role, for example, may be purposely limited to that of source and disseminator of the day's news. One well known nineteenth century editor, James Gordon Bennett of the *New York Herald,* exemplifies the influence which an editor can exercise merely in the role as newsman. Likewise, William Goodard, Charles Dana, and William Rockhill Nelson all played influential leadership roles, primarily as newsmen. Most newspapers of influence, however, have engaged in more advocacy with at least a portion of their resources devoted to editorial columns or editorial pages. The editorial page was the strength and driving force of such publications as Lawrence Godkin's *New York Evening Post,* Henry Watterson's *Louisville Courier-Journal,* and Harvey W. Scott's *Portland Oregonian.*

An editor may desire, of course, to become more actively involved in the important issues about which he writes, engaging in crusades as Franklin or becoming personally involved in the political process as Horace Greeley, publisher of the *New York Tribune.* Greeley, though an excellent editorialist, was also an active, if eccentric, crusader, becoming involved in public issues, in civic movements, and in politics—even as a presidential candidate. In smaller communities the editor may exercise influence and power more in his role as wise counselor and grassroots philosopher who knows and understands thoroughly the interests, desires, needs, motivations, and ambitions of his readers than in his role as editorialist. The influence of such editors as William Allen White of the *Emporia* (Kan.) *Gazette,* Ed Howe of the *Atchison* (Kan.) *Globe,* and more recently, Henry Beetle Hough of the *Vineyard Gazette* on Martha's Vineyard, all of whom became national figures despite the smallness of their newspapers, can best be explained in terms of their close identification with their readers and their communities.

The annual Pulitzer Prize in journalism awarded for editorial writing is evidence that the American editorialist continues to perform his historic role as crusader and advocate. The Pulitzer citation reads:

> For distinguished editorial writing, the test of excellence being clearness of style, moral purpose, sound reasoning, and power to influence public opinion in what the writer conceives to be the right direction, due account being taken of the whole volume of the editorial writer's work during the year.

Henry Watterson of the *Louisville Courier-Journal* won that award in 1918. William Allen White of the *Emporia Gazette* won it in 1923; Frank I. Cobb of the *New York World* was named by the Pulitzer Committee the following year. The Pulitzer award, called the "Cadillac of prizes," has also been awarded to some distinguished editorialists during the past decade, some of whose work has been used to illustrate various persuasive writing techniques throughout this book.

Awards to weekly newspaper editors have also demonstrated that editorial advocacy and courage in journalism is not dead even in the small towns. Hazel Brannon Smith, editor of the *Lexington* (Miss.) *Advertiser,* for example, has won both the Pulitzer prize and the Lovejoy award for courage in journalism for her exposés of corruption in Southern politics and the mistreatment of black prisoners in Mississippi. Gene Wirges, editor of the *Morrilton* (Ark.) *Democrat,* successfully challenged the abuse of power and corrupt election practices in the county where that paper circulated, though he lost his newspaper in the process. Tom Gish, editor of the *Mountain Eagle* of Whitesburg, Ky., who has campaigned for better working conditions in the coal mines and for legislation to protect the environment from destructive practices by mine operators, was named the Lovejoy award winner for courage in journalism in 1976.[2]

A careful examination of newspapers, either those published in the past or present-day publications, leads to the obvious conclusion that editorial policy differs from newspaper to newspaper and the editorial role of one editor may differ greatly from that of another. It is difficult, therefore, to discuss newspaper editorial policy in any very specific way, but it is possible to examine a few basic questions concerning policy making. For example, who determines editorial policy? How is the editorial policy of a newspaper formulated? How are such policy matters implemented, and how are they communicated to the public? These and other matters relating to editorial policy will form the basis for this chapter.

The Editorial Voice

When the editorial page speaks, whose voice is it? When an editorial refers to "we" or "our" or "us" or "this newspaper," who is speaking? Katharine Graham, publisher of the *Washington Post,* has a terse answer when such a question is addressed to her. She says: "That 'we' is me." The editorial voice of any newspaper is theoretically that of the owner or publisher. The publisher has the responsibility for control of the newspaper, hires—and can remove—the editor, and can cause the editorial pages to be, and say, what he wants. In practice, however, editorial policy cannot be—and should not be—determined in such an authoritarian or unilateral manner. Speaking of the *Post,* Mrs. Graham noted that:

> The ultimate *responsibility* is obviously mine; the *authority* to run the editorial pages as I see fit is also obviously mine. But while there might have been a day when owners and publishers reserved this authority to themselves, they rarely find it possible, and still less desirable, to do so today.[3]

The making of editorial policy actually begins with the hiring of the editorial page staff, particularly the editor of the page. Mrs. Graham reports, for example, that she and Philip L. Geyelin, editor of the *Post* editorial page, walked the beaches of Martha's Vineyard for two days, discussing just about every issue they could think of, searching not so much for agreement as establishing whether they had similar values and approaches to problems and some agreement on the methods of working out any future differences. In subsequent talks she and Geyelin reached an understanding which has apparently worked out well. Mrs. Graham explains that understanding, or agreement, as follows:

> First, while we may differ on specific issues, our relationship will be successful as long as there is general accord on policy questions and on the nature and quality of the editorial page. Second, it is his prerogative as editor to make the final judgments on editorial policy—as long as what we call the "no-surprises rule" is observed. That means that he will spare me the experience of opening the paper some morning and finding that *The Post* has made a major pronouncement or change of policy about which I have not been either consulted or apprised.[4]

There are other practical considerations which often prevent publishers from single-mindedly dictating editorial policy. One is that the growth of chain ownership has brought the corporate publisher, an in-residence position often filled by a more business-oriented executive rather than a newsman. Such corporate publishers may perform managerial functions, but they are not owners. Their primary concern is not usually the newspaper's editorial voice as expressed through the editorial pages. Secondly, even the modern-day publisher-owner who operates more independently is less likely to become involved in the day-to-day editorial page production than his nineteenth century counterpart. Kenneth McArdle, associate editor of the *Chicago Daily News*, has observed that while it might be foolhardy to write editorials for a publisher with whom one wholeheartedly disagreed, that, generally speaking,

> it would be hard to be utterly out of synch with them unless you, yourself, were on the kooky side, because they tend to be rational people. Moreover, except on issues very dear to their hearts, they tend to be off meeting the payrolls and leaving the day-to-day editorializing to the people they pay to follow the news. They set the broad guidelines, and leave the rest to the editors and the editorial writers.[5]

The editorial writer, however, in contrast to the editor-publisher, must operate within whatever guidelines have been established or whatever frame of reference has been adopted by the publisher, the editorial page editor, the editorial board, or whoever is charged with formulating such policies. Often the guidelines provide the editorialist a wide degree of freedom, but there is always the risk that he will collide with them if he attempts to operate too independently. An editorial writer for the *Dayton* (Ohio) *Journal Herald* has noted that:

> The most independent among us, who labor under the most amiable and enlightened editors, and who roam almost unchecked over the entire spectrum of social and political commentary, are nonetheless faced with boundaries that may not be crossed, however tempting the view from the far side.[6]

Critics of editorial policy are as likely to express concern about restraints and pressures from outside the newspaper editorial rooms as from within. A *Masthead* symposium in 1970, for example, asked: Are editorial writers tools of the interests? Robert T. Pittman, editor of editorials of the *St. Petersburg* (Fla.) *Times;* responded that debate of such a question was pointless. The question should be, he said, "How do we spring them loose?" Pittman suggested a number of ways: (1) that newspapers be kept in the hands of news-trained managers, (2) that creative imaginative writers and editors be employed, (3) that editorial page staffs be enlarged, (4) that editorialists take a firmer stand against the establishment's social pressures, (5) that better ways to develop responsible dissent to editorial views be found, and (6) that the trend toward more public ownership of newspapers be opposed.[7] Other symposium respondents also argued that too many editorialists have become tools of special interests. A distaste for controversy, a growing provincialism, complacency about what one editor called the editorialist's voluntary servitude induced by high salaries, all these were viewed as making the editorialist a more susceptible target of special interest groups.

The editorial page staffs on the more enlightened, more enterprising newspapers, however, have a voice in the formulation of editorial policy. One of the primary forums for staff participation in such policy development on a day-to-day basis is the editorial conference.

The Editorial Conference

Some type of daily conference of the editorial staff or the editorial board is used by many larger newspapers as a matter of policy. Such meetings may provide a forum for testing editorial ideas, for plugging loopholes in editorial arguments, for mounting an editorial campaign through the input of staffers who may hold differing views based upon their own experiences and training. For other newspapers the daily conference is more of a convenient forum for charting the day's work, making assignments, and exchanging information. While the daily conference is most used by the multimember editorial staff, one of the largest newspaper editorial staffs, that of the *New York Times,* operates without a conference. John B. Oakes, former editor of the *Times* editorial page, talked individually with the various writers of the thirteen-member editorial page staff rather than engage in a formal conference. Oakes had a second opportunity to monitor the individual writer's output before sending it to the composing room.

In a 1976 symposium conducted by *The Masthead,* editors responded in various ways to the question: "The Daily Editorial Conference: Why Bother?" As expected, the larger the staff, the stronger the impulse to confer, but this was not found to be an invariable rule.

John G. McCullough, editor of the *Philadelphia Bulletin* editorial page, lamented that vacations, illnesses, and other staff absences sometimes prevented daily conferences because the *Bulletin*'s editorials suffered when the give-and-take of editorial conferences was missing. The *Bulletin* invited summer news interns to participate in editorial conferences from time to time in an effort to foster a diversity of opinion and to prevent the conference from becoming an "echo chamber" of the editor's views. McCullough, turning to his crystal ball, concluded:

> I see newspaper editorials as a sort of journalistic early warning system. We will be trying to detect trends, using the kind of radar that develops from the conference to see what is coming next. . . . We have to spot the issues as they first arise and sort of lay them out for our readers to think about. How do we do all of this? I'm not sure. But I'm sure that group discussion will help, so long as those who discuss—or confer—bring something worthwhile and varied to the session. We don't want to sit by a mill pond. We need boiling waters.[8]

Wilbur Elston, associate editor and editorial page director of the *Detroit News,* views the editorial conference as a valuable method of determining editorial policy and deciding who is going to write what for an editorial page. The value of the conference, however, depends upon the amount of freedom the individual editorialist has in picking his topics and determining what he is going to say about them, Elston argues. If a writer proposes a new policy or advocates an opinion that differs from the newspaper's previous view, then it is his obligation to offer enough evidence and arguments to convince the rest of the staff—and the editor—that the new position is a responsible and deserving one for the newspaper to take. If the majority of the participants or the editor vetoes a writer's proposed editorial, that should be the end of it, Elston notes. A major criticism of the daily editorial conference, however, is that it often produces editorials that sound as if they had been written by a committee. Elston commented upon this problem and the dilemma it presents for the editorial page editor:

> [W]hat occasionally happens is that an editorial is revised so much in the conference that the writer who proposed it no longer recognizes his brainchild and bows out as the writer. In my experience, somebody else usually volunteers to write it. But if nobody offers to write it and management really wants the view expressed, I volunteer to do so. For I believe management has the right to have its opinions expressed on the editorial page, and if nobody else is willing to do it, the editorial page editor or director should accept that responsibility.[9]

Gilbert Cranberg, editor of the editorial pages of the *Des Moines* (Iowa) *Register and Tribune,* views the editorial conference as a valuable vehicle for charting the day's work and for exchanging information. Since most of the newspaper's editorials are self-assigned, the conference is a forum for the nine-person staff to relate to others what subjects are being tackled and to enable the editor to react to the editorial proposals. Cranberg notes that:

> I ask each writer at the conference what he has in mind for the day. Most of the time topics are just mentioned; at times a writer who has not formulated his thinking on a subject will seek advice, and ideas are kicked into the pot; sometimes the conference takes on aspects of a seminar.[10]

While many of the functions performed by editorial conferences might be done without a formal meeting, several editorial page editors responded to the symposium question by pointing out certain merits flowing from the process. Reese Cleghorn, editor of the *Charlotte* (N.C.) *Observer,* found that conferences often provide "spontaneous thought" which sends one out to turn out a better editorial before the 1 p.m. deadline. Thomas Gephardt, associate editor and editor of the editorial page of the *Cincinnati Enquirer,* found the conference to be edifying, often even fun, and an ideal forum for visiting dignitaries wishing to share their views with editorial writers. But not every respondent shared such positive views. Frank H. Crane, editor of the *Indianapolis* (Ind.) *Star,* found conferences too time-consuming except for occasions when there arises a sharp difference of opinion about an editorial position. Crane quoted his predecessor who viewed the product of the daily conference as "the lowest common denominator of the thinking of the various writers." Bob Frazier, editorial page editor of the *Eugene* (Ore.) *Register-Guard,* who heads a three-member editorial page staff, saw little need for a formal conference since the three of them were in "perpetual conference" when they were in the office. Noting the demands placed on the staff to meet deadlines, Frazier observed that "you can't meet and work at the same time."[11]

Newsmen are sometimes invited to sit in on editorial conferences in an effort both to promote understanding of the editorial page function and as a method of providing access to a broader spectrum of views. Gannett's two Rochester newspapers tried this with some success in the early 1970's. Cliff Carpenter, former editor of the *Democrat* and *Chronicle,* described the two-way therapy as bringing results that were "like alternate doses of castor oil and paregoric."[12] The move toward more democracy in the newsroom and the cry for "reporter power," however, has had little effect on the overall functioning of the editorial page policy making. Paul Ringler, writing in *The Masthead* in 1972, predicted that while there may be a movement toward giving top staff people greater voice in management, including the determination of editorial policy, most American newspapers will make no significant surrender of management authority.[13]

Implementing Editorial Policy

Once the editorial policy of a newspaper has been formulated, how is it then implemented and communicated to the public? The first step is obviously the dissemination of the newspaper's stance on important public issues through its editorials, columns, and other opinion-oriented utterances. Such editorials may include those endorsing or opposing candidates for public office at the local, state, or national level. The ideological stance of the newspaper may often be determined by readers on the basis of such political endorsements to the extent that they are politically consistent. But editorial policy may be communicated in other ways as well. Through the choice of issues and problems for comment and consideration, for example, the newspaper helps to formulate the priorities readers ultimately place upon such matters. At least this is the theory of the agenda-setting function attributed to the press by recent communications research. This function, in turn, helps to communicate the newspaper's overall editorial policy to its readers.

Many newspapers, however, carry the editorial process one step further by reprinting selected editorials and columns for wider distribution to select audiences who might be expected to be interested in the subject matter treated in the editorial. The *Los Angeles Times,* for example, regularly reprints various editorials for more widespread distribution. The *Times* may also reprint the work of other staffers as it did a selection of columns by Ruben Salazar, a Mexican-American staffer killed while covering a 1970 riot. Salazar had written a weekly column focusing on the problems of the unprivileged Chicanos in the Los Angeles area. The *Buffalo* (N.Y.) *Evening News* likewise reprinted in pamphlet form thirty-six of its bicentennial editorials in 1976 selected from its American Issues Forum. Pulitzer Prize winning editorials are often reprinted for wider distribution. Such reprinting efforts tend to boost the prestige of the newspaper by expanding the audience of the editorial pages.

The opportunities for boosting editorial policy and enhancing public understanding of the newspaper's policies, platforms, goals, and commitments, however, are not limited to the publication or republication of editorials. Such opportunities range from brief editorial masthead statements to costly advertising campaigns and special service sections prepared for national distribution. The masthead statements may be little more than a declaration of editorial independence, such as those in the *St. Louis Globe-Democrat* or the *Chicago Daily News,* or a simple statement such as the *Chicago Tribune*'s masthead credo:

> The Newspaper is an institution developed by modern civilization to present the news of the day, to foster commerce and industry, to in-

> form and lead public opinion, and to furnish that check upon government which no constitution has ever been able to provide.

. . . or Joseph Pulitzer's *St. Louis Post-Dispatch* "platform" statement:

> I know that my retirement will make no difference in its cardinal principles, that it will always fight for progress and reform, never tolerate injustice or corruption, always fight demagogues of all parties, never belong to any party, always oppose privileged classes and public plunderers, never lack sympathy with the poor, always remain devoted to the public welfare, never be satisfied with merely printing news, always be drastically independent, never be afraid to attack wrong, whether by predatory plutocracy or predatory poverty.

The problem with such statements of independence, such credos, or such platforms is that readers get used to them being there each day as a part of the masthead and never bother to give them a second thought.

Editors sometimes write editorials or make speeches in an attempt to explain the policy-making process or to illuminate their newspaper's editorial policy. John G. McCullough, editor of the editorial page of the *Philadelphia Bulletin,* for example, devoted an editorial page column to the subject, "An Editorial View—Why It Is Given." McCullough noted that:

> There have been biting references to writers who sit in 'ivory towers' and know nothing of the city, its people or its problems. There have been references to 'the one man' who gazes at an office ceiling for awhile, puts his own views and prejudices onto paper and then retreats quickly into secure anonymity.

It isn't this way at all, McCullough says. His column goes on to explain how the *Bulletin*'s editorial policy is formulated.[14]

M. Stanton Evans, editor of the editorial page of the *Indianapolis Star,* chose a meeting of the Mid-America Press Institute dealing with editorial pages to espouse his views on the proper function of an editorial page. It is to give voice to the corporate opinion of the newspapers, speaking both to and for the community, Evans argued. An editorialist can't "ad hoc" it every day; he needs to operate from a position, have a point of view, a perspective, striving to be consistent, Evans told editorialists attending the weekend institute. This editorial policy standard should be applied to the Republicans as well as the Democrats, and it should be applied to all levels of an issue—local, state, and national.

Reader advocates, reader service editors, ombudsmen, and media critics often deal with matters of editorial policy in their columns addressed to readers. Francis Wood, reader service editor of *Newsday,* for example, engaged in a continuing series on how that newspaper formulated its editorial policies and covered the news. Selected columns from the series were reprinted in a tabloid format in 1974 as a public service. In 1975 the *Minneapolis Star* published a twelve-page reprint section containing stories published in the *Star* between August 25 through September 6. The series, which explained the operation of all the news media, both print and electronic, in the Twin Cities, was described as a "journalistic first," at least in Minnesota.

Sometimes the dissemination of editorial policy takes the form of special brochures or pamphlets. A brochure entitled "We Submit" was published in 1969 by Scripps-Howard newspapers to set out the editorial viewpoints of Scripps-Howard editors and editorial executives on twenty-five major issues. The series had been published in *Editor & Publisher* over a six-months period to publicize the editorial policies adopted by Scripps-Howard newspapers. Seventeen editors of Knight newspapers were given the opportunity to report on the editorial function of their newspapers in a pamphlet published in 1970 entitled "A Matter of Conscience." The pamphlet must have been of interest to Knight newspaper readers; it has served as an excellent teaching aide in editorial writing. Another Knight brochure, this one entitled "The Eagleton Case: A Story of Initiative and Responsibility," explained why the Knight newspapers did not publish the story of Senator Thomas Eagleton's past psychiatric problems until the reporters had the opportunity to check with both Senator Eagleton and Senator George McGovern for verification and explanation, even though it cost them an exclusive story.

Landmark newspapers outline the scope of Landmark's operations and its newspaper philosophy in a brochure entitled "Landmark Communications." The Gannett group publishes its *Gannetteer,* a magazine devoted to keeping the staffs of that group's seventy-three newspapers informed as well as members of the public interested in the Gannett holdings, Copley newspapers formerly published a quarterly review for journalists entitled *Seminar.* Indeed, there are numerous methods which may be used by newspapers in disseminating editorial policy.

Ethics and Fair Play

One of the questions continually plaguing editorialists is how newspapers can best insure fair play on their editorial pages. The formulation of such groups as Accuracy in Media and the National News Council has only emphasized the battle being waged within journalism for higher ethical standards. Various national news organizations, including the American Society of Newspaper Editors, the Associated Press Managing Editors Association, the Society of Professional Journalists (Sigma Delta Chi), and the National Conference of Editorial Writers, have joined in the "patrolling of the precincts." One of the fairness concerns of the NCEW, as well as others, is to insure editorial page access for readers who wish to reply. This aspect of the problem has been treated in Chapter 12. Another aspect of the larger ethical problem is the matter of avoiding conflicts of interest by editorialists, both local staffers as well as those writing for national syndicates. The NCEW, after much debate, finally revised its "Basic Statement of Principles" in 1975 urging that:

> The writer should be constantly alert to conflicts of interest, real or apparent, including those that may arise from financial holdings, secondary employment, holding public office or involvement in political, civic or other organizations. Timely public disclosure can minimize suspicion.

And, the "Principles" state, "Editors should seek to hold syndicates to these standards."

The "full disclosure of association" issue arose after the NCEW objected to the News Council about syndicated columnist Victor Lasky who failed to make clear to editors using his column that he had received a $20,000 fee from the Committee to Re-Elect the President in the 1972 presidential campaign. The National News Council subsequently figured in editorial comment and what has been described as "tart correspondence" in the case of three other syndicated columnists involving charges of failure to disclose their association—Tom Braden, William Buckley, and Ann Landers. While the findings were not entirely satisfactory to the complainants, it brought from the News Council the view "that every journalist should either refrain from commenting upon matters in which he or she has a familial or financial interest or make those interests so clear there can be no misunderstanding."[15]

Many editorialists, however, oppose the efforts of NCEW or any other group to impose ethical standards related to fair play. "If an editor doesn't know what fair play is," one respondent to a national survey noted, "neither NCEW nor anyone else can help him." The overwhelming consensus of the 1972 survey was that NCEW should keep out of a judgmental press council-type role, confining its standard-setting efforts strictly within some kind of informational, or at most inspirational, limits.[16]

Robert N. Fishburn of the *Roanoke* (Va.) *World News* views editorial fairness as, at best, an "iffy" matter. He noted that the *News* had found that:

> if we have a broad enough range of opinion;
> if we do not pontificate too often;
> if we admit our mistakes and misjudgments in print;
> if we lay claim to fallibility;
> if we seek out and print letters;
> if we actively solicit "viewpoint" columns on issues;
> if we are polite on the phone;
> if we avoid writing down; and
> if we, in editorials, include counter-arguments, even though we may not accept them, we avoid much criticism of unfairness.[17]

Livening Up the Editorial Page

It is important that the editorial page is produced each day under a consistent set of guidelines which flow from a concerned, enlightened, responsible editorial page policy. It is important that readers are aware of this general policy as it relates to the illumination and advocacy they are exposed to each day. It is important that the editorials have something to say; it is also important that such messages are clearly and persuasively written. Research and reflection as discussed in Chapter 5 should provide suggestions about the climate needed for the nurturing of editorial ideas. The techniques of writing and the principles of persuasive writing as discussed in Chapters 6 and 9 should provide the needed guidance for writing more persuasively. What other steps should the editor consider to make the editorial pages more meaningful, more readable, more lively?

Editorial page editors from Gannett newspapers, responding to an "Editorially Speaking" feature in the *Gannetteer,* had a number of interesting suggestions. Tom Reay, executive editor of the Rockford, Ill., newspapers, encourages guest columnists and "reader editorials," the latter submitted on coupons printed once a week. Jeff Frank, editorial page editor of the *Ithaca* (N.Y.) *Journal,* attempts to keep editorials and commentary current, even if it means writing editorials early in the morning on an overnight news development. Bill Branche, editorial page editor of the *Niagara* (N.Y.) *Gazette,* argues that the editorial page should not only emphasize local subjects, such editorials should tell it the way it is regardless of hurt feelings.

Christy Bulkeley, editor and publisher of *The Saratogian,* Saratoga, N.Y., had a simple but effective formula for editorial persuasion: "Say what needs to be said. Say it the most effective way possible. Say it more often than you think should be necessary." Pinckney Keel, editorial director of the *Nashville* (Tenn.) *Banner,* says that even a conservative-leaning editorial page should be liberal in its use of white space, large "punchy" heads, and boxed display of letters to the editor.[18]

The op-ed page can also provide diversification for local and national subjects as well as needed space for columns, letters to the editor, or other editorial features. The op-ed page, indeed, can be the most typographically pleasing page in the newspaper. The editorial cartoon, which is beyond the scope of this study, is an important graphic feature of most editorial pages and should serve to catch the reader's eye as well as supplying a needed ingredient of humor.[19]

Editorial pages can be further livened up, of course, by the use of better packaging and display techniques. The need for such packaging has been urged by Edgar T. Zelsmann, president of Carl J. Nelson Research, Inc., a readership survey and research firm. To bolster declining readership of editorial pages Zelsmann recommended at a session of the Mid-America Press Institute that label heads be eliminated in favor of two-line heads on editorials, that editorials engage in less "doomsaying" in favor of at least some lighter material, that humor panels and provocative editorial cartoons be used more extensively, and that letters to the editor be encouraged.[20]

The proper packaging of the opinion product is, without doubt, an important modern-day concern, just as packaging is important in other areas of marketing. It is important that the editorial page be both pleasing in appearance and readable. It is important that emphasis be given to locally written editorials through the use of larger type sizes and/or wider column measure. It is important to seek an orderly but varied format which provides generous white space inviting readers onto the page. A well-placed cartoon and other graphic materials should help catch the eye of the reader. A thoughtfully designed op-ed page is needed which supplements the editorial page. Such packaging concerns may be of even more importance if the newspaper is to continue to compete in the marketplace against the more sophisticated packaging of the news magazines, the journals of opinion, and the great diversity of television commentary. Editorial packaging, however, can go only so far in livening up a page if the content is so dull and bland that a reader looking for analysis, illumination, and ideas is turned off. The content of the page must deal with provocative issues in a persuasive manner if the page is truly to remain alive and interesting. John S. Knight, editorial chairman of the Knight eleven-newspaper chain, commenting upon criticism of newspapers by former Vice President Spiro Agnew, noted:

> An editor, who must or should take vigorous editorial positions on the great issues of the day, is not meant to be loved. If he seeks affection and popularity, he should be in public relations. Newspapermen who formulate policy must base their conclusion upon the facts at hand. The unvarnished truth is frequently unpleasant reading since it so often differs from the reader's preconceived notions of what the truth should be.[21]

There is nothing which will liven up an editorial page more readily than speaking up on "the great issues of the day," particularly local issues. This type of subject, plus a well-packaged editorial page, will both encourage readership as well as enhance persuasibility.

Looking to the Future

The evidence of technological change in the 1970's is nowhere more evident than it is in the communications industry. Recently it was microwave channels and digital communications which expanded the newsman's capability to link a central computer to remote bureaus and operations. In addition, it has provided the means for facsimile distribution to satellite plants and to receive newsphotos electronically.

Today may be viewed as a crossroads of new opportunities; for example, the development of the space shuttle capable of establishing massive broadcasting satellites in space, of the fiber optics technology bringing virtually unlimited communications capabilities for point-to-point transmissions, and, finally, of electronic delivery and retrieval devices, permitting information to be supplied directly to the home.[22] There is little doubt that today's video display terminal places the newspaper editorialist in a far greater persuasive role than at any time since the industrial revolution.

But the challenges which face the editorialist may also be greater. Researchers, for example, are having increasing difficulty explaining who reads a newspaper and why. One study concludes that the young adults of today were caught up in the vortex of rapid social change of the late 1960's and early 1970's, leaving society in a state of flux. These many new currents tug in one direction upon these young people while the more familiar and older currents pull in the opposite. These contradictory demands also pose a problem for newspapers. Ruth Clark, senior vice president of Yankelovich, Skelly, and White, Inc., noting that the research findings related to these contradictions are not simple, summarized them as follows:

> (1) Today's newspaper readers are a lot less loyal, far more demanding, and far more interesting than ever before.
>
> (2) The new values provide a good environment for innovation and change.
>
> (3) Neither habit nor duty can be counted upon to produce regular reading. It's what the paper does for the reader that particular day that counts. Obligation to read is old hat.
>
> (4) Reading a paper has to be an interesting, useful, and pleasurable experience. No one wants to work at it anymore.
>
> (5) Readers don't make the same distinctions between hard and soft news as the business does. News is anything that is interesting, relevant, and meaningful to the individual reader.
>
> (6) Readers expect to have a lot more in the paper than they will probably read. They'll select and pick what they want, provided it is made easy for them to do so.
>
> (7) Personalization is high on the agenda. Readers want to know more about their newspaper as well as the people in it.
>
> (8) Readers want to know more about themselves as well as about others.
>
> (9) Readers' standards of morality are stricter for newspapers than for themselves.
>
> (10) Technology is back in vogue, and newspapers have a wonderful technological story to tell in terms of reader benefits.[23]

It is clear that editorial pages, if they are to be read by the generation of young people emerging from the decade of the 1960's, will, more than ever before, have to be better written, be more interesting, and be more relevant from the perspective of such readers.

There is also evidence that editorial pages are being increasingly designed to meet these needs. A University of Georgia researcher, for example, reported that almost two-thirds of those responding to an editorial survey which he conducted indicated that their newspaper had turned more toward local issues and topics on the editorial page. Many newspapers also reported that they were taking stronger stands on local issues with less emphasis upon "rhetoric" and more personal writing. Shorter, easier to read editorials, with a definite trend toward more humor, were also reported by a number of newspapers. Most of the respondents were positive in discussing the future of editorial pages; some suggested, for example, that editorialists generally were producing "more light and less heat," taking more responsible positions, and turning out less pretentious work. A frequently reported comment related to the need for improving methods of helping readers understand the issues, a theme of the Yankelovich research on the needs of readers.[24]

Most projections into the future may be merely extensions of trends from the past. A number of trends, therefore, may indicate changes which may be expected in the future on the nation's editorial pages. The growing complexity of public issues, for example, has already forced editorialists to strive for a better understanding of such problems through better research and more specialization. Where the small size of the staff makes specialization impractical, syndication will likely play an increasingly important role in providing the needed editorial page materials. Less anonymity on the editorial page, a trend already underway, can be expected to accelerate as editorial page editors strive to remind readers their editorials and columns are produced by real people, not computers or "bloodless functionaries of a remote institution."

The open forum function of the editorial pages will likely become more important in the continuing effort to make the page more relevant to readers with greater emphasis being placed on the publication of letters to the editor, guest columnists, and opinions from outside sources. As the news columns become increasingly more interpretative and analytical, it will become more important for editorial pages to break away from standard molds and become more flexible and lively. There will be more emphasis placed upon good writing in the future. As one editorialist has noted, "There is still much truth in the cliché that there is nothing wrong with the editorial page that can't be cured by writing better editorials." These are among the trends in the opinion function of newspapers.

Almost a decade ago an advertising executive, engaging in a bit of editorializing, concluded his analysis of changing news interests in a paragraph which provides a challenge for the newspaper editorialist today. Leo Bogart, executive vice president and general manager of the Bureau of Advertising, said:

> Newspapers are still the greatest medium yet devised for making all the people of a community alive to the common interests and problems they face each day. This happens only through the newspaper's unique and now often challenged capacity to explain and even to *create* news as well as to report it, to evoke excitement, to arouse and channel indignation, to force civic crises and to present thoughtful solutions. We all know that there is a profound difference between reportage and journalism. An evolving communications technology is rapidly finding new ways to compete with the newspaper's function as a routine record of the day's events. But no technological change can ever challenge the newspaper's command of big ideas, its traditions to deep inquiry, sweeping synthesis, and inspired advocacy. Tomorrow's newspaper must be not merely a register, but a tribune, not merely a ledger, but a clarion.[25]

If the American newspaper is to remain a tribune and clarion, it must continue to rely upon the proper functioning of the editorial page.

NOTES for Chapter 13

[1] Willard G. Bleyer, "The Beginning of the Franklins' *New England Courant," Journalism Quarterly* 4 (June 1927): 5.

[2] For a discussion of these and other community editors singled out for their editorial courage, sometimes in the face of serious political and economic pressures to silence them, see Howard R. Long, ed., *Main Street Militants* (Carbondale, Ill.: Southern Illinois University Press, 1977).

[3] Katharine Graham, " 'We': A Preface," in *The Editorial Page,* ed.: Laura Longley Babb (Boston: Houghton Mifflin, 1977), pp. 1–7.

[4] *Ibid.,* p. 5.

[5] Kenneth McArdle, "The Real Pressure Is to Make Sense," *The Masthead* 22 (Spring 1970): 8–9.

[6] Harold Piety, "Tools of the Interests? Of Course We Are!" *The Masthead* 22 (Spring 1970): 13–14.

[7] Robert T. Pittman, "How to Free Editorial Writers," *The Masthead* 22 (Spring 1970): 10–11.

[8] John G. McCullough, "Consulting Some Other Oracles," *The Masthead* 28 (Summer 1976): 5–6.

[9] Wilbur Elston, "Writers Need Topics, Not Orders," *The Masthead* 28 (Summer 1976): 9–10.

[10] Gilbert Cranberg, "Skull Sessions Over Lunch," *The Masthead* 28 (Summer 1976): 10–11.

[11] For other views concerning editorial conferences, see "The Daily Editorial Conference: Why Bother?" A symposium compiled by William P. Cheshire, *The Masthead* 28 (Summer 1976): 3–11.

[12] Cliff Carpenter, "When Newsmen Sit in on Edit-Page Planning," *The Gannetteer*, October 1970, pp. 23–24.

[13] Paul Ringler, "Can Staff Participation Help a Newspaper to Survive and Prosper?" *The Masthead* 24 (Fall 1972): 21–24.

[14] For a reprint of the column, see John G. McCullough, "An Editorial View—Why It Is Given," *The Masthead* 24 (Spring 1972): 16–18.

[15] See "Statement on General Ethics" approved by the National News Council, December 10, 1974.

[16] For a discussion of the survey results, see Millard C. Browne, "How Can Newspapers Best Ensure Fair Play?" *The Masthead* 24 (Fall 1972): 9–16.

[17] Robert N. Fishburn, "With Apologies to Kipling—an Iffy View of Fairness," *The Masthead* 24 (Fall 1972): 10.

[18] "Editorial Pages: How to Make Them Meaningful and Entertaining to the Reader," *The Gannetteer*, "Editorially Speaking" Section, July 1975.

[19] For a discussion of editorial page humor, see "Editorial Page Humor: A Status Report," a symposium compiled by Richard B. Childs and Herb F. Robinson, *The Masthead* 29 (Spring 1977): 3–11.

[20] Edgar T. Zelsmann, "Studies Reveal Editorial Shortcomings," *The Masthead* 29 (Spring 1977): 39.

[21] "Quotation to Ponder" from a speech before the City Club of Charlotte, N.C., as reported in *Parade Magazine*, November 7, 1971.

[22] For a discussion of the newspaper of the 1990's, see American Newspaper Publishers Association, *Research Institute Bulletin* 1266, August 19, 1977.

[23] Ruth Clark, "Our New Role in the Marketplace: A Reader's View," American Newspaper Publishers Association, *Research Institute Bulletin* 1265, August 16, 1977, pp. 238–46.

[24] Ernest C. Hynds, "Local Emphasis Seen for Editorial Pages," *Editor & Publisher*, February 12, 1977, p. 18.

[25] Leo Bogart, "Changing News Interests and the News Media." *Public Opinion Quarterly* 32 (Winter 1968–69): 450–74.

Index